THE ULTIMATE BUSINESS SUPERPOWER

SCOTT MARTIN

Published in the United States by Insurgent Publishing, LLC.
PO Box 8043, Aspen, CO 81612

www.insurgentpublishing.com

Ordering Information:

Insurgent Publishing books are available at special discounts for bulk purchases for sales promotions or corporate use. Special editions, including personalized covers, excerpts of existing books, or books with corporate logos, can be created in large quantities upon request. For more information, please contact the publisher by email at admin@ insurgentpublishing.com.

Although every precaution has been taken to verify the accuracy of the information contained herein, the author and publisher assume no responsibility for any errors or omissions. No liability is assumed for damages that may result from the use of information contained within.

ISBN: 978-1-940715-15-5

Cover design by 100Covers
Interior design by FormattedBooks

Printed in the United States of America
10 9 8 7 6 5 4 3 2 1

To James Fawcett

FOREWORD

Prolific author and superstar copywriter Scott Martin's new book THE ULTIMATE BUSINESS SUPERPOWER reveals how to write copy the right way and for the right reason – not to entertain people with your wit or win creative awards, but for the only reason that ever matters: to move the sales needle and bring in leads, orders, and money by the truckload! Scott is a master at writing this kind of money-making copy and this book shows you his winning secrets. Chapter 2 on the most common marketing mistakes and how to avoid them is by itself worth 100X the price of the book.

– Bob Bly. McGraw-Hill calls Bob Bly "America's top copywriter." The Direct Marketing Association awarded him the Gold Echo, and AWAI voted Bob Copywriter of the Year. He writes a column for Target Marketing magazine, has taught copywriting at New York University, and is the author of 100 published books, including The Digital Marketing Handbook (Entrepreneur Press) and The Copywriter's Handbook (Henry Holt).

CONTENTS

INTRODUCTION

Here's a conversation I have up to five times a day. This conversation has taken place at trade shows, at social gatherings, at sporting events, during meetings with marketing people, on airplanes, on ski lifts, and in various bars and hostelries in different towns and cities around our planet.

"So, Scott...what do you do?"
"I'm a direct response copywriter."

Then comes this blank look, not unlike the look on someone's face after they have been asked an especially difficult trivia question. The conversation pauses for several seconds as the person who asked the question tries to figure out what a direct response copywriter is and does.

This conversational paralysis has impacted a wide variety of people... young graduates just out of college...CEOs of large companies...HR specialists...headhunters...even people who work in advertising and marketing at the highest levels...executive vice presidents and the like.

Many people think I have some type of legal role, specifically protecting people's copyrights and related intellectual property. No. It's not the © thing. I'm in copywriting NOT copyrighting. There's a huge difference. Copyrighting is a legal discipline.

Only one person I meet in five hundred, give or take, instantly knows what a direct response copywriter does, and more importantly, can do, for a company.

And this upsets me, not because I have a whopping ego, but because the work of an experienced direct response copywriter can transform the fortunes of a business of any size. My work for one of my clients has generated $220 million in revenue in six years. The owner of this company started his nascent business by shipping items from his dining room. I was the fourth person he contracted. The company grew to 58 employees and was acquired by one of the biggest media companies in the world.

I helped launch three dietary supplements for another company. These supplements have generated well over $300 million in sales. You've likely seen their ads on TV.

Part of me likes the mystery of my chosen profession. But another part of me is genuinely upset that business decision makers give me the "blank stare" when I tell them I'm a direct response copywriter.

Dan Kennedy, the noted marketing specialist, called direct response copywriting the "ultimate business superpower."

SUPERPOWER?

Really?

And the ULTIMATE business superpower?

"Isn't that going over the top with the hype?" you might be asking.

No.

And I'm going to prove it in this book.

This "superpower" was generating over $1.5 million a month for a tiny company just north of Dallas. The product was a book that sold for $19. A book that sells 10,000 copies is a huge success for a typical book publisher. We were selling 78,000 books every 30 days.

For another client, my superpower has created over $200,000 in sales in one day. The project will ultimately generate over $1 million in the next three months.

Many of my competitors—I prefer to call them colleagues because we're generally cordial—have enjoyed even more success with this superpower. There's a newsletter company in Connecticut called Bottom Line. It used to be called Boardroom. My colleagues generated well over $2 billion in sales in just 15 years for Boardroom.

One entrepreneur in California sold over $2.5 billion in merchandise by using this superpower, mainly through TV advertising late at night. Nobody pays attention to those ads, right?

Those of us who use this business superpower are anonymously and quietly generating tens of millions of dollars in revenue every day for companies around the world. These companies are growing and prospering. The owners are building vast wealth. These companies are hiring people and helping those people prosper. These companies are driving growth in the economy.

Name another group of professionals who can create this level of measurable revenue, growth, and prosperity every day—and by themselves, simply choosing words and putting those words in a certain order. So now you can fully understand why part of me gets a little upset when people give me the blank stare when I tell them I'm a "direct response copywriter."

You can understand why I call direct response copywriting a SUPERPOWER. You'll soon discover why I call direct response copywriters "The Greatest Salespeople You've Never Heard Of."

And one more thing: the investment in the work of a direct response copywriter is a FRACTION of the revenue generated. Let me give you an example. For one of the clients above, my fees equate to .0023% of total revenue. Maybe I should have called this book Give Me Ten Cents; I'll Get You a Dollar, or even more accurately, Give Me a Fraction of 1 Percent of Your Revenue, and I'll Make You Wealthy Beyond Your Wildest Dreams. But that title is too long.

Yes, my fees, and the fees of many of my colleagues, may seem high to some, but the smartest businesspeople, as I'll describe later, gleefully pay these fees and consider the investment a total bargain.

And everything is totally measurable down to the penny. The numbers are right there in black and white. I write some copy, the client mails it or makes it live on the Internet, and they know precisely how much revenue my copy has generated. DOWN TO THE PENNY.

There are lots of business theories and movements out there. Some are trendy. Some are not. What's big as I write?

- Emotional intelligence, a.k.a. "EQ"
- "The Tipping Point"
- Engagement
- Principles
- Blink
- TED Talks

I'm sure you can name more. But let's take a look at EQ. It's nice enough, I suppose. I haven't read any of the books but some people I know seem to dig it.

But here's the problem with EQ and everything else that's so super-trendy: THERE'S NO WAY TO MEASURE ANY OF IT. Someone who is into EQ can say, "It really helps me deal with people more effectively."

That's nice. But I can say, "What's the precise ROI?" I can say, "you can measure the impact of my work."

End of that conversation.

With direct response copywriting and its parent discipline, direct marketing, you can measure EVERYTHING TO THE PENNY. Nobody else in marketing or business can make this claim and back it up.

So, You Have a Choice

You can ignore this book and do something else like bake cookies and watch old Bonanza episodes on Netflix...or...you can pay close attention to what I'm going to reveal so you can understand what a direct response copywriter does and how you can put this superpower called direct response copywriting to work for your business.

I can think of 97 things I would rather do than write yet another book. I've already written or edited 17 books. That's enough, right? I write quickly, but books still take a lot of time. And just so you know, nobody has parked a Brinks truck outside my apartment and said, "Scott, take as much cash as you like out of the truck to write this book." Writing a book is a speculative venture, at best. I wrote a book about Caddyshack in 2006. I just received my first royalty check, and it was for $145.16; that's better than nothing, but not by much.

So...why am I writing this book? My first answer is: **TO HELP YOU GENERATE WHOPPING AMOUNTS OF MONEY** so you reach your financial and career goals faster and with much less effort.

Companies will often hire, at huge expense, marketing consultants and advertising agencies and get nothing in return. These agencies and consultants cannot, and will not, measure ROI unless they're in direct marketing. On the other hand, direct response copywriters closely measure ROI and are totally accountable. Yet companies will hire advertising agencies and marketing consultants who have zero interest in measuring results. It makes no sense...unless you're the advertising agency or marketing consultant.

My primary motivation for writing this book is to introduce the astonishing financial impact a direct response copywriter can have on a business. Once you understand my work, you'll want to start using a direct marketing model and you'll want to hire a direct response copywriter... maybe five. But good luck finding them. Fortunately for you, I show you how to find direct response copywriters later in this tome.

I'm not goofing around when I call direct response copywriting "The Ultimate Business Superpower." It's not hype. It's not brash hyperbole. I'm going to back it up with a ton of proof. People who are smart enough to hire direct response copywriters already have this proof and lots of it...in their bank accounts.

The Answer to That Question

There are lots of different ways to answer the question: "What does a direct response copywriter do?" Here are just a few of my answers over the years.

- I motivate your potential clients and customers to try products and services that will help them reach their goals.
- I'm a salesman using words on a page to sell.
- I help companies earn tens of millions of dollars, quickly.
- I write junk mail...although I don't call it junk mail; I call it "gold mail" because it can create so much revenue.
- I help companies sell more products and services, more often, at higher prices, by harnessing the power of the written word and proven sales psychology and techniques.
- As a writer, I choose words and put them in a certain order so the reader tries a product or service or calls a toll-free number...or takes another carefully measured action that leads to a sale.
- I help companies dramatically increase the value of the business so the owner, or owners, can eventually sell the business and reach their personal and financial goals.
- I'm in advertising and direct marketing.
- I write ads for the web, newspapers, magazines, radio, TV, and other places to help my clients get fabulously wealthy.

It's not easy; in fact, it can be extremely difficult to explain my work. Just the other day, I said to a friend, "Nobody really fully understands what I can do." But here's the reality: right now, as you read this book, someone somewhere is reading copy I have written. The words I write are motivating that reader to buy a product or service. Sometimes the product or service costs thousands of dollars.

In this book I'm also going to introduce you to direct marketing, which is the most powerful, accountable, and fun form of marketing.

Then I'm going to take you inside my office and show you how I use words, photos, and graphics, to generate all that cash for my clients. I will also detail, as I just mentioned, how to find, hire, and keep direct response copywriters. They're hard to find for people outside direct marketing. I know where they are.

This book will help:

- Business owners
- Marketing managers
- Advertising agency owners and executives who are seeing the fast decline of the branding game and understand they have to start showing actual ROI to clients.
- Marketing professors at top MBA schools—really!
- Students
- Fundraisers
- The employees of big, wealthy, and highly-respected business consultancy companies, like McKinsey, whose associates claim to know everything about business but who have no idea what a direct response copywriter is.
- People considering entering this business
- And many others.

I'm also going to reveal...

Why You Haven't Heard of Direct Response Copywriting

By now, you may be asking yourself...or I hope you are... "Why is a direct response copywriter such a mysterious figure?"

There are many answers to this question. Here are just a few.

- There isn't a single university or college course that teaches direct response copywriting or even direct marketing. I know a direct marketer who taught a direct marketing course at Tulane University in New Orleans, but he left academia to run a direct marketing consultancy and earn serious money without the nonsense that routinely comes with academia.[1]
- When people think about advertising, they usually think about witty and clever ads on television. That's not direct marketing. That's "general advertising," where the goal is to create awareness. I will show you why general advertising is a whopping waste of time and money for 99.9999 percent of businesses.
- People have seen or heard the work of a direct response copywriter, but they don't realize that someone actually has to write the TV ads, the web pages, the radio ads, the direct mail, and other forms of direct marketing.
- The number of direct response copywriters is extremely low, primarily because you can't learn how to be a direct response copywriter at university. However, there are 205 law schools in the United States, and they pump out 34,000 new potential lawyers every year. In fact, there are over 1.2 million lawyers in the United States. There are fewer than four hundred direct response copywriters with more than five years of proven experience IN THE WORLD and a chunk of them work for one company. There are thousands who call themselves direct response copywriters, with many more trying to break into the business. Many of the most experienced and accomplished direct response copywriters no longer write copy; they teach other copywriters. I would estimate there are 200,000 copywriters on the planet but only a tiny fraction are direct response copywriters. There's a huge difference, as you'll soon discover.
- Very few companies hire full-time direct response copywriters... although they should. You'll find 10-20 copywriters at a large

---

[1] Just prior to publication, I learned of a copywriting course taught at Augsburg University in Minneapolis.

corporation and around 5-10 at a mid-sized advertising agency but, again, no direct response copywriters.

- Surprisingly—or perhaps not—even marketing academics rarely understand the world of the direct response copywriter. Academics and famous theorists, many of whom have never actually sold anything ever, want to publish articles about curious theories and love to use buzzwords and buzz-phrases like "tipping point" and "brand-centric" and "splinterization" and "brand equity." Whatever all that means.

- Academia generally shuns direct marketers and direct marketing because our world is accountable. We're seen as crass and full of hype. Few people want to be accountable in business. We do.

- Advertising agencies rarely hire direct response copywriters because most advertising agencies don't want to go anywhere near direct marketing. Once again, that's because they don't want clients measuring results and ROI. Many advertising agencies want to create "image" and "brand awareness" and other such nonsense, none of which can be measured. The least favorite phrase at most advertising agencies is direct marketing. Why? Because direct marketing is a blood sport replete with failure, persistence, victories, and accountability.

And finally, here's another reason there aren't many experienced direct response copywriters around…and why you haven't heard of a direct response copywriter. It's not an easy profession.

In theory, there are no barriers to entry. You just need a laptop, a phone, and a business card saying, "Erica Smith, Direct Response Copywriter"… and, suddenly, you're a direct response copywriter.

But it's tough to break in and tougher to maintain a practice. Let's remember, we're accountable. My clients measure the results of my work to the penny. Direct response copywriters cannot hide behind awards, accolades, and pats on the back from colleagues and bosses for creativity. My copy has to generate revenue for my clients or they fire me.

When I produce revenue for a client or company, the client keeps me around. But if the copy doesn't generate revenue and/or leads, I get booted out. Very few people in any business actively seek this level of raw accountability.

Why Do Many Direct Response Copywriters Routinely Earn More Than Doctors, Lawyers, and "C-Suite" Executives?

A direct response copywriter is a writer—but more importantly, a direct response copywriter is a salesperson.

I once worked for a commercial real estate company as the director of communications. One of the brokers brought the owner of the company a deal worth over $10 million. The broker earned a $500,000 commission, approximately. And that was in the early 1990s.

In commercial and investment banking, some of the employees are essentially salespeople. They earn a lot of money for the bank and they get paid accordingly, sometimes into the millions every year.

Direct response copywriters are salespeople. The smartest marketing companies understand the value of hiring the top direct response copywriters and give them the opportunity to earn tens of thousands of dollars per project, even paying royalties and commissions into "two-comma" territory. Gleefully.

Marty Edelston was a newspaper advertising salesman who founded the company I mentioned earlier, Boardroom. This company became a publishing empire with help from Brian Kurtz, one of the most accomplished direct marketers of the last 30 years. Please read his excellent book, *Overdeliver*.

Brian and Marty sought, and found, the world's top copywriters and gave them the opportunity to earn millions in royalties. When Boardroom sent a royalty check to one of their stable of copywriters, Marty Edelston included a personal note saying "thank you" to the copywriter. Edelston paid the copywriters a dime, actually much less, and the copywriters gave him a dollar. No wonder he wrote thank you notes.

The world's greatest living direct response copywriter, Gary Bencivenga, before he retired, used to charge $25,000 per project, plus a royalty...and that was in the mid-1990s. Today, he would likely charge $100,000 plus a royalty. Companies lined up to hire Bencivenga, and I'm sure they would line up again today. Why were companies so eager to hire him? Because he brought them vast amounts of money. He brought revenue but he also helped to increase the value of their business. The new customers he brought to his clients were worth millions in lifetime value. And he also built a company's brand, without ever thinking about branding. More on this controversial subject later.

The smartest minds in marketing understand the value of a direct response copywriter and are happy to pay what may seem like whopping fees. This book will help you understand why you should join these marketers and stop people in your company from paying big fees to unaccountable advertising agencies, branding people, and so-called "marketing consultants" who love vapid concepts like emotional intelligence.

With the demand for direct response copywriters being high, and the supply being extremely low, it's no surprise that many direct response copywriters earn more than most doctors and lawyers. They should.

The Difference Between This Book and Other Business Books

There are lots of books about direct marketing and I recommend you read them all. There's a list of my favorite direct marketing books in the appendix. We're fortunate in direct marketing that many of our greatest practitioners have written books. And these books are choc-full of excellent advice based on what has actually worked and what has not. Spend $1,000 on these books and the return on your investment will be stratospheric. Make your colleagues read this book and the ones in the appendix.

Direct marketing is the ONLY business discipline where you directly measure results. Direct marketers know, to the penny, the impact of marketing spend. There are lots of business books about theories and "the latest greatest" way to run a business.

There's emotional intelligence, which I just mentioned. Look at all that Malcolm Gladwell stuff. There are thousands of tomes about leadership and team building. There's one about something called OKR, which claims to have some measurability, but does not when compared to direct marketing. There are books about corporate culture. There are books about branding, of course.

People in business digest these books and become proponents of the various philosophies. I know people who love the EQ theories but NONE OF THIS can be measured in any tangible way. Yet in direct marketing and direct response copywriting, we measure everything. The unit of measure?

MONEY. The stuff you can actually take to the bank. Can you take emotional intelligence and "the tipping point" to the bank? Good luck with that.

Sadly, there's some snobbery here. The so-called "thought leaders" plus the CMOs and other people who speak at marketing conferences and get media attention look down their noses at direct marketing. There are some exceptions, of course, but people in business gravitate toward the "next big thing" because it makes them look "with it" and forward-thinking. People in branding and other areas of marketing see direct marketing as so old and so past it. Yet right now, there are direct marketers and direct response copywriters taking in massive revenue using direct marketing techniques.

Oh well. I'll be over here making the cash register ring while the "thought leaders" and other brain-waves are talking about unproven theories that have never worked and never will.

But Wait! There's More!

You won't get the information in this book from ANY business professor at ANY university or business school. You won't get it from so-called "marketing experts" who have never really sold anything and are famous for being famous. You won't get it from some vacuous TED Talk. And you won't get it from even the top business newspapers, magazines, and websites. I know a famous marketing "expert" who speaks at least 15 times a year at marketing conferences, including his own. He tells audiences around the world NOT to use direct response copywriters because they write too much copy. He's totally wrong.

And, sadly, he's not the only marketing consultant who tells people that direct marketing is dead. You'll discover why you MUST ignore these speakers and consultants if you genuinely want to generate millions in revenue and dramatically increase the value of your business.

A lot of what you'll find in this book will seriously annoy people in "general" advertising—the unaccountable form of marketing that focuses on branding and awareness. I'm not the first writer to expose the faults in branding advertising and get a little giddy about direct marketing; David Ogilvy never really liked general advertising, even though he worked successfully in that field. I will talk more about Ogilvy later in this book. If you happen to work in general advertising then I will convert you to direct marketing.

Ultimately, this book is about YOU and YOUR success in business.

Strap yourself in. It's going to be a wild ride as you discover the "hidden" profession of direct response copywriting and how YOU can harness this genuine business superpower to grow your business, reach your financial and personal goals, plus give you a whopping advantage over your competitors.

Even better, if you meet a direct response copywriter in a bar, airplane, or hotel, you will know exactly what they do. Which is nice.

Part 1
CHANGING YOUR MARKETING MINDSET

CHAPTER 1

The Power of Direct Marketing.

You know what marketing is. But what is direct marketing? You'll find a number of different definitions.

Here's mine.

Direct marketing is selling directly to current and potential consumers through various media, including mail, TV, radio, telephone, and the Internet. Direct marketing uses proven, ethical techniques to gain the attention of prospective customers. Direct marketing then requests an instant response from the potential customer. Direct marketing closely measures this response and constantly strives to improve response to generate more revenue, more often.

Notice a key word I included in the second sentence: RESPONSE. That's why many people call direct marketing direct response marketing and it's why I call myself a direct response copywriter.

You've seen examples of direct marketing and direct response copywriting, likely without realizing it. In fact, you see examples every day. You also see plenty of general advertising that simply tries to improve product awareness. It's important to understand the difference.

Think about the last time you watched prime time TV. Maybe you saw a 30-second advertisement for a company that provides retirement services. You likely saw happy smiling older people enjoying their dream retirement, driving sports cars, walking on the beach, visiting art galleries in Lichtenstein, and so on. But there was no specific call to action at the end of the advertisement. The ad ended and it was on to the next ad. Maybe you saw those popular ads for Dos Equis beer. You saw slightly over-the-top ads featuring "The Most Interesting Man in the World." Funny and entertaining, but, at the end of the ad, there's nobody asking you to call a toll-free number, visit a website, or rush into your local liquor store.

Now think about some late-night TV.

You've seen a three-minute commercial selling some type of household product, like a blanket, a set of knives, a dietary supplement, acne cream, or some type of cleaning solution. These ads have a tried and tested structure, which I'll reveal later in this book. The ad ends by telling you to call a toll-free number RIGHT NOW. That's a pure example of direct marketing. A direct response copywriter wrote the advertisement.

Let's look at your mail. Sometimes you'll get a postcard from a political candidate. You'll see a photo plus some words telling you where the candidate stands on various issues. That's general advertising. But other mail you receive is more likely to be direct response, listing the benefits of the products or services and then telling you take a specific action, most likely calling a toll-free number. Direct mail remains a powerful way to generate millions in revenue with a relatively small investment.

What about the Internet? Most websites and webpages are filled with fluffy copy replete with clichés, hype, and vagueness. I define hype as unproven claims usually accompanied by a lot of exclamation marks!!!!!!!!!

Other webpages get your attention with a headline, provide benefits backed up with proof, and finally, tell you to CLICK HERE NOW or BUY NOW at the end of the page. These webpages are pure direct response. I've written thousands of these pages and they have generated hundreds of millions in revenue (over $400 million in the last six years for my clients).

One of Golf's Great Innovators Has Solved this Problem

Remember Barney Adams? He was the founder of Adams Golf and he also invented those awesome "Tight Lies" clubs that FINALLY made it easy to hit fairway woods. He also made other great clubs.

After selling Adams Golf to TaylorMade, Barney Adams turned his attention to improving "old school" putter shafts and created an all-new putter shaft using the latest technology. After all, driver and iron shafts are packed with technology these days, and putter shafts had been largely ignored.

The new putter shaft is called THE STABILITY SHAFT and it's now available to Revolution Golfers.

Now ... let's take a look at THE STABILITY SHAFT in more detail.

Introducing THE STABILITY SHAFT ... The Putter Shaft FINALLY Gets a Much-Needed Overhaul ... And It Will Immediately Help You Sink More Putts

Here's an example of copy from a promotion I wrote for a golf product. In the direct response model, we're directly generating measurable revenue.

Join us for a
global meeting
of the minds.

PUT OUR TAILORED INSIGHTS TO WORK FOR YOU.

To make confident decisions about the future, middle market leaders need a different kind of advisor. One who starts by understanding where you want to go and then brings the ideas and insights of an experienced global team to help get you there.

Experience the power of being understood.
Experience RSM.

rsmus.com

THE POWER OF BEING UNDERSTOOD
AUDIT | TAX | CONSULTING

RSM US LLP is the U.S. member firm of RSM International, a global network of independent audit, tax and consulting firms. Visit rsmus.com/aboutus for more information regarding RSM US LLP and RSM International.

A classic example of a branding advertisement. It looks good. A little bit of copy, most of it vague. "The Power of Being Understood." Please tell me what that means. The goal of the ad, if there is one, is to create awareness of the company's name.

How direct response advertising can increase your sales and profits

Even if your company has never used direct response, read what Ogilvy & Mather has learned from half a billion coupons

Ogilvy & Mather has created more than $150,000,000 worth of direct response advertising—in mail and media—for the American Express Company, Burpee Seeds, Cessna Aircraft, Nationwide Insurance, Shell Oil, Sears, Roebuck and other clients.

In the process, we have learned that direct response advertising can help sell $750,000 jet airplanes as well as 25¢ packets of flower seeds.

Here are a few of the ways Ogilvy & Mather uses this most *accountable* form of advertising as part of our clients' marketing programs. Some of them may be useful to you.

1. Direct response can be your "secret weapon" in new product introductions. Cessna Aircraft used direct mail in its introduction of "Citation," a new $750,000 business jet. Ogilvy & Mather began mailings to a list of key corporate executives and their chief pilots long before the first "Citation" was in production.

Sales leads in response to these mailings helped "Citation" become the world's largest selling business jet in just one year.

2. A remarkably efficient way to reach your best prospects. Today Mercedes-Benz diesel-engine cars sell well in America. But ten years ago, it was difficult to identify and reach the limited number of high-potential prospects for the diesel cars.

Ogilvy & Mather compiled a list of people who matched the demographic profile of *existing* diesel-car owners, then sent them an 8-page letter. As a direct result of the letter, Mercedes-Benz sold 716 diesel cars within eight weeks.

3. How to land your most profitable new customers. Ogilvy & Mather has developed special acquisition programs designed to acquire new credit customers for our clients on a highly selective basis.

These programs combine sophisticated list segmentation techniques with a remarkably precise formula that identifies the profitable customer; establishes his real value; and reveals how much should be spent to acquire him.

PRESENT VALUE FORMULA

$$PV = \int_0^s (a \cdot r \cdot m \cdot e^{-t/\lambda} - a \cdot r \cdot d \cdot e^{-t/\lambda} \cdot {}_{a}C_{g} \cdot e^{-t/\lambda}) e^{-\rho t} dt - Sc^{-\rho L} - M - RC_p$$

This is an example of a "present value" economic model. This model—programmed with ten trends and approximations and discounted rates—reveals the true cost of acquiring a new credit customer and predicts the net profit he will return over the next 5 years.

4. How to build a bank of localised leads for your sales force. The pinpoint accuracy of direct mail makes it the ideal medium for obtaining sales leads exactly where you need them most.

Our computerized "Commodity Futures List Bank" supplies *localised* leads to Merrill Lynch representatives from Saskatchewan to San Francisco.

5. Direct response can make television dollars work harder. Television commercials for American Express Credit Cards end with a request for a direct response by phone. This produces tens of thousands of applications for the Card.

Ogilvy & Mather has also improved response to direct mailings by timing mail drops to coincide with television advertising.

6. Direct response is an indispensable element in successful travel advertising. Direct response, in mail as well as other media, has proven to be a key ingredient in marketing travel.

The secret is to close the sale by mail—or to obtain a highly qualified lead—instead of wasting a fortune mailing expensive booklets and pamphlets.

Ogilvy & Mather coupon advertisements for Cunard have paid out four times over in immediate ticket sales.

A direct mail offer of free London theater tickets produced response rates as high as 26 percent for the British Tourist Authority.

7. You can now sell high-ticket items direct by mail. Today's ever-increasing distribution of credit cards has revolutionized marketing by mail.

Credit cards now make direct mail practical for selling sewing machines, calculators, color television sets and many other products costing hundreds, even thousands, of dollars.

As sales costs escalate, more and more manufacturers will turn to this new way of selling direct to the consumer.

How to capitalize on new profit opportunities in direct marketing.

Today, more and more major corporations are considering direct marketing in their search for new sources of profit. It pays to look before you leap into this highly specialized business.

Ogilvy & Mather has found that the odds for success improve if you can use your own customer list and retail packages as an entrée into direct marketing.

One mail marketing business we helped develop now does fifty million dollars in annual sales.

Techniques that work best in direct response advertising

8. Challenge dogma. Ogilvy & Mather has found that it often pays to challenge dogma and test for breakthroughs. Our tests show that:

• An inexpensive offset letter can often out-pull far more costly computer letters.

• "On-page coupon-envelopes" can be more cost efficient than expensive preprint inserts.

• An innovative *letter* can be more important to your success than a big, beautiful 4-color brochure.

Note: These examples are not offered to create new dogma but to emphasize that *it pays to test.*

This innovative "personal" letter from Yves Yves Whiskovitz—created from hundreds of letters actually written by the great composer—substantially increased response for a new record client.

9. How to make long copy succeed. Tests show long copy usually, but not always, pulls more orders than short copy in direct response advertising.

Specifics are the key ingredient in successful long copy. Glittering generalities turn readers off. Beware of long copy that is lazy. Supply facts and figures. They impress the reader and help close the sale.

10. The way you position your offer can double your response. We recently split-run double your response against a successful Burpee advertisement that featured a $1 offer in the headline.

All three new advertisements improved response. The one shown below increased results 112 percent.

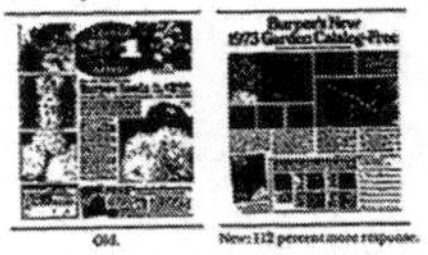

Old. New: 112 percent more response.

The reason: The new advertisement offered a free catalog—and clearly positioned Burpee as America's leading breeder of new flower and vegetable varieties for the home gardener.

11. It pays to demonstrate. Product demonstrations are not easy to do in direct mail. But they are worth the effort. They can be exceptionally effective.

Ogilvy & Mather's mailing for Cessna's "Citation" jet enclosed a recording that contrasted the "Citation's" low noise levels with competitive jets—and even an electric blender.

The record proved Cessna's case; words alone could only have made a claim.

12. Asking the reader to quiz himself increases response. Inviting readers to take a quiz involves them with your advertising.

This can pay handsome dividends, as this split-run test shows.

WHICH AD PULLED BEST?

The advertisements on the right included the sender to quiz himself—as we are doing here by asking you topics in which ad pulled best. (The "quiz," of course, by 126 percent.)

13. The "close" is crucial in direct response. The reader who makes a mental note to "mail the coupon later" usually never does.

One survey showed that less than a third of the readers who *intended* to send in a coupon actually did so.

Ogilvy & Mather uses a four-point checklist to ensure that our copy does all it can to get the reader to tear out the coupon before he turns the page.

14. The position of your advertisement can make the difference between profit and loss. Tests show that the back page of a publication, or the back of one of its sections, can pull 150 percent better than inside pages.

POSC—page opposite third cover in magazines—is another winning position. You can often buy it without paying a premium.

15. New direct mail techniques. The efficiency of mailings can be substantially improved through new techniques.

These techniques—"merge-purge," "hotline" mailings, timing sequence—produce more response for every dollar invested.

16. Separate the wheat from the chaff. List segmentation concentrates your dollars where they will do the most good.

List segmentation—by both demographic and psychographic factors—becomes critical to profit as direct mail costs go up and up.

Take full advantage of computer technology and sophisticated segmentation procedures—zip code analyses and consumer criteria grids.

They now make it practical to single out your best prospects.

Separating the wheat from the chaff is the secret to successful direct mail.

17. Pretesting copy can reduce costs and improve response rates. Ogilvy & Mather's Research Department has developed inexpensive techniques that rank copy promises *before* mail or media testing.

This saves time and money—and increases your chances for success.

COPY PROMISES CAN VARY WIDELY IN APPEAL

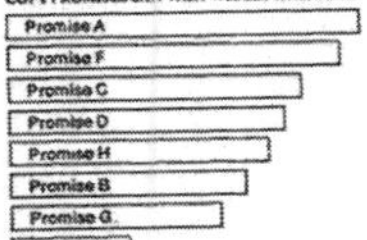

Promise A
Promise F
Promise C
Promise D
Promise H
Promise B
Promise G
Promise E

"Promise Test" research ranks your selling points before mail or media testing. In the above example (from an actual test for winning record client) the promise provided by the weakest one.

18. Success can be exported. Ogilvy & Mather has found that direct response principles which work in the U.S. are frequently just as effective when applied abroad.

We export these principles to 57 Ogilvy & Mather offices in 30 countries, and coordinate international campaigns through New York.

Example: A series of new direct response advertisements and mailings, initiated in New York and carried out by our Paris office, tripled response for one of the leading book clubs in France.

19. The most accountable form of advertising. Claude Hopkins titled his famous book "Scientific Advertising."

He emphasized that direct response the most *accountable* form of advertising. It allows you to measure precisely what every dollar invested returns in sales and profits.

We use coupons and sales conversion rates to evaluate the specific contribution direct response advertising makes to our client's marketing programs. Results show direct response has increased sales and profits in almost every case.

An Invitation

Ogilvy & Mather's Direct Response Division employs three dozen people who specialize in this demanding discipline.

The body of our experience—which can only be hinted at in the space available here—is revealed in a slide presentation: "What Ogilvy & Mather has learned about direct response advertising and marketing."

To arrange a presentation, please mail the coupon today.

Ogilvy & Mather

Barry Blau, Managing Director
Ogilvy & Mather, Direct Response Division
2 East 48th Street, New York, New York 10017

I would like to arrange for a special presentation of "What Ogilvy & Mather has learned about direct response advertising and marketing."

Name	
Company	
Title	
Address	
City	State Zip
Telephone	

Here's an ad from David Ogilvy's agency. It's a direct response print ad selling the services of his agency. How many agencies produce brilliant direct marketing like this? Almost zero.

If you want to see an orgy of general/branding advertising then watch The Super Bowl. You'll see clever and witty advertising for anything from tortilla chips to beer. I have only ever seen one direct response advertisement during the Super Bowl and it was for GoDaddy. The ad told viewers to visit the company's website to see a free video.

The 24 Pillars of Direct Response Marketing

By now, you're getting a sense of the difference between direct response marketing and general, or branding, advertising.

Here are the "pillars" of direct marketing in more detail.

ONE. Building marketing around very specific goals. Many companies say, "We're going to spend 3.5% of last year's revenue on marketing." Direct marketers set a goal that's often linked to personal and business goals. Then they spend what they need to reach those goals based on detailed metrics.

TWO. Traffic, a.k.a. potential clients and customers. Every piece of direct response advertising must have an audience. You can rent or buy databases, also called lists, of potential clients for direct mail. You can build your own database online or use another company's email database. Many online direct marketers advertise heavily on websites like Google, Yahoo, and Facebook. Advertising networks help companies advertise on websites like The Weather Channel. It's easier than ever to buy highly targeted traffic. But it's vital to have someone buying the traffic who is an expert or you will quickly waste a lot of money.

THREE. Research. You have to know your audience and you have to know what they will buy and how much they are willing to spend. Demographic information is valuable but psychographic information is more important. I ask my clients to send over absolutely everything they have about their clients. "Back up the truck," I tell them, when it comes to information I need to write their direct response ads.

FOUR. Front end acquisition. It's the process of finding new customers and bringing them into your fold so you can sell them more products, more often. Most direct marketers recommend a breakeven financial strategy when it comes to front end acquisition.

FIVE. Back end sales. Once they have acquired clients and customers through front end marketing, they make their money on "the back end" by selling services and products to this database.

SIX. RFM - Recency. Frequency. Monetary. RFM is the analysis of customer value. It is a technique used to determine quantitatively which customers are the best ones by examining how recently a customer has purchased (recency), how often they purchase (frequency), and how much they spend (monetary).

SEVEN. A scientific approach. The seminal book in direct marketing is *Scientific Advertising* by Claude Hopkins. The book is available free on the Internet but you can also find annotated and curated versions that explain some of the theories. Hopkins published the book in 1923, and every word is relevant today. Direct marketing is 90 percent science and 10 percent creativity.

EIGHT. The offer. It's not discounting. Essentially, the offer is: here's what you get when you hand over your money. Stating the offer clearly is the heart of every direct marketing promotion. Here's an example of a bad offer: sunlamps in the Sahara Desert. A good offer: premium quality golf balls for 60% of what others charge. Or clean, cool water for a person who is crossing the Gobi Desert.

NINE. Creativity. Some of the most hardcore direct marketing people I know don't think that creativity has a role in direct response. There's room for creativity but only in small doses. Creativity in direct marketing is the clear presentation of the offer with the copy, graphics, and proof elements. Creativity is NOT coming up with new strategies and it's NOT originality. See #10.

TEN. Using what's worked before. We all know what works in direct marketing. These pillars work. So we use them. Technology changes. Media changes. People don't. The same direct marketing strategies that worked two hundred years ago will work two hundred years from now.

ELEVEN. A focus on what people really want. What do people want? Clever, funny advertising? No. They want solutions to problems and they want to feel better about themselves. They want to...

- Look great
- Feel great
- Have more money

- Have more sex
- Beat aging
- Drive a nicer car (than their neighbor)
- Help people they like
- Get where they want to get
- Enjoy financial security
- Overcome health issues
- Be smarter
- Have more free time
- Gain freedom from daily hassles
- Work less
- Be better and look better than other people
- Live where they want to live

I'm sure you can think of other factors that motivate people to take action, but, in general, people wake up thinking, I want to feel better about myself today. Always remember: the most important person to someone is himself. I'm constantly answering the question the potential customer is asking: "What's in it for me?"

TWELVE. Matching the benefits of the product or service to people's desires and vice versa. Eugene Schwartz wrote extensively about this, specifically that you can't persuade people to buy a product they don't want, like sunlamps in the Sahara. Direct marketing is a method of channeling people's desires into wanting to try the product or service the company is selling. It's one reason I like to use the word "motivating" instead of "persuading."

THIRTEEN. Overcoming objections. Even if a potential customer has serious joint pain and the product you're selling deals successfully with that problem, the customer will be skeptical and have objections like "I don't know the company" or "I can't trust the ingredients." Every direct response copywriter must overcome every potential objection.

FOURTEEN. A willingness to fail. Every direct marketer has failed spectacularly. But direct marketers pick themselves off the floor and keep going. They learn from their direct marketing mistakes. When something works, they try to make it work even better. Branding advertisers don't measure anything of any value so how can they know what to improve?

How do they know what actually works? They say they have ways to measure impact but they don't.

FIFTEEN. Proof. General advertisers love to make big claims, usually without any type of proof. One of my clients sent me a list of 42 ways to prove claims made about a product. I'll detail this list later in the book but here's an example of one common proof element: before and after photos or videos showing the product actually works.

SIXTEEN. Telling the truth. You'll find liars and scammers in business, politics, education, and in marketing—every walk of life. Some people think direct marketing is one big scam. Scammers are not direct marketers. I don't work with clients who ask me to make things up. I put products and services in the best possible light but I always tell the truth. The top direct marketers tell the truth and back up their claims with proof elements discovered during research.

SEVENTEEN. A guarantee. Every direct marketer backs up the product or service with a guarantee. One of my clients offers a 365-day guarantee and the company stands behind it. Returns are usually between 2-3% of sales.

EIGHTEEN. Direct response copywriting. Direct marketers understand the value of a direct response copywriter. The top direct marketers actively seek the top direct response copywriters. Serious marketers fully understand that, without direct response copy, they will sell absolutely nothing.

NINETEEN. Active...not passive. Direct marketers go after the customers they want. They don't wait for them to appear. The biggest marketing mistake people make is to use advertising and marketing methods that rely on hope and image, and yet 99.99 percent of people in business make this mistake.

TWENTY. Accountability. Everything is measured to the penny in direct marketing. We're accountable in direct marketing.

TWENTY-ONE. Testing. This pillar should probably be higher up on the list. Direct marketers test like crazy. It's much faster to test on the Internet than direct mail. Testing reveals what works and what fails. John Caples wrote a superb book about direct marketing titled *Tested Advertising Methods*. It details what works and what doesn't based on real results and actual revenue.

TWENTY-TWO. A constant desire to improve. Direct marketers are never satisfied. They are constantly trying to beat their best efforts. And the top direct marketers I know are constantly educating themselves by reading books, attending seminars, and participating in peer groups.

TWENTY-THREE. Generating recurring income streams. You can have success selling individual products and one-time services but the ultimate prize in direct marketing is different—a lot of people paying a monthly fee or regularly buying products.

TWENTY-FOUR. Treating customers the right way. Here's what Gary Bencivenga wrote:

"I believe in selling with integrity. The strongest ads tell the truth dramatically. You don't have to lie, shortchange your customers, sully your good name, or cut corners. Treat your customers by the Golden Rule and they will reward you with much more gold."

Does It Have to Be Obnoxious?

Direct marketing can be loud and brash, obnoxious even. And there are plenty of obnoxious people in direct marketing. But direct response advertising does not have to be annoying. In fact, it shouldn't be. I can get attention without being stupid, brash, or loud. How? By providing valuable information and clearly stating the offer and answering the primary question in the customer's mind: "What's in it for me?"

But direct marketing is not about being tepid. It's also about the first word in direct marketing: DIRECT.

Now that you understand more about direct marketing, it's time to reveal the typical, and expensive, marketing mistakes you must avoid.

One additional word about direct marketing. There are other ways to market your product or service and these can generate revenue. But the numbers PROVE that direct marketing is the most powerful, accountable, and effective form of marketing. NOTHING can beat even the mediocre implementation of direct marketing. Yet, shockingly, intelligent business people fail to use direct marketing either through ignorance, lies provided by so-called experts, or the mistaken belief that clever advertising will lead to awareness that will lead to a stampede of buyers who are desperate for their product or service.

CHAPTER 2

Marketing Myths, Marketing Mistakes, Marketing Lies, and Why You Should Fire Your Advertising Agency IMMEDIATELY.*

* Unless your agency practices direct marketing at an elite level.

When I meet businesspeople, they have a lot of misconceptions about advertising. These misconceptions lead to a loss of revenue. So, let me attack these misconceptions.

This exercise is vital when it comes to understanding direct marketing and the value of a direct response copywriter. I'm also going to detail marketing mistakes and describe why branding advertising agencies fail their clients. If you're a merchant of branding, a 'brand equity specialist,' perhaps, you might want to look away.

Let's start with common myths.

Myth One. People don't read anymore. Garbage! Or as a former school principal at one of my schools would say: "PURE, UNADULTERATED BALDERDASH!"

And for the record, the origins of the word "balderdash" come from 16th Century England. Balderdash is a nasty and disgusting drink.

When people are genuinely interested in what you have to offer, they will demand as much information as possible; in fact, they won't be able to find enough information. There's a popular magazine devoted to running...called Running. Why? Runners want as much information as possible about, you guessed it, RUNNING.

Running may seem like a simple form of exercise to most people, including me, but to serious runners it's different. Runners want as much information as they can possibly get about running, which is why there's a magazine about their hobby, plus numerous websites and books all devoted to running. Runners even send monthly newsletters to each other. The subject? Surprise, surprise...running!

Think about your favorite hobby or passion. Can you get enough information about it? No.

Later on, I will detail why tons of copy always beats very little copy when it comes to actual money earned. People read more than ever.

Myth Two. The more that people in your office like your advertisement or website, the better the advertisement or website. It's not about whether your ad or website is pretty. It's about two things:

- Will it create the desired response?
- How much money will it make for the company?

Having an ad, website, or even a direct marketing campaign that looks good is fine, but looking good is not the point. The point is to create marketing that motivates targeted prospects to take the action you want them to take. The action could be motivating the customer to crack open their wallet and pull out their credit card and buy; or it could be motivating someone to call a toll-free number to order; or it could be motivating the customer to provide some contact details so you can follow up later and make the sale.

Here's a brutal truth in direct marketing.

Ugly wins.

Do you want to win design awards and have people tell you that your advertising looks good? Or do you want the phone to ring with people eager to buy your products? Do you want a pretty website or a website that generates money?

I remember sitting down one day with a company in Connecticut. They hired me for a day so we could talk about improvements to one of their direct mail pieces. It was a mortgage and refinance company. The founder of the company started his business by mailing one thousand letters to people he thought would need/want a mortgage or similar financial product. It became a multi-million dollar company.

The mailing they were using was super ugly but it was working really well. They wanted me to beat that mailing and by "beat" I mean make some changes to boost response and revenue.

Just before lunch, three young graphic designers and a copywriter arrived from Manhattan. They had produced a beautiful new mailer with "clever" copy.

The marketing director loved the new look and she asked me what I thought.

"It will be a disaster," was my reply. "Your current winner is ugly. Let's work on the copy and the offer so we can test it and try to beat the current winner. Let's stick with ugly because ugly wins."

The young graphic designers and the copywriter were not happy with me. Nor was the marketing director. The word "apoplectic" comes to mind. I never heard from that company again. I'm confident the great-looking piece failed and a slightly tweaked version of the "ugly" piece likely gave them an increase in revenue.

You must design the advertisement specifically for the people you know or believe will purchase your product or service. The goal is to motivate people to take an action that leads to a sale.

Myth Three. If I target the entire country, I will get more sales. Companies with billions in sales, like Budweiser, need to reach tens of millions of people every time they advertise. Are you a company with billions in sales? No? Then you must get targeted and find the people who want and/ or need your product plus can afford it. You can find these people through Internet advertising and direct mail. You turn them into customers by harnessing the power of direct marketing and direct response copywriting. I just spoke with a potential client who has a database of one thousand companies they know will be good targets for the highly specialized service they provide. That's my type of company.

Myth Four. Don't offend anyone and don't exclude anyone. Direct marketing excludes people who are not good prospects for a product or service. You don't want to be rude or offensive but you don't want phone calls and emails from people who will just waste your time. I make a point on my website to tell price shoppers to go away and not contact me. My clients are looking for a copywriter who can actually get results and they are willing to pay for my experience, track record, expertise, and ability to generate cash.

Myth Five. If my competitors are doing it, then I should do it too. If all your competitors' ads generate epic results, go ahead and imitate them—but without plagiarizing. Most advertising I've seen, however, is literally doomed to fail or produce subpar results. Why imitate that?

Myth Six. Word-of-mouth advertising is the best type of advertising. But it can also be the worst. Let me illustrate. I regularly think about a woman I met in a ski lodge in Colorado. She would sit in the lobby, talking, non-stop, for hours, about local restaurants and other businesses. This woman was the type of person with an opinion about everything. She routinely interrupted people just to provide the amassed with her views. She would say awful things about most restaurants in the town. She would have glowing reviews of a few restaurants but there was more vitriol than bonhomie. I knew the restaurants she was slagging and they are excellent. The bad recommendations from that woman? That's word-of-mouth advertising, my friends.

Myth Seven. A picture is worth a thousand words. Open up a flashy magazine like Vogue or Vanity Fair and you'll see lots of ads that subscribe to the myth above: ads with extremely small amounts of copy plus a photo of a model, or models, wearing beautiful clothes. But there's a problem here. Have you ever watched someone going through a magazine like this? They fly through, not paying much, if any, attention. If the photo was truly worth a thousand words, then the reader would stop and pay as much attention as they would to one thousand words of convincing and attention-grabbing direct response copy. There's a definite place for photos, videos, graphics, and related images in direct response advertising but they must be used to augment and complement the sales message in the copy. Advertising that's only copy can successfully sell. Advertising that's only photos will NEVER sell as well as advertising that's only words.

David Ogilvy, who founded the agency Ogilvy and Mather, wrote a series of full-page newspaper ads that were all copy. Here's one of them.

How to create advertising that sells

by David Ogilvy

Ogilvy & Mather has created over $1,480,000,000 worth of advertising, and spent $4,900,000 tracking the results.

Here, with all the dogmatism of brevity, are 38 of the things we have learned.

1. The most important decision. We have learned that the effect of your advertising on your sales depends more on this decision than on any other: *How should you position your product?*

Should you position SCHWEPPES as a soft drink—or as a mixer?

Should you position DOVE as a product for dry skin or as a product which gets hands really clean?

The results of your campaign depend less on how we write your advertising than on how your product is positioned. It follows that positioning should be decided before the advertising is created.

Research can help. Look before you leap.

2. Large promise. The second most important decision is this: what should you promise the customer? A promise is not a claim, or a theme, or a slogan. It is a *benefit for the consumer.*

It pays to promise a benefit which is unique and competitive. And the product must *deliver* the benefit you promise.

Most advertising promises *nothing.* It is doomed to fail in the marketplace.

"Promise, large promise, is the soul of an advertisement"—said Samuel Johnson.

3. Brand image. Every advertisement should contribute to the complex symbol which is the brand image. Ninety-five percent of all advertising is created *ad hoc.* Most products lack any consistent image from one year to another.

The manufacturer who dedicates his advertising to building the most sharply defined personality for his brand gets the largest share of the market.

4. Big ideas. Unless your advertising is built on a BIG IDEA it will pass like a ship in the night.

It takes a BIG IDEA to jolt the consumer out of his indifference—to make him *notice* your advertising, *remember* it and *take action.*

Big ideas are usually *simple* ideas. Said Charles Kettering, the great General Motors inventor: "This problem, when solved, will be simple."

BIG SIMPLE IDEAS are not easy to come by. They require genius—and midnight oil. A truly big one can be continued for twenty years—like our Eyepatch for Hathaway shirts.

5. A first-class ticket. It pays to give most products an image of quality—a first-class ticket.

Ogilvy & Mather has been conspicuously successful in doing this—for Pepperidge, Hathaway, Mercedes-Benz, Schweppes, Dove and others.

If your advertising looks ugly, consumers will conclude that your product is shoddy, and they will be less likely to buy it.

6. Don't be a bore. Nobody was ever *bored* into buying a product. Yet most advertising is impersonal, detached, cold—and dull.

It pays to *involve* the customer.

Talk to her like a human being. Charm her. Make her hungry. Get her to participate.

7. Innovate. Start trends—instead of following them. Advertising which follows a fashionable fad, or is imitative, is seldom successful.

It pays to *innovate,* to blaze new trails.

But innovation is risky unless you pretest your innovation with consumers. Look before you leap.

8. Be suspicious of awards. The pursuit of creative awards seduces creative people from the pursuit of sales.

We have been unable to establish any correlation whatever between awards and sales.

At Ogilvy & Mather we now give an annual award for the campaign which contributes the most to *sales.*

Successful advertising sells the product without drawing attention to itself. It rivets the consumer's attention on the *product.*

Make the product the hero of your advertising.

9. Psychological segmentation. Any good agency knows how to position products for *demographic* segments of the market—for men, for young children, for farmers in the South, etc.

But Ogilvy & Mather has learned that it often pays to position products for *psychological* segments of the market.

Our Mercedes-Benz advertising is positioned to fit nonconformists who scoff at "status symbols" and reject flimflam appeals to snobbery.

10. Don't bury news. It is easier to interest the consumer in a product when it is *new* than at any other point in its life. Many copywriters have a fatal instinct for burying news. This is why most advertising for new products fails to exploit the opportunity that genuine news provides.

It pays to launch your new product with a loud BOOM-BOOM.

11. Go the whole hog. Most advertising campaigns are too complicated. They reflect a long list of marketing objectives. They embrace the divergent views of too many executives. By attempting too many things, they achieve nothing.

It pays to boil down your strategy to *one* simple promise—and go the whole hog in delivering that promise.

What works best in television

12. Testimonials: Avoid irrelevant celebrities. Testimonial commercials are almost always successful—if you make them credible.

Either celebrities or real people can be effective. But avoid *irrelevant* celebrities whose fame has no natural connection with your product or your customers. Irrelevant celebrities steal attention from your product.

13. Problem-solution (don't cheat!) You set up a problem that the consumer recognizes.

Then you show how your product can solve that problem.

And you prove the solution.

This technique has always been above average in sales results, and it still is. But don't use it unless you can do so *without cheating;* the consumer isn't a moron, she is your wife.

14. Visual demonstrations. If they are honest, visual demonstrations are generally effective in the marketplace.

It pays to *visualize your promise.* It saves time. It drives the promise home. It is memorable.

15. Slice of life. These playlets are corny, and most copywriters detest them. But they have sold a lot of merchandise, and are still selling.

16. Avoid logorrhea. Make your *pictures* tell the story. What you *show* is more important than what you say.

Many commercials drown the viewer in a torrent of words. We call that logorrhea (rhymes with diarrhea).

We have created some great commercials *without* words.

17. On-camera voice. Commercials using on-camera voice do significantly better than commercials using voice-over.

18. Musical backgrounds. Most commercials use musical backgrounds. However, on the average, musical backgrounds reduce recall of your commercial. Very few creative people accept this. But we never heard of an agency using musical background under a new business presentation.

19. Stand-ups. The stand-up pitch can be effective, if it is delivered with straightforward honesty.

20. Burr of singularity. The average consumer now sees 20,000 commercials a year; poor dear.

Most of them slide off her memory like water off a duck's back.

Give your commercials a flourish of singularity, a burr that will stick in the consumer's mind. One such burr is the MNEMONIC DEVICE, or relevant symbol—like the crowns in our commercials for Imperial Margarine.

21. Animation & cartoons. Less than five percent of television commercials use cartoons or animation. They are less persuasive than live commercials.

The consumer cannot identify herself with the character in the cartoon. And cartoons do not invite belief.

However, Carson/Roberts, our partners in Los Angeles, tell us that animation can be helpful when you are talking to children.

They should know—they have addressed more than six hundred commercials to children.

22. Salvage commercials. Many commercials which test poorly can be salvaged.

The faults revealed by the test can be corrected. We have *doubled* the effectiveness of a commercial simply by re-editing it.

23. Factual vs. emotional. Factual commercials tend to be more effective than emotional commercials.

However, Ogilvy & Mather has made some emotional commercials which have been successful in the marketplace. Among these are our campaigns for Maxwell House Coffee and Hershey's Milk Chocolate.

24. Grabbers. We have found that commercials with an exciting opening hold their audience at a higher level than commercials which begin quietly.

What works best in print

25. Headlines. On the average, five times as many people read the headline as read the body copy.

It follows that, if you don't sell the product in your headline, you have wasted 80 percent of your money. That is why most Ogilvy & Mather headlines include the brand name and the promise.

26. Benefit in headlines. Headlines that promise a benefit sell more than those that don't.

27. News in headlines. Time after time, we have found that it pays to inject genuine *news* into headlines.

The consumer is always on the lookout for new products, or new improvements in an old product, or new ways to use an old product.

Economists—even Russian economists—approve of this. They call it "informative" advertising. So do consumers.

28. Simple headlines. Your headline should *telegraph* what you want to say—in simple language. Readers do not stop to decipher the meaning of obscure headlines.

29. How many words in a headline? In headline tests conducted with the cooperation of a big department store, it was found that headlines of ten words or longer sold more goods than short headlines.

In terms of *recall,* headlines between eight and ten words are most effective.

In *mail-order* advertising, headlines between six and twelve words get the most coupon returns.

On the average, long headlines sell more merchandise than short ones—headlines like our "At 60 miles an hour, the loudest noise in this new Rolls-Royce comes from the electric clock."

30. Localize headlines. In local advertising it pays to include the name of the city in your headline.

31. Select your prospects. When you advertise a product which is consumed only by a special group, it pays to "flag" that group in your headline—MOTHERS, BED-WETTERS, GOING TO EUROPE?

32. Yes, people read long copy. Readership falls off rapidly up to fifty words, but drops very little between fifty and five hundred words. (This page contains 1909 words, and you are reading it.)

Ogilvy & Mather has used long copy—with notable success—for Mercedes-Benz, Cessna Citation, Merrill Lynch and Shell gasoline.

"The more you tell, the more you sell."

33. Story appeal in picture. Ogilvy & Mather has gotten notable results with photographs which suggest a story. The reader glances at the photograph and asks himself, "What goes on here?" Then he reads the copy to find out.

Harold Rudolph called this magic element "story appeal." The more of it you inject into your photograph, the more people look at your advertisement.

It is easier said than done.

34. Before & after. Before and After advertisements are somewhat above average in attention value.

Any form of "visualized contrast" seems to work well.

35. Photographs vs. artwork. Ogilvy & Mather has found that photographs work better than drawings—almost invariably.

They attract more readers, generate more appetite appeal, are more believable, are better remembered, pull more coupons, and sell more merchandise.

36. Use captions to sell. On the average, twice as many people read the captions under photographs as read the body copy.

It follows that you should never use a photograph without putting a caption under it; and each caption should be a miniature advertisement for the product—complete with brand name and promise.

37. Editorial layouts. Ogilvy & Mather has had more success with editorial layouts than with "addy" layouts.

Editorial layouts get higher readership than conventional advertisements.

38. Repeat your winners. Scores of great advertisements have been discarded before they have begun to pay off.

Readership can actually *increase* with repetition—up to five repetitions.

Is this all we know?

These findings apply to most categories of products. But not to all.

Ogilvy & Mather has developed a separate and specialized body of knowledge on what makes for success in advertising *food products, tourist destinations, proprietary medicines, children's products*—and other classifications.

But this special information is revealed only to the clients of Ogilvy & Mather.

Ogilvy & Mather

2 East 48th Street, New York, N.Y. 10017

An ad with no photos. Copy sells, not photos. Images are proof elements to back up the claims in the copy.

A picture is worth a thousand words?

NO.

In fact, I was just in New York City and went to a photography exhibit. Each photo needed around three hundred words of copy to explain what was happening in the photo.

Myth Eight. A marketing professor at a business school knows how to market. Let's head to Durham, North Carolina, specifically to Duke University and its Fuqua School of Business.

Marketing Course 807 is called Marketing Strategy, and the instructor is Christine Moorman. She's the T. Austin Finch Senior Professor of Marketing at Duke. Who is/was T. Austin Finch? Maybe Ms. Moorman will tell me one day.

From the course description:
"...the customer focus of the course means that capabilities are evaluated relative to their contribution to customer value and not as inherently valuable."

If you can tell me what that means, please let me know.

Ms. Moorman is the author of the book *Strategy from the Outside In: Profiting from Customer Value*. She's a lifetime academic. The book won the American Marketing Association Foundation's Berry-AMA 2011 Book Prize for the best book in marketing. She's published a TON about marketing but, based on her resume, she's never actually held a full-time job in marketing or sales. She's never spent any time in the real marketing battleground, getting her nose bloodied and her teeth kicked in, getting rejected and failing. Has she actually sold anything? Has her income depended on her ability to sell products and services? Has she put words down on a page, words that have motivated someone to pull a credit card out of their wallet and hit the "Buy now" button? I see no evidence to answer "yes" to any of these questions. Academia is fine but I'm going to learn a lot more from people who have actually sold stuff. So will you.

Her colleague, Carl F. Mela, spent five years in corporate marketing departments, according to his resume. That was back in the 1980s. Here's my experience of 99.9999 percent of corporate marketing departments: you will not find much in the way of direct marketing.

Accomplished academics at Duke for sure. But what do these professors really know about the daily, get-smacked-in-the-teeth, we-must-generate-money-this-week grind of everyday marketing and sales? Perhaps they will enlighten me.

And in case you think I'm picking on Duke's highly ranked business school, which I might be, let's fly to the West Coast, specifically to Stanford, the currently ranked #2 business school in the United States.

Professors Jennifer Aaker and Baba Shiv, while accomplished academics and writers, list no actual working experience on their resumes. I'm not certain they've spent much time deep in the muddy trenches of real-world marketing and sales.

If you're serious about serious marketing, pay close attention to marketers who know how to sell and have experienced significant success, and failure, in the real world of direct marketing. Later in this book, I'm going to point you towards books and resources by people who actually know how to produce revenue and profits through direct marketing.

Academics who specialize in marketing think at the "ethereal" and "strategic" level. And that may be fine for some. But you NEVER find serious direct marketers in academia. And you certainly won't find any direct response copywriters at Harvard.

Here's why: direct marketers and direct response copywriters are too busy generating cash.

There's one exception I know: Mark Roberge, a professor at Harvard Business School. Mark is a direct marketer and sales specialist. They're really fortunate at Harvard to have Mark on their faculty.

Ron Popeil started a company called Ronco. The company has generated over $2 billion in sales through direct response marketing. Is there a university professor who has achieved this remarkable result?

No.

Popeil provides textbook examples of how to sell products using perfectly executed direct response techniques. So, am I going to follow a university professor who hasn't sold a thing...or am I going to pay close attention to Ron Popeil? You know the answer.

In 2011, I attended the Dan Kennedy information marketing conference in Atlanta. About one thousand people attended and I estimate the event generated at least $5 million in "back of the room" sales. At one point, people were literally running to the "store" to buy a $1,000 iPad loaded with everything Kennedy has ever written.

If you really want to understand real-life marketing and you really want to maximize your results, then emulate the world's most successful direct marketers. Fortunately, hundreds of these marketing rock stars have made their wisdom freely available.

And when I say "freely," that's exactly what I mean—it's FREE. You'll find gobs of extremely valuable direct marketing advice, from experts like Dan Kennedy, available for no charge. Here's proof from Dan Kennedy's website.

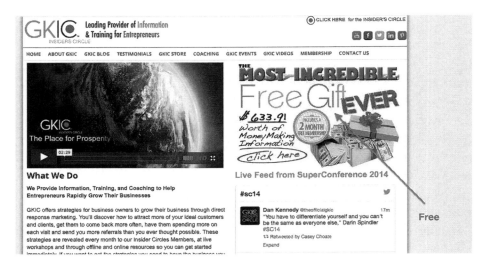

Your Duke MBA will cost $59,550 per year in tuition and expenses or you can download money-making information from an accomplished marketer—for free. Hmmmmmm...

If you're going to follow marketing advice, make sure it comes from people who have generated massive results. My copy has helped to generate over $400 million in sales for my clients in the last six years. Many other direct response copywriters have achieved similar results. I don't publish academic papers. Nor do I teach marketing or marketing writing at a business school. No, like my fellow direct response copywriters, I'm busy motivating people to pull a credit card out of their wallet and hit the "Buy now" button so they can try a product or service that will help them feel better about themselves.

I have a degree in English and Comparative Literature, and the skills I learned help me today. However, I learned the art and science of direct response copywriting two ways.

First, I wrote copy and measured the results. I quickly discovered what works and what fails. And like every serious direct response copywriter, I'm still learning.

Second, I have invested extensively in my own marketing and copywriting education. I have attended seminars, bought manuals, and taken one-on-one coaching from the top direct response copywriters. I was in a mastermind group for three years. Brian Kurtz ran the group and he routinely brought in many of the world's top direct marketers to speak with the group. I was NOT the smartest person in the room by far, which was exactly how I wanted it. If I went to Duke and sat in a marketing class, I'd know more about real-world marketing than everyone there, including the academics.

But perhaps the ultimate value comes from reading the books written by the giants of direct response advertising and marketing.

Copywriter and author Bob Bly has an excellent list of must-read books. And Brian Kurtz recently wrote his own list. But let me give you seven books to get you started. There are more books listed in the appendix.

Both lists include *Scientific Advertising* by Claude Hopkins. Published in 1923, the book is available for free on hundreds of websites. Still salient today, *Scientific Advertising* demands advertisers measure results.

The Complete Idiot's Guide to Direct Marketing by Bob Bly. I've never been a fan of a series that automatically insults the intelligence of the reader but this book provides a tremendous introduction to direct marketing from an extremely experienced and accomplished marketer and writer.

The Ultimate Sales Letter by Dan Kennedy. The book simplifies the art of writing copy. I use the headline templates from this book almost every day. Kennedy used the principles in this book to generate hundreds of millions in revenue.

Cunningly Clever Marketing by Andrew Wood. Another great introduction to direct response marketing.

Breakthrough Advertising by Eugene Schwartz. A more complex book but one to tackle after you've read the others.

Tested Advertising Methods by John Caples. An excellent introduction to the power and importance of testing as it relates to direct response copywriting.

Overdeliver by Brian Kurtz. A great introduction to direct marketing techniques based on Brian's successes in direct marketing.

Bop around the Internet and you'll find marketing webinars online; plus, you can attend seminars and listen to MP3s and podcasts.

When assessing the potential value of the content, simply look at the credentials of the author. Are they an academic with a lot of pieces in magazines and journals published by, and for, other academics? Or is the author someone who is, or has been, right in the middle of the real action, winning some victories but also getting beaten up and failing from time to time? Has the author actually sold anything in person?

You'll see a lot of bizarre definitions of marketing on business school websites. Here's mine: the goal of marketing is to sell as much stuff as possible while spending as little as possible in order to generate cash plus increase the value of the business.

Not beating around the bush there.

Here's the definition from Harvard.

"Marketing is critical for organic growth of a business and its central role is in creating, communicating, capturing, and sustaining value for an organization."

Hmmmmm...

My mentor in direct marketing, Andrew Wood, doesn't have an MBA. Andrew began his remarkable—and highly profitable—marketing career when he owned a karate school in Southern California. He had no students. So he went to the library and took out every book they had about direct marketing.

In a few years, in his early 20s, he owned a chain of over two hundred karate schools.

If you have a passion for generating revenue, then educate yourself every day. Rely on the work of marketers like Andrew who have actually sold products and services in the real world. Avoid "gurus" who have never walked into a business and been soundly rejected. Totally avoid academics who have never actually sold anything.

Myth Nine. Direct marketing has to be obnoxious. You'll see plenty of super-obnoxious ads from direct marketers. But you'll also see plenty of presentable and toned-down ads from direct marketers. Some direct marketers like to be a little loud...especially if being loud works. Other direct marketers turn the volume down. Selling a cleaning product? You need to be loud. Selling life insurance? You need to tone it down.

Myth Ten. Creative talent is cheap. Many marketers say, "I'll just go online to a commodity site. You can find copywriters, graphic designers, and other talent on sites like Fiverr and Upwork." And that's understandable, especially if you have to keep your costs low. But you won't find the top talent on those sites.

There's a publishing company in South Florida that pays its top copywriter well over $3 million a year. Why? Because that copywriter generates well over $30 million a year for the company. They give him ten cents. He gets them a dollar.

Remember, direct response copywriters have a superpower: the ability to choose and organize words that motivate potential customers to try products and services. The smartest business owners in the world understand this superpower and will gleefully pay for it. It's expensive, until the money starts rolling in, and then it's the greatest investment you'll ever make, the greatest bargain.

Myth Eleven. To generate more sales, I need to discount the price. I'm going to discuss pricing in greater detail later in this book. Pricing is part of what we call "the offer." The top direct response copywriters write copy but they also understand how to present the price so that you NEVER have to discount. In fact, one of my goals as a direct response copywriter is to help my clients get significantly higher prices for their products and services. This skill, by itself, is a reason to hire a direct response copywriter. Again, I'll talk more about pricing later but one of your major goals should be the avoidance of discounting.

Myth Twelve. Social media is marketing. Facebook. Twitter. YouTube. Snapchat. You know all the social media channels. There are two types of advertising on social media. One that's genuine marketing. One that's not. So, "social media is marketing" is only half a myth. Posts, and likes, and general "banter" on social media are NOT MARKETING. For example, a company like Mercedes Benz can post content on its Facebook page, or add videos to its YouTube channel and these generate interest in the products. But "generating interest" is not measurable, and all marketing must be measurable when it comes to revenue. What's measurable on Facebook? Those ads that you pay for. I've written thousands of them and my clients can directly measure ROI. Why bother with "generating interest and awareness" when you can use a measurable form of marketing that generates MONEY? Look...there's something to be said for a strong presence on social media. I get it and it can help generate awareness for small businesses, especially when it comes to events. But remember that social media is a total weakling when compared to the full muscularity of direct marketing.

Myth Thirteen. If the advertising is funny and smart, it's AWESOME. NOBODY loves a good laugh more than me. I especially love those ads for Dos Equis featuring "The Most Interesting Man in the World." Anyone who has studied David Ogilvy's work knows this: these ads are a lot like the "man in the Hathaway shirt" ads. Look them up and you'll see what I mean. Good swiping, boys and girls.

Either way, the Dos Equis ads are funny and popular. Sales increased 22% after the ads started running in 2009. Total growth in sales, according to USA Today, is 34.8%. Impressive figures... But let me spoil the party, if I may.

- Yes, there's a link between sales and the ads running, but it's not definitively measurable.
- What is the actual revenue generated? Sales are up 34.8%, but what really matters? Revenue. 34.8% of not much is not much.
- Did the increase in revenue offset the tens of millions the company obviously spent on buying super-expensive TV time? What was the actual ROI? What about the cost of acquiring a new customer? What about lifetime value?

These are not questions advertising agency people want to hear. These are not questions that marketing people at beer companies want to hear.

But these are questions I have as a direct marketer and direct response copywriter. You should ask the same questions about your marketing.

Myth Fourteen. I must have a celebrity endorsement. Two years ago, I started to ask a question. What's the ROI on celebrity endorsements? I found a study, admittedly an old one, that calculated the ROI. The conclusion based on the data? It's never worth it; ROI is neutral, at best.

I bought a certain type of ski because some "rockstar" skiers I know use those skis. So, this type of celebrity endorsement influenced my decision. Thus, you might think it's a great idea to have a celebrity endorsement. But again, you have to look at actual data and numbers. What did the company pay those "rockstar" skiers? Can the ski company directly measure results based on actual data? The answer will be "no." Celebrity endorsements can be the last resort of a marketing team or advertising agency that's in dire trouble and under pressure to make something happen.

But in the medical field, especially in dietary supplements, one way to differentiate a product in a crowded space is to have an endorsement from a doctor. This can work. And what about the hugely successful George Foreman Grill? These two celebrity tactics have more to do with direct marketing and direct response copywriting than pure celebrity endorsements. The doctor provides what we call a proof element. The endorsement from George Foreman differentiated the grill from other grills. A grill, my friends, is ultimately a grill.

And remember the huge potential negative impact of the celebrity gig. What happens when the celebrity gets into some "slight turbulence" or some "dissipation" and crashes? Think about Tiger Woods and his troubles. Think about hundreds of other products endorsed by celebrities who got into trouble. Think that money was worth it? Nike paid Tiger Woods almost $100 million but today it's out of the golf club business. It was a dismal failure for Nike even though they produced some decent equipment.

Myth Fifteen. I don't need to hire an expensive copywriter. I'll just write everything myself. Anyone with a pen can write. This means anyone can write copy. You need a pen, paper, a personal computer, laptop, whatever. So a lot of people decide to write their own copy. I'm totally fine with this provided they have extensively studied direct response copywriting. In fact, it can make sense, in very rare occasions, for some business owners to write their own copy. Why? Because they know their customers better than anyone. I just worked on a brochure for a golf company. The owner of the copy supplied some copy I thought was excellent. I didn't change a word of the portions I liked.

But think about what we're trying to achieve in business. We're trying to maximize revenue and profit. Here's where business and direct marketing are a perfect match. In direct marketing, we're always trying to maximize response. **Translation: we're always trying to maximize the revenue and profit for the client.**

You can write your own copy or hire a copywriter who doesn't really understand direct marketing and direct response copywriting and you might get some OK results. Maybe. But you can invest some money, and, with the right traffic, the right offer, and some testing, you'll end up with a lot of money in your bank account.

Brian Kurtz helped to build Boardroom, the newsletter publisher, from pretty much zero to $150 million a year (maybe more) with help from some of the world's top direct response copywriters. Here's what he writes about creative talent.

"Never be a cheapskate with copy and creative...it's just not the place to cut costs...it's the place to invest in world-class resources. Don't leave this make-or-break area of your business to amateurs."

Enough said.

● ● ● ●

I have listed just a few of the common myths in the worlds of advertising, direct marketing, and sales. I could list 100 more.

But here's the most important point: if you're a business owner and/or involved with any type of marketing or selling, then you must question everything you have learned. You must ultimately move, as quickly as you can, toward the direct marketing model. There is absolutely no excuse to stay with your current strategy and tactics unless you're already making whopping cash through the near-perfect execution of direct marketing. And if you're achieving this, then you have a direct response copywriter on your team. Even if you're enjoying some success, you're never satisfied; you're constantly trying to improve.

Most advertising agencies will tell you something totally different—as you will discover in the next section of this chapter.

WARNING TO PEOPLE IN 98 PERCENT OF ADVERTISING AGENCIES: You WILL NOT Like This Part of This Book...

Here we go. Strap in.

If you're a business owner, or if you're involved in the marketing of a product or service, then you might be working with an advertising or marketing agency. Or you might be thinking of working with one. Maybe you're working with a marketing consultant. Maybe you're working with an agency with offices from Manhattan to Sydney.

I've worked with a number of advertising agencies and consultants over my 33 years in the copywriting world and here's what I've discovered: 98 percent get it completely wrong—while you pay for their rancid incompetence.

Yes...I know. This statement will not endear me to many advertising agencies and my chances of getting any work from 98 percent of agencies has entered negative territory. I don't care. I'm not here to get work from these agencies. I'm here to help you generate more revenue and profit, plus build the value of your business. The 2 percent of agencies that actually understand direct marketing and direct response copywriters will totally understand what I'm about to write.

Before I describe what really happens in that 98 percent of the advertising world, let me return to something I wrote in the first chapter of this book, specifically that blank stare I receive when I tell people I'm a direct response copywriter. I get this stare from people who work outside the marketing world and I fully understand why my doctor isn't familiar with my trade. But I also get this "blank stare" from people who run advertising agencies and have worked in and around agencies for many years. I'll explain why in a minute. But first, let me describe the work of an advertising agency.

Tasks completed by an agency can include:

- Creation of branding materials like logos and graphic standards for the brand.
- Market research.
- Brochures and marketing collateral.
- Placement of advertisements in publications, on the Internet, and in other traditional media like radio and television.
- Website creation and development.
- Creation of advertisements.
- Marketing plans.
- Graphic design, copywriting, photography, and related creative services.
- Lead generation.
- Public relations.

These are the primary services offered by 99.3% of advertising agencies. By now, you may have noticed something... I DID NOT MENTION DIRECT MARKTING.

Why?

Because most advertising agency owners do not want to go anywhere near the raw accountability that comes with the pure execution of direct marketing.

Advertising agencies make their money two ways. They charge fees for the services above and, in some cases, they still receive a 15% commission for the placement of advertising in media. Some get their fees in the form of a retainer as the "agency of record."

For example, a large multinational advertising agency might charge $5 million to create a series of TV commercials for a large multinational company. The advertising agency then receives a commission for each advertisement they place on TV stations around the world. The commission comes from a discount provided by the media companies. The stated price for an ad might be $1,000 but the company selling the ads will only charge the agency $850. The advertising agency then charges the client $1,000. This spread can add up.

Here's another example. An agency might produce a printed brochure you can take to a trade show. Or they might produce a beautiful-looking website. Everyone can be delighted with both but here's the problem: nobody knows if the brochure and website actually generate money for the client. They certainly generate money for the agency. But the agency does not want to be accountable for actual results. If sales increase, the agency is delighted and takes the credit.

Here are the issues I have, and you should have, with advertising agencies.

- The commission structure gives the advertising agencies a whopping incentive to spend your money, and lots of it, without any accountability.
- Agencies rarely, if ever, want to go anywhere near pure accountability. If sales increase, agencies will take credit. But if sales are flat or they decrease, the agency will blame "factors out of our control" like political upheaval in Barcelona or a snowstorm in Seattle ... or a virus.
- The agency world is extremely self-congratulatory. Agency types love to gather at least once a year to hand out awards, and lots of them, to other agency types. Enter the offices of an advertising agency and you'll find a lot of trophies and plaques. These awards are for "creativity" or something similar but rarely, if ever, for actual results like revenue gained for clients. But the smart company owner or smart marketing manager will ask to see evidence of data-based results and will ignore all the awards handed out at black tie awards dinners.
- Because many companies are increasingly looking for measurable results, the branding world has created tools that claim to measure results. For example, I was on a conference call the other day and one of the speakers was talking about a tool that measures the impact of content on "brand health." These tools might sound clever but the only measurement tools that matter to me are the ones that measure revenue. Apply these tools to branding advertising and the revenue will be zero.
- Most agency heads HATE direct response. "It will ruin your brand reputation," they will bleat. But here's what they really hate about direct marketing. One...it's accountable. Two...you can't get media placement commissions. Three...it works.
- It's all about the brand...and jargon. In direct marketing, "branding types" are the enemy. They constantly talk about "making a

company stand for something through its brand" and they use words and phrases like "brand authority" and "brand equity" and "brandicity"...and they love jargon and gibberish. They want to sound clever and "with it" and super-trendy. But here's what's really happening: they are running away from being accountable.

- Most agencies are totally horrible at marketing themselves. Much of the WORST copy I have read comes from the marketing materials produced by advertising agencies...digital and printed. I have spent hours and several thousands of dollars on my copywriting website. My website ranks #1 or #2 for most search terms related to my work and the site itself has generated over one thousand leads in five years, and these leads have helped to generate hundreds of thousands in fees. There is close to 70,000 words of content on my website.
- It's extremely rare to find people in advertising agencies who genuinely understand direct marketing...or who want to understand.
- I understand why certain massive companies hire advertising agencies for branding and image work. These companies want to get their name out there to the world and have millions, billions even, to spend on keeping their name above others. But we're really only talking about 1,000 companies...if that. For the other millions of companies, direct marketing is the only form of genuinely accountable and truly effective marketing.

Why pay for work from an advertising agency that's not going to be accountable? There is no good reason. Here's a test I'd like you to conduct if you're currently working with an advertising agency, or if you're about to hire one: ask the person you're working with if they have read *Scientific Advertising* by Claude Hopkins. If the answer is "no," then move on. If the answer is "yes," then ask them about using a direct marketing approach to your advertising. If you hear anything except "great!" then issue forth the red card.

If your advertising agency shuns direct marketing and direct response copywriting, issue forth the red card.

David Ogilvy is one of the most famous advertising people of all time. He held a number of jobs before entering advertising: farmer, door-to-door salesperson, writer, researcher, and cook in a hotel.

His agency, Ogilvy and Mather, is famous for creating brand images and building brands. But Ogilvy was actually a direct marketer. He used direct marketing to get clients. Deep inside his agency you'd find his secret weapon: his direct marketing department where he could show his clients actual results, to the penny. He held a deep love for direct marketing and direct marketers. He was suspicious of the other agency types, who, as he said, "worship at the altar of creativity." If you want proof, go to YouTube right now and type the following into the search box: "David Ogilvy we sell or else." **This video proves all of what I just wrote.** It's a video branding types hate.

David Ogilvy: We Sell or Else
218,783 views   👍 1.5K 👎 9   ↗ SHARE   ⊟₊ SAVE   •••

The video that 99.9 percent of advertising agencies don't want you to see:
"WE SELL OR ELSE." David Ogilvy beats up "general advertising" and
writes a love letter to direct marketers. Watch this video three times a week.

● ● ● •

Ogilvy is a hero to the branding agencies yet, in this epic video, he slams them.

Here's a transcription. A quick note: Ogilvy speaks in the "male" tense. I'm sure there were plenty of female copywriters out there at the time.

● ● ● •

"I wish I could be with you today, in the flesh, as they say. Unfortunately, I'm in India. Ever been in India? It's very hot. If you don't mind, I'm going to take off my coat.

You know, in the advertising community today, there are two worlds. Your world of direct response advertising and that 'other' world, the world of 'general' advertising.[2] These two worlds are on a collision course. You direct response people know what kind of advertising works and what doesn't work. You know to a dollar. The general advertising people don't know. You know that two-minute commercials on television are more effective—more cost-effective—than 10-second commercials or 30-second commercials. You know that fringe time sells more than prime time.

In print advertising, you know that long copy sells more than short copy. You know that headlines and copy about the product and its benefits sell more than cute headlines and poetic copy. You know to a dollar.

The general advertisers and their agencies know almost nothing for sure because they cannot measure the results of their advertising. They worship at the altar of creativity, which really means originality, the most dangerous word in the lexicon of advertising.

They opine that 30-second commercials are more cost-effective than two-minute commercials. You know they're wrong. In print advertising, they opine that short copy sells more than long copy. You know they're wrong. They indulge in entertainment. You know they're wrong. You know to a dollar. They don't. Why don't you tell them? Why don't you save them from their follies?[3] There are two reasons. First, because you're impressed by the fact they're so big and so well paid and so well publicized. You're even perhaps impressed with their reputation for creativity—whatever that may mean. Second, you never meet them. You inhabit a different world.

The chasm between direct response advertising and general advertising is wide. On your side of the chasm I see knowledge and reality. On the other side of the chasm, I see ignorance. You are the professionals. This must not go on. I predict that the practitioners of general advertising are going to start learning from your experience. They're going to start picking your brains.

---

[2]   Most call "general" advertising "branding" advertising.

[3]   I'm following your salient advice, Mr. Ogilvy.

I see no reason why the direct response divisions of agencies should be separate from the main agencies. Some of you may remember when the television people in agencies were kept separate. Wasn't that idiotic? I expect that direct response people will become an integral part of all agencies. You have more to teach them than they have to teach you. You have it in your power to rescue the advertising business from its manifold lunacies.

When I was 25, I took a correspondence course in direct mail. I bought it out of my own pocket from the Dardanelle Corporation in Chicago. Direct response is my first love and later it became my secret weapon. When I started Ogilvy and Mather in New York, nobody had heard of us. But we were airborne within six months and grew at record speed.

How did we achieve that?

By using my secret weapon: direct mail. Every four weeks, I sent personalized mailings to our new business prospects. And I was always amazed to discover how many of our clients had been attracted to Ogilvy and Mather by those mailings.

That was how we grew.

Whenever I look at an advertisement in a magazine or a newspaper, I can tell at a glance whether the writer has had any direct response experience. If he writes short copy, or literary copy, it is obvious he has never had the disciplines of writing direct response. If he's had that discipline, he wouldn't make those mistakes.

Nobody should be allowed to create general advertising until he's served his apprenticeship in direct response. That experience will keep his feet on the ground for the rest of his life. The trouble with many copywriters and general agencies is they don't really think in terms of selling. They've never written direct response.

They've never tasted blood.

Until recently, direct response was the Cinderella of the advertising world. Then came the computer and the credit card, and direct marketing exploded. You guys are coming into your own. Your opportunities are colossal. In the audience today there are some heads of general agencies. I offer you this advice. Insist that all your people—creative, media, account executives—are all trained in your direct response division. If you don't have such a division, make arrangements with a firm of direct marketing specialists to train your people. And make it a rule in your agency that no copy is ever presented to clients before it has been vetted by a direct response expert.

Ladies and gentlemen, I envy you. Your timing is perfect. You've come into the direct response business at the right moment in history. You're onto a good thing. For 40 years, I've been a voice crying in the wilderness, trying to get my fellow advertising practitioners to take direct response seriously. Today, my first love is coming to its own. You face a golden future.

● ● ● ●

My thoughts about this short but powerful video.

- Whenever I get into a verbal battle with a branding type, I send them a link to "we sell or else," and that's the end of the argument. Everyone in branding loves David Ogilvy. They can argue with me but they can't argue with Ogilvy.
- I'm not precisely certain when he filmed the video, but Ogilvy worked for his agency in India in the early 1980s.
- Ogilvy was right about the differences between direct response and "general" advertising but, clearly, the chasm never really closed. Direct response remains the "Cinderella" on Madison Avenue and in the branding world. Maybe that's finally starting to change.
- Pay close attention to what Ogilvy says about measuring results and how it relates to know-how.

"We sell or else" is one of the most perfect marketing videos ever recorded.

Who to Work With

If you're going to work with an advertising agency or marketing consultant, partner with those who live and breathe direct marketing. Make sure a direct response copywriter will write your copy and be part of the team helping you increase your revenue. These direct marketing agencies exist. Let me give you two examples.

My friend and mentor Andrew Wood runs an agency that primarily targets golf courses, hotels, and resorts. However, he will work with pretty much any business. His agency is totally built around proven direct marketing and sales principles. He and his group routinely help clients around the world significantly increase revenue. Clients must listen to Andrew and follow his recommendations and when this happens, his clients experience huge results.

Andrew has read and digested well over three hundred books about marketing and sales. He's an excellent direct response copywriter. Andrew has spent his own money on marketing himself and his businesses.

Then there's another friend and mentor, Will Swayne, from Brisbane, Australia. He runs a digital marketing agency plus sells his own products online. Will started his advertising career in Japan where he wrote ads for a direct marketing company that grew from zero revenue to well over $50 million a year by using direct marketing principles. Will is a direct marketer who spends his own money to learn about direct marketing from people like Dan Kennedy and Perry Marshall. He reads books and materials about direct marketing. He insists on copy from direct response copywriters and he trains his writers to write copy that converts at high levels.

Because Australia is a relatively small country, Will has a wide range of clients, from financial planners to plumbers. If he worked in America, he'd probably specialize in a certain niche. He helps his clients generate leads and he makes this promise to them: if you're not happy with the results, you can leave at any time and not pay us a penny more. That's called ACCOUNTABILITY.

Brian Kurtz is not a consultant. That's partly because he doesn't like the word "consultant." In Brian's mind, and mine, sometimes, people tend to see consultants as people who are useless and essentially unemployable. That's not totally fair. Either way, let's call Brian a direct marketing specialist.

Is Brian someone who will come to your office and offer vagueness and jargon? Will he talk about awards for creativity?

NO!

Brian helped develop Boardroom into a $2 billion company (at least) and it's a powerful success story in the publishing business. He's a 35 (plus) year student of direct marketing, all based on his successes and failures at Boardroom. He knows how to market: he motivated five hundred people, including yours truly, to attend a two-day marketing seminar that cost $3,500 a ticket.

What I'm saying is that Brian knows how to market, based on direct marketing principles. He hired the world's top direct response copywriters when he was at Boardroom. He understands the power of direct marketing and direct response copywriting. He gets quasi-emotional when talking about direct marketing. I get the same way.

She's not part of an agency but Katie Yeakle runs a highly successful direct marketing enterprise called American Artists and Writers, better known as AWAI. This company, based in Delray Beach, Florida, earns millions by providing training to direct response copywriters. She and her team know how to sell high-priced products and services to people who want to become copywriters or to copywriters who want to be more successful.

I consider Katie an "elite-level" direct response marketer. If she ever left AWAI, then a company would be super smart to hire her. She's worked with many of the world's top direct marketers and direct response copywriters.

Andrew, Brian, Katie, and Will are part of that .007 percent of marketers who truly understand direct marketing. You want to hire them and people just like them if you want actual measurable results from your advertising. They're not trying to win awards. They're not about phrases like "brand equity" "and brand health" and other such piffle. They're all about direct marketing and using direct marketing techniques and strategies to help companies like yours.

If you're serious about hiring an advertising agency, make certain they're a direct marketing agency. You want measurable results, measurable to the penny. You want a direct response copywriter on your team. You don't want awards, vague platitudes, jargon, pretty ads, and overall muppetry.

Some companies take a more "a la carte" approach to direct response, seeking the top specialist in each discipline. For example, a company might find the top direct response copywriters, the top list brokers, the top traffic buyers, the top graphic designers, etc. This approach can work provided you can coordinate all the freelancers and specialists. In fact, I recommend you try this approach first.

Finally... Be a Good Client and Accept Failure. Really!

Everyone in direct marketing fails.

We have our successes. But we have our failures. We know precisely what works and precisely what fails because we have the guts to measure the results. We've "tasted blood" as David Ogilvy said in the video I just mentioned.

In the world of "general" or "branding" advertising, there's no real or reliable way to gain precise measurement of results. So there's no real way to know if your advertising is succeeding or failing. And that's, as I mentioned earlier, exactly how the branding agencies want it. In direct marketing, we have failures but we learn from these and we don't repeat the mistakes.

Trust your direct marketing agency or direct marketing specialists or direct response copywriter. Let them fail. Eventually, they will get the strategies and tactics correct and they will help you earn a fortune.

Your Next Step

It was important to provide you with an introduction to direct marketing. Why? Because to understand the work of a direct response copywriter, you have to understand direct marketing.

There's a slight caveat here. NOBODY truly understands direct marketing. Yes...there are practitioners who I consider "elite" in the field. But here's one reason I say they perform at that level: they're constantly learning and trying to improve. I work in the golf industry periodically and I'm also a part-time ski instructor. I've worked with top golfers and I train with other ski instructors, many of whom have been teaching for upwards of 50 seasons. The top golf instructors and skiers I know are still trying to "figure things out." They're always trying to improve significantly.

CHAPTER 3

Advertising Methods Rated and Ranked

B efore I assess different forms of advertising and marketing, let's remember what we're trying to achieve here. We're trying to generate as much revenue and wealth as possible, in a measurable way, so we get the most efficient and productive use of marketing spend in order to reach financial and personal goals.

Why use marketing methods that are, at best, mediocre, especially when that goal above is so important? I'm going to help you answer that question for yourself by focusing on various forms of advertising and marketing and why you should avoid them, or why they are rarely effective.

WORD OF MOUTH. A friend tells you about a restaurant in Aspen they like. A friend tells you about a bar in New York they like. The concierge at a hotel gives you some dining options. A friend tells me about a golf course I have to play.

PROS. It's free and it can generate revenue...even great lifetime business.

CONS. What about people who tell their friends NOT to visit a business? That, my brothers and sisters, is word of mouth advertising. It's not a reliable form of marketing. It's not measurable. It can bring the WRONG form of customer. Some of my fellow copywriters rely on word of mouth but potential clients who have arrived at my doorstep through referrals have usually been bad clients. Not bad people, but the wrong client for me. You're not in total control with word of mouth plus it's extremely passive. It's free and you get what you pay for. And what about the concierge who recommends a certain restaurant because he/she gets free drinks there?

GOOGLE ADWORDS, FACEBOOK, AND PAY-PER-CLICK ADVERTISING. Tens of thousands of direct marketers use this method.

PROS. It's a form of direct marketing. It's measurable. It's a proven winner. The great "old school" direct response copywriters would have loved these platforms. It's aggressive because you're going after the customers you want.

CONS. Google AdWords is a powerful tool but you MUST know what you're doing or you can quickly waste tens of thousands of dollars, maybe more. Ditto Facebook display advertising. I write thousands of ads for Google AdWords and the display networks so it helps to have a direct response copywriter when you're advertising on these platforms. You will also need to hire a specialist who truly understands PPC advertising. It's complex.

PRINT: NEWSPAPERS AND MAGAZINES. Even though we've had the Internet since the early 1990s, newspaper and magazine advertising remains a viable option for many companies. I divide print into display ads in the first two-thirds of the publication and classified advertising in the back of the publication. You know the difference.

PROS. Use a direct response approach, and print can work. You'll need to test ads. It can be super easy to reach the right market. A fly-fishing magazine can work extremely well for people who sell fly fishing stuff. It can also be one of the most cost-effective ways to advertise. With fewer people advertising in print, it can be easier to stand out.

CONS. It's a total waste of money if you don't use a direct marketing model. Frequent advertising in the larger publications can be expensive although it's coming down in price and the right media expert can help you find the bargains.

PUBLIC RELATIONS. You try to get articles written about your business in newspapers and magazines plus on websites and social media. You also try to get positive pieces run about you on TV and radio. You can hire an agency that specializes in PR to run a PR campaign. Many PR firms can help with publicity on social media sites and other platforms.

PROS. A positive piece of publicity will never hurt you. You can put the logo of the TV station, radio station, or magazine or newspaper on your website, providing some valuable proof. You can get a bump in business from good publicity. An expert-level PR agency can minimize the impact of bad news. You can include the good articles or pieces on your website and this can be a useful proof element.

CONS. It's not direct marketing. It's unreliable and inconsistent. You're never in full control of the message. I would not even call it marketing or advertising. I don't know a single serious direct marketer that uses public relations.

PERSON-TO-PERSON...BELLY-TO-BELLY...HAND-TO-HAND

COMBAT. A company has salespeople who constantly chase after potential customers. Then they strive to sell even more to the customers. The salesperson is not dead. Results are measurable and it's an extremely pure form of direct response marketing.

PROS. Great salespeople can produce superb results if they have a great database of potential prospects, great products, excellent training, plus the support of the company. It helps hugely when the company can also supply warmed-up leads through direct mail or the Internet. Many of the world's top advertising people and copywriters started a career by selling products door-to-door. Exhibit A: David Ogilvy. I have worked in sales. I've sold backpacks and outdoor gear...advertising...publishing services. And, of course, I sell my copywriting services.

CONS. It can be hard to find and keep top-quality salespeople. They must be bulletproof plus understand every sales technique. This type of direct marketing is more prevalent in the business-to-business world where price tags can be extremely high. But it's hard to argue with direct person-to-person selling. But even the greatest person-to-person salesperson can only be in one place at one time. A live salesperson can make one sale. A direct response copywriter can make tens of thousands of sales.

SOCIAL MEDIA. Facebook posts. Twitter. Etc. There are two approaches to social media: paid advertising and routine posts in the news feeds.

PROS. Display advertising on Facebook is a powerful direct marketing tool for many companies. You need a direct response copywriter plus a media buying expert to make it work. You can also use social media to get opt-in emails. However, posting posts on social media IS NOT MARKETING.

CONS. Way too many companies think that getting "likes" and posting on Facebook is advertising. It is not. There is no reliable way to determine ROI from posts on social media. It's good for awareness but that's not direct marketing. Plus you have to deal with the anarchy of negative comments. Once again...FACEBOOK POSTS ARE NOT MARKETING.

TELEMARKETING. You know all about telemarketing.

PROS. It still works. It's a form of direct marketing and totally measurable.

CONS. It's brutal on the callers and brutal on the potential customers. It's also increasingly illegal.

EMAIL MARKETING. You build an opt-in email database or you rent an email list.

PROS. Still the most cost-effective way to generate traffic to an offer page or website. Totally measurable down to the penny. You need a direct response copywriter to test different emails. With so many bad/spammy emails out there, it can be easy to cut through the garbage by writing useful emails.

CONS. Renting lists is borderline spam. You have to build your email database and this will take time and money. You need a top-quality acquisition funnel to acquire emails.

"SCOTT BRINGS ME MONEY..." A case study.

One of my clients is a restaurant located in what I describe as the worst restaurant location on the planet. It's tucked underneath a nail salon on the back side of a suburban shopping center.

Friends own the place and I wanted to help them. So I set up, using direct marketing principles, a simple promotion known as "free dinner on or near your birthday."

It's NOT exactly an original concept. But here's how it works. The patrons sign up for free dinner and they get an email just before their birthday with the invitation and details. I also periodically send emails detailing events at the restaurant. Some emails are just plain silly. For example, I sent an email on April Fool's Day saying the restaurant would be expanding underground using Japanese tunneling technology.

Right at the beginning of the promotion, people started coming in with their birthday emails. Some came alone but most brought two to three people. Other people brought big groups. Three good things are going on here. First…the promotion brings people to a restaurant that's hard to find. Second…it's a great way to build and maintain a database. Third…new people discover the restaurant.

The manager had advertised in several different publications but never had a sense of whether the ad spend was producing results. With the birthday promotion, the manager can see and feel tangible results. "Scott brings me money," she says. It's all thanks to the power of direct response marketing and direct response copywriting. It's not me.

INBOUND MARKETING/SEO. The subject of a controversial book titled, you guessed it, *Inbound Marketing*. Here's the theory: you build a website and optimize it for the search engines, primarily through content.

PROS. It has worked for me. My site ranks extremely well in the search engines and this has generated significant traffic to my website. I then use direct response copywriting to convert the visitors into leads.

CONS. Depending on your niche, it can be extremely difficult to rank highly in the search engines. Plus you can be at the mercy of the search engines and the infamous "algorithm change" that search engines like Google organize periodically. It's extremely passive and not a pure form of direct marketing. You get the leads you get…not always the ideal customers.

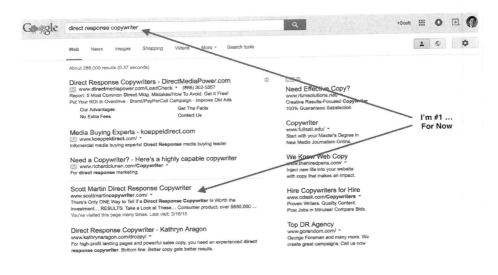

I rank highly for certain search terms. But for how long? It's not always a predictable and reliable way to generate traffic.

TRADE SHOWS. CONFERENCES. SEMINARS. This marketing method involves visiting large and small events to meet potential customers.

PROS. This can be a good way to generate leads and maybe make some direct sales. After all, if you sell ball bearings and you visit an engineering conference, you might be in the right place. But you must take a direct marketing approach and get leads and keep pounding away at prospects with direct marketing techniques.

CONS. Not a pure form of direct response marketing and it can be extremely passive. A total waste of time if you fail to gather data from leads and/or don't follow up.

RADIO AND TV. Placing commercials on television and radio. There are two types of commercials: branding commercials and direct response commercials.

PROS. When you get direct response commercials right, they can generate huge revenue. Are you hearing or seeing the same direct response ads over and over? They're working.

CONS. There's no way to measure the true effectiveness of branding advertising. The media can be extremely expensive even though the reach can be extensive. Fewer and fewer people are watching traditional TV and listening to traditional radio.

HIRING A CELEBRITY. A company will often hire a celebrity to endorse a product or service. The celebrity appears in advertising saying, "I love this product and you will too." You've seen, read, or heard these ads.

PROS. Potential customers will often buy a product because of the celebrity endorsement. I use a certain brand of skis because two skiers I admire use these skis.

CONS. What if you HATE the celebrity? Are you buying the product? NO! Celebrity endorsements can backfire if the celebrity gets bad publicity. Some celebrities have bucked the trend and used a personal endorsement to sell products...like the George Foreman Grill...but it's rare. And the success of the George Foreman grill had more to do with direct marketing than a celebrity endorsement. What about ROI? A study showed that celebrity endorsements never produce a positive ROI when you include the cost of the endorsement and the cost of media. People buy products and services based on what's in it for them...and not the endorsement of a celebrity. You're better off investing celebrity endorsement money in direct response marketing, specifically customer acquisition. It's more powerful plus you can measure results down to the penny.

OTHER CRAZINESS. Advertising on busses and trains. Advertising in train stations. Billboards. Sponsoring Events. Ads in airports.

PROS. Every now and then I see a superb direct response ad on a train or bus. But that's extremely rare. If you're going to use an "off the wall" form of advertising then find a way to measure the results using a dedicated phone number or web address.

CONS. Most ads in the "miscellaneous" section are extremely difficult to measure and a waste of money for most businesses.

DIRECT MAIL. Still the purest form of direct response marketing. You buy or rent a database of prospects. You create an offer. You hire a direct response copywriter to create the copy for the letter. You print the mailing then mail it to prospects. You measure the results.

PROS. It's extremely measurable. And it's easier to find highly targeted databases of prospects. Direct mail remains a powerful marketing tool that way too many businesses ignore. I even know business owners who have enjoyed significant success going to door-to-door with flyers, door hangers, and the like. That's a form of direct mail.

CONS. Postage and dealing with our brothers and sisters at The United States Post Office.

As I sit here in mid-2020, there are just seven forms of pure direct marketing.

1. Direct mail.
2. Direct marketing ads in newspapers and magazines.
3. Online/pay-per-click like the advertising networks, Facebook, and Google. These ads go to sales pages.
4. Salespeople making direct contact with current and potential clients.
5. Email marketing.
6. Direct response commercials on radio and TV.
7. Telemarketing/text advertising.

Ignore every other form of marketing and focus on the methods above...if you're serious about maximizing your revenue and the value of your business.

But Wait! What About Mobile?

Advertising on mobile devices has increased in the last few years and will continue to increase as more people get their information from smartphones and tablets.

The biggest challenge with mobile marketing is simply the size of these devices. It's difficult to get the full sales message across on a phone, though it's easier on a tablet. However, there's no need to panic. The fundamentals of direct marketing remain the same.

Part 2
THE ANONYMOUS
SALESPERSON

CHAPTER 4

How to Spot the Work of a Direct Response Copywriter

R emember when I said that, out of five hundred people I meet, only one will instantly know exactly what a direct response copywriter does? I find this curious and amusing because almost everyone has seen or heard the work of a direct response copywriter. And, of the hundreds of people I meet who think my work, and the work of my fellow direct response copy- writers, is a tad "over the top" and of no interest to them, ALL of them have bought a product or service thanks to direct response copy—words on a page written to motivate them to try a product or take the next step in the sales process.

You've seen the work of a direct response copywriter. And there's a 99 percent chance you have made a buying decision based on this work. You might say, "Oh...I would never buy anything based on what you're talking about." But you have and I'm going to prove this by showing you some of my work...and the work of famous direct response copywriters. And I don't consider myself famous, in case you're wondering. I'm a successful direct response copywriter, in that I've generated millions in revenue for my cli- ents, but I don't speak at events, appear on panels, have my own YouTube channel, and the like. I'm "under the radar" to use a shocking cliché.

To help you understand the work of a direct response copywriter, I'm going to show you some of the various forms of media where you will see direct response copy.

Direct Mail

People call this "junk mail," but I call it "gold mail" because, when written correctly to the correct audience, it can generate millions for the sender.

Direct mail comes in a wide variety of formats and sizes. Here are just a few...

- Postcards.
- One-page letter.
- Two-page letter.
- Longer letter.
- Flyer.
- Postcard pack.
- Magalog.
- Direct mail "package" including a multi-page letter, lift note, brochure, and reply card.
- Catalog.
- Sample pack.

Let me define a couple of pieces of direct response jargon: lift note and magalog. A lift note is a one-page letter that accompanies the direct mail package and tells the reader why they should read the main letter in the package. It's called a "lift note" because it's proven to "lift" (increase) response. A magalog is a sales piece that looks a lot like a magazine. The word "magalog" is a cross between magazine and catalog. Magalogs are major productions and the goal is to provide you with valuable information about a problem, challenge, or opportunity, then motivate you to purchase the product or service that solves the problem.

Here's a letter I wrote for a roofer. This generated tens of thousands in revenue for the client. He was extremely delighted with the leads this letter generated.

● ● ● ●

ENVELOPE

"Open now to discover why everyone in your neighborhood is getting a new roof."

IF YOU HAVE HOMEOWNER'S INSURANCE, YOU COULD GET A NEW ROOF AND NEW SIDING ... FREE

Dear Neighbor:

Have you been driving around the neighborhood asking, "Why is everyone getting a new roof?" Recently, a powerful hailstorm pounded your area, severely damaging thousands of homes. Insurance companies have been paying to repair the damage to roofs, gutters, and siding...in most cases covering the entire cost. **Your neighbors are getting new roofs, AND many are getting work and materials for the cost of their deductible...or less... Many are getting a free new roof.**

I'm Tom Coleman, with TSC Roofing, a LOCAL company with a 25-year record of helping thousands of homeowners.

Do you qualify for a free new roof? Call me right now at (7xx) 2xx-xxxx, and I'll inspect your roof, siding, and gutters... for no charge and with no obligation.

When I find storm damage, I will contact the insurance company on your behalf. This increases your chance of a successful claim by 90 percent, AND **you will not have to spend hours dealing with your insurance company.**

When your insurance company gives the "green light," we'll use top materials installed by professional roofers backed by a rock-solid guarantee. **In most cases, you'll get a new roof ABSOLUTELY FREE.**

DO NOT make the mistake of thinking, "My roof looks fine, so it must be OK." Your neighbor's roof looked fine. Why was it replaced? An expert inspection revealed material damage that could quickly lead to expensive leaks. Do you want water suddenly cascading into your living room?

It's VITAL you get an inspection now. Your roof could start leaking at any time. And the chance of getting your insurance company to pay for crucial repairs decreases significantly the longer you wait. Call me right now at (7xx) 2xx-xxxx, and we'll schedule your free roof inspection today.

Sincerely,
Tom Coleman, Insurance Replacement Specialist, TSC Roofing

P.S. Hire a LOCAL company... Workers from as far away as Denver, Colorado are lurking in your neighborhood. Call a local company for peace of mind... (7xx) 2xx-xxxx. The inspection is free.

"I was previously denied by my local agent. Tom was great in getting approval and my roof completed. Total Service Company is TOP rated—I checked prior to getting my roof completed. Tom made it happen for me!! I got my new roof!!"
P. Parrish, Charlotte resident

The company was based in Charlotte, North Carolina.
Because I gave you a roofer letter, I need to provide you with a roofer joke.

I was with a woman who is a friend.
We met a roofer and my friend found the roofer to be very handsome.
I said to the roofer: "my friend finds you to be very attractive. She'd like to know: Are you married or shingle?"

And here's the front cover of a magalog I recently wrote.

Thirty years ago, there was a lot more direct mail. The Internet dramatically reduced the volume of direct mail but it's making a comeback. Why? It's becoming more expensive to gain traction on the Internet, especially in crowded categories. Also, it's easier and more cost-effective to get a highly targeted database of potential customers through a mailing list. Let's say you sell expensive scissors created for elderly people who only have a left arm. You could buy or rent, in the next 24 hours, a mailing list of wealthy people over 70 with no right arm who have bought scissors and other expensive tools in the last 24 months. Yes, I'm exaggerating just a hair, but, thanks to technology, you can find extremely targeted databases, also known in direct marketing as lists.

Email

Yes…you hate emails, especially "spam" emails but do you really hate every email? No…of course not. That's because when you receive an email and it's about something of great interest to you, you read and digest every word and will take the action the email asks you to take.

Here's an example of a direct response email.

● ● ● ●

Email 1.

Subjects

How to let Amazon put money in your pocket

Earn thousands from the eBook craze

$3 billion Kindle market… Get your piece of the action

50 Shades of…GREEN!

Body

You can make upwards of $2,000 a month selling just ONE eBook through Amazon's Kindle platform.

Click the link below to discover more.

http://www.numberonebooksystem.com/challenge/

There's a MASSIVE opportunity right now for writers and people who sell information.

$989,832,832 worth of eBooks were sold in 2011.

Could be more than $3 BILLION (with a 'B') this year.

More than $15 million "Shades of Grey" eBooks have sold.

Amazon is bending over backwards to promote eBooks...which means they do 99% of the promotional work for you.

Discover more now. Click here.

To your Amazon publishing success,

John Smiths
Kindle Author

P.S. Even if you don't think you have an eBook ready to go...think again. These eBooks don't have to be long. In fact, you probably have content on your hard drive that you can turn into an eBook.

You can start this weekend and be selling on Kindle in 3 days. Click here to see how I did it.

P.P.S. It's especially important to jump into this market NOW. Incredible growth is taking place in the eBook market, and there are several categories just waiting to be dominated...by YOU.

CLICK HERE NOW TO EARN MONEY THROUGH AMAZON KINDLE'S PLATFORM.

● ● ● ●

Email 2.

Subjects

Writers Wanted!

Experts Wanted!

Let Amazon put $2,000 a month in your pocket

Make money from the eBook craze

$3 billion Kindle market... Get your piece of the Kindle action

50 Shades of Grey information

5 Reasons to Love Kindle...

Body

Right now, I'm earning $2,000 a month selling just ONE eBook through Amazon's Kindle platform. It's passive "set and forget" income.

Click the link below to see how I'm doing this.

http://www.numberonebooksystem.com/challenge/

Kindle is revolutionizing the publishing business and provides a MASSIVE opportunity for writers...and people who sell information.

Here's proof.

$989,832,832 worth of eBooks were sold in 2011.

Could be more than $3 BILLION (with a 'B') this year.

I'm sure you've heard of the *Fifty Shades* books...like *Fifty Shades of Grey*...

Should be "50 Shades of Green" if you ask me!

More than $15 million *Fifty Shades* eBooks have sold, according to industry magazine, *Publishers Weekly*.

In the United Kingdom, Amazon sells 114 eBooks for every 100 printed books.

Publishing will never be the same.

NEW writers are breaking through and earning significant money from eBooks.

My name is John Smiths and I'm one of these writers.

I took my first eBook to well over 100 sales a day...in 3 days.

Right now, I have several eBooks that sell more than 100 "copies" a day.

I'm happy to show you how... Just click here to get started. I provide a significant amount of free information about this subject.

Even a complete beginner can sell 10–20 eBooks a day...once you understand how to make the most of Kindle.

5 Reasons to Love Kindle...

1. You don't need a big email database.
2. You don't need to spend money promoting your book.
3. You get paid quickly.
4. You get published instantly.
5. The income is passive... Just sit back and watch the money float into your account...

Any age or background. You could be 9 or 99. Any location.

If you really want to be successful on the Kindle platform, you MUST know some incredibly important "secret tunnels," shortcuts, and hidden techniques. Amazon does not tell you about these techniques.

But I will...for free...

Here's the place to get started.

To your Amazon publishing success,

John Smiths
Kindle Author

P.S. Even if you don't think you have an eBook ready to go...think again. These eBooks don't have to be long. In fact, you probably have content on your hard drive that you can turn into an eBook.

You can start this weekend and be selling on Kindle in 3 days. Click here to see how I did it.

P.P.S. It's especially important to jump into this market NOW. Incredible growth is taking place in the eBook market and there are several categories just waiting to be dominated...by YOU.

CLICK HERE NOW TO EARN MONEY THROUGH AMAZON KINDLE'S PLATFORM

● ● ● ●

And here's an email from Levi's. Another copywriter wrote this email. I would organize their emails very differently and I would measure results extremely closely.

OUR 3 FAVORITE
LOOKS THIS MONTH

Sadly, scumbags and reprobates around the world send millions of spammy emails every day and this gives emails and direct response copy a bad name. It's so inexpensive to send email compared to direct mail that spammers will keep spamming. But email is so important for official business today that email will continue to be a force in marketing. But you must have a direct response copywriter write your emails for maximum revenue.

Pay-Per-Click Ads

When you visit a major, or even minor, website, you'll see advertising. And when you visit search sites like Google, Bing, and Yahoo, you see advertising in the form of a few lines of copy.

Let's take a look at some examples.

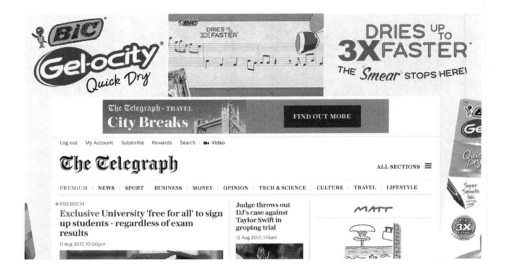

The above site is for The Daily Telegraph and you'll see some advertising at the top of this page...ads for pens. Let's take a look at another example, this time from The Weather Channel.

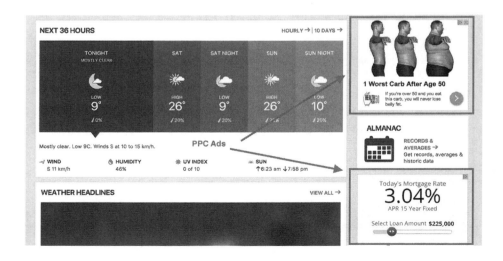

And when I search on a search engine like Google, ads like those below appear. The advertiser gets charged for each "click" on their advertisement. The price depends on a formula determined by companies like Google.

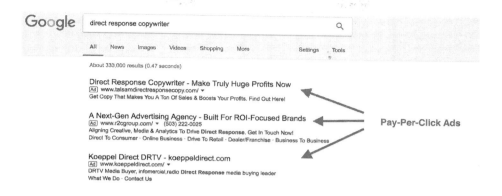

Facebook also sells this type of pay-per-click advertising. Here are three examples...in the red boxes.

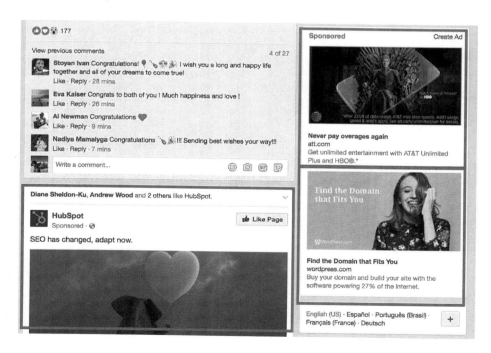

You'll find these pay-per-click ads on other popular and even less well-known websites. I write these ads for some of my clients and I use direct marketing principles, specifically headline templates. I'll talk about headlines later in this book.

Opt-In Pages

An opt-in page is a form of landing page. A landing page is so called because it's a web page where you "land" after clicking a link in an email or an online ad.

The goal of the opt-in page is to provide some type of information that motivates the potential customers to provide information. The information could be your first name and email address. It could be a lot more information. The company that gathers this information will then contact you by phone, by email, or maybe by regular mail. Opt-in pages are a lead generation exercise.

I have written hundreds of opt-in pages. These are extremely effective at helping companies generate leads, nurture leads, and build their own databases. Once people opt in to a database, they can opt out. So it's not a spammy exercise when you follow the rules.

Advertorials

The nomenclature pretty much describes this type of advertising: it's part editorial, part advertisement. The advertisement looks like an article, or near enough, but it's an advertisement. In fact, you'll see many magazines and newspapers put the word "advertisement" above the advertorial.

You'll find advertorials in print publications but you'll also find them online. Here's an example.

The online version of the advertorial is the "landing page," and the advertorial will motivate you, if the writing is good, to click through to a full-on sales page, as described below.

You might think that print advertising is dead...newspapers and magazines. Precisely the opposite is true. I know several marketers who are making a small fortune advertising products and services in print, primarily using advertorials.

I've recently seen advertorials in The New York Post. I've recently seen advertorials in The New York Times. I've recently seen advertorials in The Daily Telegraph in London. I've recently seen a lot of advertorials in the tabloid newspapers in the United Kingdom.

The advertorial formula follows the same formula as other forms of direct response copywriting. The call to action at the end of the advertisement is usually to call a toll-free number.

Online, the advertorial works because it provides some valuable information before the reader visits the sales page. What's a sales page? You're about to find out below.

Sales Pages

A sales page is a web page created to motivate the potential customer to try a product or service. You've been to many sales pages without realizing you're on a sales page. When I write a sales page, it's usually a long one, with somewhere between 3,000 and 15,000 words. Yes, that's a lot of copy. There's an old saying in direct response copywriting: the more you tell, the more you sell.

There are lots of elements to a successful sales page.

- Headlines.
- Proof.
- Leads.
- Photos and graphics.
- Guarantee.
- Close.
- P.S.
- Sub-heads.
- Lists.
- Videos.
- Details of the offer.
- And more.

Here's the top part of a sales page.

**An EXCLUSIVE Offer With a Special
Low Price Just For Revolution Golfers**

Click the image below for a special video.

**Everything You Expect from a
Premium and Super-Durable Tour-
Level Ball ... For HALF the Price**

And then a little further down.

22 Reasons to Add the Vice PRO and/or the Vice PRO SOFT to Your Golf Improvement Arsenal

People are loving the **Vice PRO** and the **Vice PRO SOFT** golf balls and you probably will too ... here's why ...

1. **A premium golf ball WITHOUT the premium price** by going straight to you ... a member of the Revolution Golf Family.

2. **Tour-level distance** with every club in your bag thanks to the construction.

3. **Superior control** with every club in your bag.

4. **Great touch and feel** for a magical short game around the greens.

5. **Tons of spin** around the green for maximum control with every short game shot.

6. **Hit all the shots you want to hit.** Smack it down the fairway. Baby draw. Soft "feathery" fade into a tight pin. Low spinner. Lob. Bump and run. Standard pitch ... every shot in your arsenal is easy to hit thanks to the design, engineering, and construction.

7. **Every bit as good** as the premium golf balls? You be the judge...

8. **You can try it for free.** If you don't like the Vice PRO and/or the Vice PRO SOFT, you can get your money back thanks to the Revolution Golf 365-day guarantee. You take no risk.

9. **Golf Digest Hot List accolades** – every bit as good as the premium golf balls ... according to the experts.

These pages can generate millions in revenue. They need the right copy, the right list, and the right offer.

Radio Advertising

I'm sure you've heard those ads on the radio that ask you to call a toll-free number three times at the end of the ad. These are direct response ads written by a direct response copywriter. You've also heard clever and witty radio ads with no specific call to action. These are branding ads.

Direct Response TV Advertising

On prime-time TV, you will see 30-second commercials, usually entertaining, poignant, or funny. Later at night, or sometimes during the day, depending on the channel, you'll see longer ads, sometimes up to three minutes. The ads are often for some type of home gadget or something similar. You'll likely hear and see the words, "BUT WAIT, THERE'S MORE!" and you'll be told to call a toll-free number RIGHT NOW.

The former are branding ads. The latter are direct response ads and these have created billionaires.

You will also see much longer ads, known as infomercials. These can last up to 30 minutes. Again, a direct response copywriter writes the copy.

VSL

VSL stands for video sales letter. It's basically a narrated PowerPoint presentation and these can last from 25 to 60 minutes.

I've written these for health products and also for financial information products. I've used VSLs to sell my own information products.

Stealth Direct Response Copy

I've included the "usual suspects" where you can see the work of a direct response copywriter. But I've also written copy for speeches, blogs, forums, displays, and what we call "display ads" on sites like Facebook and Google.

The medium doesn't really matter. The basics of direct response copy-writing are always the same. The medium changes. The fundamentals are the same.

QVC

When I'm on the road, I usually watch QVC in my hotel room. Why? It's not because I want anything they sell. They usually sell women's items like clothes, jewelry, and skin care creams. I don't wear women's clothes. I don't wear women's jewelry...or any jewelry...and the only skin cream I use is sunscreen because I'm outdoors a lot.

But I watch QVC with a huge smile on my face. In fact, I'll be in the hotel room, muttering things like "I love that" or "what a great proof element."

QVC provides a non-stop lesson in textbook direct response copywriting. Go on...prove me right by switching on the TV right now and paying close attention.

Here's what you'll see.

- There's a headline in the script to grab your attention.
- Enthusiasm – a crucial part of direct marketing.
- Proof in abundance – this could be a "before and after" display or an attractive model showing off a dress.
- Scarcity – look at that counter showing how many they've sold or how many they have left.
- The irresistible offer.
- A solid guarantee.
- Personality in abundance – this could be the creator of the product or just the person making the pitch.
- TOTAL CLARITY – you know PRECISELY what you're getting for your money.
- A clear explanation of the benefits.
- The super-clear CTA, which is usually to call the phone number, where, I'm certain, there's probably an upsell...or two...or three.

QVC is ALL ABOUT direct marketing and they clearly have some of the top direct response copywriters on their team.

EVERY Advertisement Should Be a Direct Response Ad

There are two types of advertising. Image or "creative" advertising and direct response advertising. The vast majority of companies use image advertising and "creative" copy. There's no accurate way to measure the response. But many of the most successful companies use direct response marketing and the work of a direct response copywriter. You can measure the results to the penny. Then you test and hone your message so you generate even more revenue.

Why would anyone use "image" advertising when direct response marketing is much more efficient, effective, accountable, and powerful?

Over the Next Several Weeks, Here's Your Assignment: If You Want to Make More Money...

Whenever you're watching TV, or surfing the web, or listening to the radio, or reading a newspaper or magazine, make a point to discover and understand the difference between direct response ads and branding ads. Pay close attention to the structure of the direct response ads and you'll start to see a pattern.

Ask yourself this question: "How could I advertise my business using direct response copywriting?" Or... "How would a skilled direct response copywriter market my products and services?"

It's pretty simple. If you want to be super successful, then you MUST make the switch from "image" advertising to direct response marketing. And you MUST have a direct response copywriter on your team.

CHAPTER 5

14 Reasons Why Advertising Agencies, Marketing Executives, and Companies Never Use Direct Marketing and DO NOT Want to Hire Direct Response Copywriters.

This chapter is admittedly a bit risky on my part. I'm listing reasons why people DO NOT hire direct response copywriters.

THAT'S ME.

But once you understand these reasons, you'll understand why you should hire a direct response copywriter.

By this stage of this book, you know how crazy I am about direct marketing and direct response copywriting. But that's secondary to a question I hope you're now asking: **"Why doesn't everyone use direct marketing all the time?"**

It's an excellent question because direct marketing is the only form of marketing where the results are totally measurable. And you'd think that every company would want to see exactly what's working, and what's not, right down to the penny.

But no, companies continue to pump millions of billions of dollars into branding advertising.

Whatever.

Let me give you 14 reasons why companies, of all sizes, rarely use direct marketing and direct response copywriting. Warning: these may upset and shock you especially if you feel that "branding" advertising is superior to direct response marketing. I'm not here for the people who won't hire direct response copywriters. I'm here for you. You bought this book because you're ambitious and want to succeed. To achieve this success, you need to hear the truth about marketing so you don't waste time and money on branding and general advertising.

Here are the reasons.

ONE. Most people DO NOT want to be accountable. Direct marketing is totally accountable and people rarely want to be accountable. Direct marketers relish accurate data and results, even when there's bad news. My clients closely monitor the results my copy produces. I like this situation because it's an opportunity to prove my worth to my clients. I have written over 400 sales pages for one client. Would they hire me if my copy failed? NO! I have worked extremely hard to learn how to write the type of copy that motivates people to take specific actions...including pulling a credit card out of their wallet and buying products. I relish the accountability of direct response marketing.

TWO. The advertising agency model. Many advertising agencies like to sell pretty websites, pretty ads, and all things "creative" because there's no accurate measurement. When sales are up, the people running the advertising agency take all the credit. When sales are down, they blame outside factors like the weather, wars in foreign countries, viruses, the price of bananas in Brazil, gas shortages, or political upheaval in the United Kingdom. But even if sales are up, there's no accurate accounting of ROI. Agencies don't want to hire direct response copywriters because we're not "creative" and we're seen as crass and loud. It's raw snobbery and it's the clients who suffer.

THREE. The awards culture. People in marketing love awards and awards dinners. The awards culture says, "If the ad wins an award, it must be brilliant and superbly effective." But nobody ever points out, "The awards are handed out by people who don't really know what they're doing and don't understand direct marketing and ROI." Every mid- to large-sized city in the United States has some type of advertising awards dinner at least once a year. And there are publications like Communication Arts, which are replete with "award-winning" advertising and design that look wonderful. But ask the question, "What's the ROI?" and you'll get blank stares or a mumbled, "Well...it's all about getting brand awareness out there." Direct response copywriters don't win awards. They generate revenue. You can take revenue to the bank. Try depositing that award with the bank teller.

Let me give you two examples of award-winning ads.

 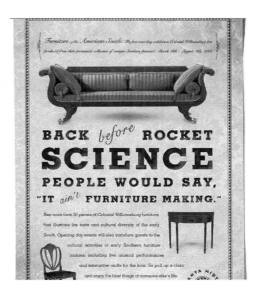

Award-winning advertising. But what's the ROI? Where's the money?

If you understand these ads and what they're trying to achieve, please let me know.

FOUR. The MBA factor. As I mentioned earlier, professors at MBA schools rarely understand direct marketing and sales. Why? Because they're academics and most haven't ever sold anything and they've never been seriously involved in direct marketing. These are the "educators" who teach MBA candidates. And it's the MBA candidates who run most marketing departments at most companies...from Fortune 100 companies to mid-sized companies.

I've told marketing directors, many of them with an MBA, that I'm a direct response copywriter and I have typically received that "blank stare" indicating they don't know what I do. Yes, some MBA marketing programs spend time focusing on data but that's just one tiny part of direct marketing.

FIVE. Lack of education. To be totally fair, it's not easy to find an organized direct marketing education. You can find seminars, books, and manuals...and lots of them...but, as I write, there's no organized course in direct marketing or direct response copywriting at any college or university. So, with a lack of educational opportunities, it's no surprise that only a small percentage of people in business seriously understand direct marketing and want to use direct marketing or speak with a direct response copywriter.

SIX. The "guru" factor. I rarely spend time following popular and trendy business gurus. Many have enjoyed success with their books and their speaking engagements but they know very little about hardcore direct marketing and direct response copywriting, at least based on what I've seen of their work. These and other gurus have significant influence on business thinking and if they promoted direct marketing, more companies would use direct marketing. But it's easier to talk about ethereal concepts like "the tipping point" and "the purple cow" instead of non-trendy but highly effective concepts like upsells and other tactics that actually drive and deliver real revenue. These people sell "the next big thing" when it's the "old thing" called direct marketing that actually generates billions in revenue.

SEVEN. The "trendy" factor. Gurus, marketing people, speakers, and others in business love to focus on "what's next" and "originality." Why? Because it makes them look cutting edge and thus...really smart and "with it." Direct marketing isn't trendy. The technology platforms change but the fundamentals of successful direct marketing have been exactly the same for centuries. They work as I write and will continue to work as long as humans continue to be humans. Social media is super trendy. Social media is NOT marketing; it's a direct marketing advertising platform for certain companies.

EIGHT. The "snob" factor. Marketing and advertising people, typically the ones who think they know everything about marketing, view direct marketing as a dirty backwater. Hire a direct response copywriter who hasn't won any awards? "No way! We're way too brilliant for that here in the agency and branding world! GO AWAY you horrible little direct marketers and direct response copywriters and go sell your junk on late-night TV" is the thinking.

NINE. Corporate Culture. I was recently sitting in a meeting full of marketing people, many with big titles like Executive Vice President of Global Marketing. The company has about one thousand employees and is part of a much larger enterprise. Someone in the room asked me to explain how and why direct response copy works. I only had 15 minutes and I was given no preparation time. No problem. I can, as I'm sure you've discovered, speak at length about direct response copywriting...without repeating myself and without much in the way of preparation. I showed the assembled an especially successful sales page and the assembled looked at me like I was a Klingon.

"Really? That stuff works?"

"Yes, really. Tens of millions for this one company, in fact."

The corporate culture in big companies and direct marketing rarely mix. There's no excuse for this. If I were the CEO of a company and all the marketing people were branding types who didn't want to implement direct marketing strategies, I'd fire them all and hire direct marketers.

TEN. Irrational fear/erosion of brand equity. In direct marketing, "branding" is concept we never think about. Branding comes from the world of ranching where ranchers and cowboys would "brand" their cattle with some type of specific mark, primarily to thwart cattle thieves and other miscreants. People who work in advertising and marketing, many with whopping salaries and big titles, like to talk at length about branding. They use bizarre words and phrases like "brand equity" and "brand-centric marketing" and "brand identity" and "brand health" and other such piffle. A company's brand is essentially what a potential or current customer believes when they see a company logo or think about the company while they are doing the dishes or something similar.

I used to work for a large company in the newspaper and information business. One of the executive vice presidents...I think he was in circulation...used to hold these meetings where managers and others were expected to attend. I was a manager so I had to show up. I remember this mega-dolt talking, at length, about the newspaper's brand. He talked about the McDonald's brand meaning "a reliable hamburger experience" and other such marketing twaddle.

And then the person in charge of the company decided it would be a great idea to hold a company-wide series of three-day meetings to, among other things, redefine the company's brand.

Nobody ever focused on what's really important to a newspaper company: selling advertising and motivating people to subscribe to newspapers and information platforms.

Look...there's a place for "branding" in the marketing universe. I'm about to hire a graphic designer to create a logo for my little company. I named my series of copywriting training videos "The Aspen School of Copywriting." Why? Because Aspen has a certain high-end cachet, plus it also happens to be the town I call home.

But branding can be misleading...and confusing. People who live outside Aspen might think of the town as a playground for the mega-wealthy. It can be. But the Aspen I know is extremely different. It's a real town with working people and real lives.

Sadly, the world of marketing is replete with people obsessed with branding and branding buzzwords; they believe that direct marketing can damage a company's brand.

There's a company in San Francisco that specializes in branding. The company is called Salt. I'm sure they are extremely pleased with their copy and so won't mind if I quote the following, from their flashy website.

"They dictate your market share, product viability and life span. They're your stock price, media buzz and critical mass. They're judge, jury, metric, evangelist, or critic. They're your customers, your prospects, and your influencers. They call the shots and set the rules. And they alone will decide whether your brand is iconic or generic, relevant, or unworthy.

"At Salt, we work with leaders to identify what makes their brands essential to these powerful people: today's consumers. We find intersections of growth among business strategies, market opportunities, and customer insights. When a brand is focused and engaged, it creates a multiplier effect by making the most of every consumer interaction, across channels, across touchpoints, across boundaries. It enables you [to] tell more powerful and compelling stories, create richer expressions, and deliver genuine engagement. In today's hyper-connected world, that's how you reach people—and more importantly, how they reach you."

This is an example of copy that doesn't say...anything.

Here's some copy from one of the largest advertising agencies in Charlotte, North Carolina, where I used to live. Again, I'm sure they think the copy is brilliant and won't mind the inclusion.

"Our award-winning Creative group engages customers by developing inventive ways to bring each brand's personality and positioning to life. Beginning with a research-based understanding of customer attitudes and behaviors, our designers, writers, and developers create compelling, integrated experiences."

Total gobbledygook. Notice the focus on awards and the capital "c" for creative. And what's a "compelling, integrated experience?" I have no idea and I've been writing copy all my professional life.

Compare and contrast my copy on my home page.

"My goal is to help you sell your products and services. I'm NOT trying to earn applause from the 'copy police' or to win advertising awards. I'm here to help you increase your sales."

WHO DO YOU WANT TO WORK WITH?
The company that promises "integrated experiences" or "product viability" or the person who promises MORE MONEY?

Here's what I do as a direct response copywriter: I choose words and images and organize them to motivate customers to try products and services.

That's a highly simplified version of a complex process, but, you have to admit, it's clear.

What do YOU want? A room full of overpaid and highly educated so-called marketing experts talking at length over expensive coffee, at your expense, about the hyper-ethereal notion of a brand...or do you want REVENUE and PROFIT that you can actually measure?

I know what I want. And hopefully, you want precisely the same.

And one more thing about branding before I shut up and never mention the "b" word again. It's so important, I'm going to put this in bold type.

Your clients and customers DO NOT care about a brand. They care about themselves and their needs, desires, problems, and goals and how your product and service can help them get where they want to get plus feel better about themselves.

I've helped to build two of the biggest brands in direct marketing in the last five years. I achieved this by writing direct response copy and using direct marketing techniques. The notion you can't build a brand through direct marketing is specious. David Ogilvy, the super-famous ad man, built his brand through direct marketing.

ELEVEN. Fear of failure. One of my sales pages generated a 6% conversion rate. This means that, for every one hundred people who saw the page, six decided to try the product. It's more relevant, and important, to measure actual revenue generated. We use conversion rates to give us a benchmark we then try to beat. A 6% conversion rate is fairly high. But that means a 94% failure rate.

I know an experienced direct marketer who set up a campaign to sell a dietary supplement. He put a huge amount of work and money into the campaign. He then launched the campaign and sold exactly THREE bottles of the supplement.

In 2014, I attended a conference with four hundred of the world's top direct marketers. I spoke with Joe Sugarman, who created the famous "blueblocker" sunglasses—one of the most wonderful direct marketing success stories in the history of direct marketing. He said, "I've had so many failures, I can't even describe them fully."

Also appearing at the conference: Greg Renker of Guthy-Renker, one of the world's top direct marketing companies. During his speech, Renker described the pain of seeing a product totally fail during the launch. Each launch costs Guthy-Renker around $20 million. But when a product succeeds, it generates billions in revenue every year. The company's new products fail all the time.

Looked at cynically, perhaps, direct marketing is about failure...repeated failure...failure every minute of every day. But looked at with more positivity, direct marketing is about picking yourself up after a failure, figuring out why something didn't work, and generating millions in revenue by learning from your mistakes. And when there's success, the goal is to become even more successful.

Nobody wakes up in the morning thinking, I'm really looking forward to failing today. One major yet hidden reason that people avoid direct marketing is the failure element, which, of course, is closely connected to accountability.

TWELVE. Nobody has ever sold anything. I have sold publishing services. I have sold advertising in regional magazines. I have sold books, person-to-person. I have sold backpacks, camping equipment, and outdoor clothing. I have sold ski lessons at $900 a day. My colleagues in the world of direct response copywriting have also sold products and services. One super-successful copywriter used to sell encyclopedias door-to-door. David Ogilvy, who founded one of the most successful advertising agencies in the world, used to sell kitchen equipment door-to-door. Specifically, he sold Aga Cookers and even wrote a manual for other Aga Cooker salespeople. Find it...it's free. It's an excellent read.

I read books about copywriting, psychology, direct marketing, and, perhaps most importantly, sales. When I write, my goal is to sell. I'm a writer, yes, but I'm primarily a salesperson. I worked in a retail store and my goal was to motivate the person in the store to bring a product to the cash register.

Sometimes, even though I try to avoid this scenario, I end up in a room full of corporate marketing types. Whenever I end up in that type of environment, I look around and ask myself, "Have any of these people actually ever sold anything?" People who have never had to sell anything in order to earn a living rarely embrace direct marketing and direct response copywriters. Selling is beneath them—even though, of course, they're supposed to sell stuff.

THIRTEEN. Voice. It's rare, but sometimes I hear this feedback from a client. "You didn't really capture the 'voice' that we're looking for."
What?

Some marketers are extremely concerned with capturing the 'voice' of a product or the person who is the figurehead of the company. They want my writing to be "on brand" whatever that means. Voice is a mysterious and essentially useless concept to this copywriter. My message to people who are worried about voice is: would like me to capture the 'voice' of your brand or motivate people to try your product or service so you make money? Voice is NOT part of direct marketing and direct response copywriting.

Your customer is not interested in your voice. They're interested in themselves and what they want and/or need.

FOURTEEN. Lack of ambition and general ennui. Whenever I meet corporate marketing types, I get a sense of boredom. I walk into rooms full of people who seem eager for Friday afternoon to arrive extremely quickly so they can go to their favorite bar, go fishing, go boating, or play video games until three in the morning.

Call us crazy, if you will, and I fully understand this, but we direct marketers are typically rabid about direct marketing. We read books and other materials about direct marketing and direct response copywriting. We get together to talk about direct marketing. It's never work. It's raw fun, even when things go badly. And we're always reading more about direct marketing. Why? Because we love this discipline and want our clients to be extremely successful.

Why did I write this chapter? Was it to bash advertising agencies and marketing executives?

No.

I don't want you to fall victim to what some people call "conventional marketing wisdom."

Let me, because I'm a direct response copywriter, use a more positive approach. I wrote this chapter to motivate YOU to focus your marketing on a direct marketing approach. Why? Because I want you to join the millions of people in business who have harnessed the power of direct response copywriting and direct marketing to generate whopping wealth and become massively successful.

It's not Just Me, by the Way...

I'm not a lone voice crying in the wilderness. What I've written above has been written and stated before, not just by theorists but by direct marketers who have enjoyed whopping success in direct marketing. Some of them started in the branding world.

Who specifically? Where can you see their work?

- John Caples in *Tested Advertising*.
- Bryan Kurtz in *Overdeliver*.
- Gary Bencivenga in *Bencivenga Bullets*.
- Claude Hopkins in *Scientific Advertising*.
- The previously mentioned David Ogilvy in his video "We Sell or Else"...and *Confessions of an Advertising Man*.

Other direct marketers could produce other examples. You must understand the difference between branding advertising and direct marketing and always use direct marketing.

CHAPTER 6

The Key Fundamental of Direct Marketing. It's NOT About Persuasion. It's About MOTIVATION.

There's a book about direct marketing called *Breakthrough Advertising*, which I mentioned in Chapter 2. The author, Eugene Schwartz, passed away in 1995. The book is famous in direct marketing and Schwartz was one of the world's top direct response copywriters when he was writing. *Breakthrough Advertising* is a dense book that's difficult to understand at first, even if you've spent several years in direct marketing.

Schwartz wrote simple and crystal-clear copy but he wrote one of the most complex books ever written about marketing. It's a book that EVERYONE in marketing and business must read and understand.

I have two takeaways from *Breakthrough Advertising*. The first is what Schwartz calls "the levels of awareness and the levels of sophistication." The other key concept is that you can't create demand for a product or service. Instead, you have to channel the existing demand toward your product or service.

Let me explain.

I cannot go up to a bald man and try to sell him a hairbrush. I will fail. I might also get punched in the nose. That's because I tried to persuade the bald man he really needs a hair brush.

But when I present the bald man with something that will help him gain the hair he so desperately wants, I have a strong chance of being successful.

The bald man doesn't want hair. He wants...

- To be more attractive to potential partners.
- To feel better about himself.
- To look younger.
- To avoid being taunted by people like me who still have an abundance of hair, even at my age.

Those are just a few of the bald man's desires. My goal as a direct response copywriter is to discover those needs, wants, and desires and connect them with what the product or service provides.

What is persuasion?

Persuasion is the act of persuading, which means: "to move by argument, entreaty, or expostulation to a belief, position, or course of action."

I'm sure you can find other definitions.

But here's the crux. Persuasion is about changing someone's mind. For example, I'm not a big fan of certain foods including tripe, which is the edible lining from the stomachs of various farm animals. However, I'm very fond of sausages, which are not usually made from prime cuts of meat.

To get me to try tripe, you're going to have to persuade me to eat it; eating tripe is not something I want to engage in. However, it will be a lot easier to motivate me to try a new type of sausage. In fact, I might be excited to try a totally different sausage.

It's a lot easier to motivate me than to persuade me. Same with you and everyone else on the planet.

You might think I'm trying to persuade you to move away from branding advertising toward direct response marketing and direct response copywriters. Nothing could be further from the truth.

I'm trying to motivate you to make the switch.

You see, I know what you want.

- You want to be wildly successful.
- You want a business that's valuable.
- You want to know the effectiveness, or otherwise, of your advertising and marketing spend so you avoid wasting money and see an ROI.
- You want to hammer your competition. Probably.

- You want to get your great products and services to your clients and customers.
- You want financial security for your family and your business.
- You want clarity when it comes to marketing.
- You want to know what other companies do to be successful when it comes to marketing.
- You don't want to waste money.
- Plus...you're skeptical and suspicious of ad agency types and their lack of accountability.

These are your motivators, your core emotions. I'm simply coupling these with the features and benefits of working with direct marketers and direct response copywriters.

In fact, I had a conversation about this very subject just a few days ago. I was enjoying lunch with a group of people, including a client. The lunch was at a sumptuous country club with one of the most cosmic buffets I have ever seen...salads...pastas...a carvery...soups...an omelet station...a full table of deserts...and more.

Someone at the table said that my work was all about persuasion and I had to correct them—politely, of course.

"Persuasion," I said, "is me telling you to try something in the buffet that you don't want or like."

I asked them what they didn't like.

"Italian wedding soup."

"Persuasion," I added, "is me trying to get you to eat a bowl of Italian wedding soup. What do you especially like at today's buffet?"

"The roast turkey," came the reply.

"Then my job is relatively simple," I said. "I want you to try the roast turkey by making you aware of its presence in the buffet and also by detailing how it's the best roast turkey you'll ever try."

That's NOT persuasion. It's MOTIVATION, and there's a huge difference.

As a direct response copywriter, I'm in the "motivation" camp.

When your copy reaches the eyes, ears, and hearts of people who will be genuinely interested in what you have to provide, that's motivation. You are motivating the prospect to try a product or service that will help them get where they want to go and help them feel better about themselves.

And here's something else about persuasion/motivation. The same applies to my clients. I will NEVER persuade a potential client they need to hire me if they don't understand direct marketing and simply see copywriters as a commodity. But when a potential client is "on the bus" and understands how a direct response copywriter can totally transform their business then it's relatively easy to motivate them to contact me and begin a conversation.

Here's another reason it's all about motivation and not persuasion. People are ultimately interested in themselves and you can't persuade them to act against what they really want. Motivation is all about giving potential customers logical, proven, and sensible reasons to act in their own self-interest and try the product or service you provide.

CHAPTER 7

Four Pillars of Direct Marketing.

To be successful with direct marketing, four pillars must be present.

- PILLAR ONE. A database of potential prospects or a way to find these prospects.
- PILLAR TWO. An irresistible offer.
- PILLAR THREE. Direct response copy.
- PILLAR FOUR. Testing.

It's extremely easy to find databases, also known as lists, of potential prospects. You need a list broker to find these lists. Let's say you're selling a golf product. You can find a list of golfers with a certain income who have bought golf devices in the past. There are companies who specialize in harvesting and selling data. A really good list broker is an amazing find. They will point you directly to the people who are eager for what you sell.

In direct marketing, we define "The Offer" thus: "When you hand over your money and/or information/or something else, here's what you're going to get." Price is a factor, but there's more to the offer than price. Pricing is a fascinating subject and my role as a direct response copywriter includes helping my clients maximize revenue through pricing strategies. One of the many reasons people hire a direct response copywriter is to charge higher prices more often. It's not scamming. It's breaking through the "commoditization" effect.

This entire book is about direct response copywriting but you will sell more with direct response copy than branding copy. Plus you'll be able to measure the results. Direct marketers always use direct response copy.

Testing and constant improvement are vital parts of direct marketing. I can never accurately predict whether one ad will sell more than another ad. There's only one way to discover what will really work, and that's constant testing.

● ● ● ●

These four pillars of direct marketing success must all work together. Some copywriters will tell you it's all about the copy but that's not true. The copy must be seen or heard by people who are going to be genuinely interested in what you're selling. The offer must resonate to the point where the only option is to try the product. Everything must be tested and you must be relentless when it comes to constant improvement.

Part 3

CONSTRUCTING DIRECT RESPONSE COPY

CHAPTER 8

The Work of a Direct Response Copywriter

I n the next several chapters I'm going to detail how I write direct response copy. You might be tempted to write your own copy after reading these chapters. At least to start, I would recommend hiring a direct response copywriter with a proven track record of generating significant revenue. In the beginning, stick to what you do best and leave the copy to copywriters. It takes many, many years of writing direct response copy to become competent. Then it takes many more years to reach the elite level. Some marketers sell programs where they promise you'll be able to write "powerful copy" in just a few short weeks. That's a scam.

It's important to understand how a copywriter assembles copy and it's vital to understand the techniques I use to motivate customers to try products and services.

Why?

- One. Once you understand all that goes into writing copy, you'll understand how much work goes into direct response copywriting.
- Two. You can help your copywriter. Successful copy is a collaboration between the client and the copywriter. Help your copywriter and you'll generate even more revenue.
- Three. You should know what's going on in the head of a direct response copywriter once you've hired one...or before.

My work begins with research...and lots of it.

CHAPTER 9

Step One: Research.

Direct response copy succeeds or fails during the research phase. I must discover everything I can about the prospect, the market, the product, the competition, and much more.

Famous copywriter Gary Bencivenga asked his clients to "back up the truck" with every piece of salient research material.

The top direct response copywriters have insatiable curiosity. They must also have a solid general business sense and understand what really motivates people to buy products and services.

In a perfect world, my research comprises the following tactics and strategies.

ONE. My Preflight Checklist.

It's a series of questions I send to the client before getting into the research. Here's the checklist in full.

● ● ● ●

Name of the product/service.

Please describe the product/service in detail (features).

What is the primary problem this product/service solves?

Please describe the people in this conversation.

The person/company doing the persuading is...

The person you're trying to persuade is...

If you had to list the ONE benefit that's most likely to make someone buy the product or service, what would this be?

EXTREMELY IMPORTANT AND IN BLUE FOR A REASON... What YOU think is important about the product/service is often COMPLETELY UNIMPORTANT to the potential client/customer. Your clients/customers will tell you what's important if you ask.

What sort of social proof can you provide?

What do potential customers fear?

What frustrates potential customers?

What do prospects desire?

What do potential clients know or believe?

Please supply links to articles about you and the product or some type of article about what you offer from the media.

For example: The ACME Halitosis Eliminator recently appeared on The Oprah Winfrey Show and was even mentioned in an article in The Wall Street Journal!

Reviews... Amazon uses reviews (stars). Google uses reviews (stars)... Can you get some of these? Even three or four can be useful.

If the copy is from a specific person (e.g., the owner of company or the inventor of the product), please detail and provide a bio.

How does the copy fit into the marketing strategy/tactics?

Please list the benefits of the product/service.

What are specific numbers associated with the results this product generates?

For example...from 2000-2010, if you had invested in this stock fund, you would have generated a 2% return. But if you had used the Vector Stock Investing System, your $100,000 would be worth $312,555 today.

OR

Last month, a client saved $5,670 over list price on a home.

OR

A Vector Insulation customer reduced their July power bill...in the heat of summer, from $149.55 to $54.20.

What's the emotional trigger?

What is the unique selling proposition of the company and the product/service?

What is the value proposition of the product/service?

What would you recommend as the primary motivator (can be one or all)?

- FEAR
- GUILT
- GREED
- EXCLUSIVITY
- SOLUTIONS

What do clients especially like about the business and the product/service?

Is there are a story associated with this product/service?

What is the price of the product service? Do you want it on/in the sales page/copy or just the order form/page?

If for web...which pages are required?

- Home page
- Landing page
- Squeeze page
- About/why us
- FAQ
- Contact
- Testimonials
- Resources

Please list other pages required.

What is (are) the offer(s)?

I'm always trying to sell happiness... What makes your clients/customers especially happy about you and what will make them happy about this product?

What can you do to instill a sense of urgency so that people are motivated to buy quickly? What will generate the sense of urgency? Please include a date/expiration.

What is (are) the step(s) you want the reader to take after reading the copy?

Please describe the PSYCHOGRAPHIC of the buyer. Please describe the demographic, although the demographic is usually less important.

Psychographic factors include lifestyle, interests, attitudes, values, and personality.

Please list competitors. How is this product different/better?

What does the client/customer stand to lose if they don't get the product/service?

What is the call to action?

Is there a downsell or upsell? Please detail.

What are the other pages in the sales process?

How are people getting to the landing page or website? If direct mail... how did you define the list?

Phone/email/other contact information.

What makes you especially excited about the product or service?

What has worked before in the client's copy? What has not worked?

What are the next steps you want the reader to take? Two options work best.

Please include/attach testimonials or send a link to testimonials.

If the company has a significant history, please detail the prominent and important points and/or moments. Or include a link.

THE MOST IMPORTANT QUESTION...

The reader is reading the copy, thinking, consciously or sub-consciously, What's in it for me? The copy has to answer that question. Put yourself in the shoes of a potential customer and answer it.

Will there be sidebars? If so, please detail.

Please include a disclaimer or link.

Please attach video and/or photos, if applicable.

Are you split testing? If so, please detail what you want to test...

- Product
- Price
- Offer
- Guarantee

If you were selling the product/service and you really wanted to shock the potential customer and really get their attention, what would you say?

What are the limitations of the product/service?

As you can see, it's a detailed checklist/questionnaire. Sometimes the client will provide me with all the information. At other times, the client will provide some and then give me a sense of where to find the information I need. Other times, I will have a call with the client in order to get all the information I need from my checklist. Please use this checklist if it will help your marketing.

TWO. **Asking the Client to Sell the Product to Me.** I will ask the client to pretend I'm a potential client or customer. I ask my client to sell the product or service to me. I make sure I'm a tough sell and very skeptical. If the client has salespeople, I go through the exercise with them.

THREE. **Discovering the Objections.** What keeps people from buying the product or service? Surprisingly, it's rarely price.

FOUR. **Forums and Website Reviews.** I know one extremely successful copywriter who bases his copy around what he reads on forums. I use this tactic when it's applicable. For example, if I'm writing about an arthritis pain supplement, I will go to a forum about that subject. Maybe I'll start a discussion.

FIVE. Act the Part. I put myself in the shoes of the client or customer and imagine I'm going to buy the product or service.

SIX. Two Vital Questions. "What's in it for me?" which is what the customer is asking. I also ask, "What is the client really selling?" If someone is selling ski lessons, they're not really selling ski lessons. They're selling something else...

- The chance to ski with a new significant other.
- Feeling safer on all terrain.
- Not feeling so tired so quickly.
- Mastering different ski conditions.
- Getting to know the mountain.
- Meeting new friends in the group setting.
- Having more fun on the slopes.

When I'm selling golf products, I'm not really selling golf products. Let's say I'm selling a two-day golf school with some of the world's top golf teachers. I'm selling the "star" factor. I'm selling faster progress toward golf goals. I'm selling the amazing destination and the fun of travel.

The "what are you really selling?" question always provides some fascinating answers. Try it with the products and services you sell.

SEVEN. What's the competition up to? What's in their copy? I don't plagiarize but I certainly want to know and understand their messaging and themes.

EIGHT. RFM. Let me explain.

Recency – how recently a customer has bought a product or service.
Frequency – how frequently a customer has purchased products and services.
Money – how much money a customer has spent.

This data is vastly valuable. Advanced-level direct marketers will have this vital data. You don't have to be a mathematician to go through it but the data, when matched with the creative, details what's worked in the past.

NINE. Really Discovering the Key Emotional Motivators.

There are lots of motivators. Here are just a few.

- Financial security
- More sex ... or just some sex.
- Hit the golf ball a long way
- Look younger
- Get a better job
- Live in a great neighborhood
- Provide for children and other dependents
- Prestige
- Feel younger
- Overcome pain
- More fulfilling relationships with significant other
- Avoid divorce
- Save money
- Earn more money
- Lots of toys
- Keep up with the Joneses
- Lose weight (for lots of reasons)
- Find Heaven/Nirvana and the avoidance of Hell
- Need for love
- The fear of shame
- Pride of achievement
- Drive for recognition
- Yearning to feel important
- Urge to look attractive
- Need to feel secure

I begin each project with a long look at these "usual-suspect" motivators. In fact, I ask the client to include what he/she thinks these might be on that preflight checklist.

But I try to dive a little deeper than the basic motivators.

How?

I become part psychologist, part salesperson.

The super-smart car salesperson will strike up a conversation with a car buyer and try to get a sense of exactly what the car buyer will use the car for. "Getting from A to B" is just one answer. The potential car buyer might open up a little and say, "I'm an avid mountain biker." The salesperson can steer (ha!) the car buyer to the product that will carry bicycles easily and get the mountain biker to the trailhead.

Psychology is not my strong suit when it comes to direct response copywriting. It's an area I'm working on by reading books about the subject as they relate to my work.

Right now, to me, the psychology comes in when overcoming objections... as they relate to how a person is thinking and feeling about the product or service.

Let's go back to that mountain biker in the car dealership. The mountain biker will have objections like price, color, options, size, etc. The salesperson has to discover what these might be and overcome them. That's a case of discovering what the prospect does not want.

Your role as the copywriter is to provide the prospect with, as Gary Bencivenga writes in *Bencivenga Bullets*, "rational, logical and honest-to-goodness reasons to act in their own self-interest."

I had a conversation the other day with someone who was telling me that people buy because they're interested in, or like, a brand. Nothing could be further from the truth. People buy because a product or service gets them what they want...or will help them make progress toward a goal...or solve a problem.

TEN. Get Belly-to-Belly. If I can visit a physical business and see the sales process in action, this can provide powerful information. In golf, I love to visit a demo day and see golfers trying various equipment and asking the equipment reps about the golf clubs. This gives me excellent insight into what golfers are really thinking about.

ELEVEN. A Basic Google Search. I get a ton of information from a few hours just cruising around the web. I have to be extremely careful about the sources as there's a lot of misinformation out there.

TWELVE. Amazon Reviews. A great source of information about a product and/or category. Again, I have to be careful. Several nefarious companies place fake reviews on sites like Amazon.

THIRTEEN. Proof Elements. Anyone can say pretty much anything about anything. I can write, "This Realtor is the Greatest Realtor in the Orlando Area," but I have to back this up with proof. I spend a chunk of my research time looking for proof; it's a is a powerful weapon in the arsenal of the direct response copywriter. I discuss proof elements in detail later in this tome.

FOURTEEN. Any Type of Research Documents. There's a famous ad for Rolls-Royce cars written by David Ogilvy. The headline for the ad...

"At 60 miles an hour the loudest noise in the new Rolls-Royce comes from the electric clock."

Ogilvy said he saw this headline in a technical manual that came from Rolls-Royce. It was literally right in the documents that Rolls-Royce sent to Ogilvy.

I was writing copy for a golf video. One of the testimonials said, "I get chosen for my captain's choice team for my driving distance." This became the headline for a successful advertisement. For another golf promotion, one testimonial read, "You'll have to pull this putter out of my cold, dead hands." Thank you...that's my headline. In some ways, writing direct response copy is simply finding the gems in the research, organizing them in a certain order, and using some additional techniques.

FIFTEEN. Levels of Awareness and Levels of Sophistication. It was Eugene Schwartz who came up with these concepts. I'm not going into massive detail about these here because I want you to read Schwartz's book, *Breakthrough Advertising* but here's a basic summary.

Before writing copy, I ask a simple question: "How aware is the potential client or customer of the product or service I'm selling?" And there's another complementary question: "How aware is the potential customer or client of what the product or service provides?"

Once I have the answers to these questions, I can write the copy like it's a one-on-one conversation.

Let's go through the levels of awareness briefly.

Level 1. Prospects Are Most Aware.

Customers know the product or service. They want it. You only need to provide the name of the product and the price. Example: buy five bananas, get one free.

Level 2. Knowledge of the Product and Its Value.

Customers know about the product or service but they don't want it...yet.

Level 3. Something New in the Market.

Customers know they have a need, want, or problem, but they don't know a product exists for that need, want, or problem...yet.

For example, the head of a small company knows he/she needs to get the salespeople performing at a high level. The owner of the company knows there is sales training out there but might not know there's a series of videos available. Yes...he/she knows there is training available but not this sort of training.

Or what about bananas? Someone might think, I love bananas but I want to spend less on bananas. The banana lover might not realize there's an app that will help you track the prices of bananas at stores in their area.

Your goals here are to find the desire that lies inside the prospect and bring this desire to the forefront so the prospect goes, "I really want to try that!"

In this case, I might focus on the technology that makes the product different. We also call this a unique mechanism. You can have major breakthroughs at this level because there might be very little in the way of competition and thus the company can charge more because there isn't much supply.

Level 4. New Products That Provide Solutions.

The potential customer has a problem. You might have the solution. It can be almost any type of problem...from bad breath to not finding any dates (romance, not the fruit). This works best when you have a new solution.

Level 5. The Market Is Totally Unaware.

A difficult but potentially lucrative spot. The potential client doesn't even really understand they have a need or a problem, even though they might. On occasion, a potential client will contact me with an idea that's totally crazy and I'll think, "Nobody will ever want that." I wrote about a sports product the other day; it was the type of product that I didn't even know existed and I write a ton of sports-related copy. Advertorials, and not straight ads, can work well here.

My summary above of the 5 levels of awareness is basic, rudimentary even. You really have to spend some time reading *Breakthrough Advertising*. Everyone in marketing should understand the levels of awareness at a professorial level. Whenever I meet people with an MBA with a concentration in marketing, they have never heard of *Breakthrough Advertising*, or *Scientific Advertising*, or books by John Caples. Tragic. Marketing malpractice.

Another way of understanding this totally new language is to pretend you're in the pub and you're having a conversation and you're trying to motivate the person to try something you know will help them get where they want to get.

Now...let's get into what Schwartz calls the "Levels of Sophistication."

Sophisticated is actually one of my least favorite words. Similar words in the popular lexicon are innovative, evolved, urbane, and the like. But in ancient Greece, the sophists were people with clever but specious arguments. So I'm not a whopping fan of the word.

But let's not worry about semantics... Here are the 5 stages of sophistication when applied to marketing, according to Eugene Schwartz.

Stage 1. First in the Market.

There's a need for the product or service. And you're the first one in the market.

Stage 2. Second in the Market.

You'll have to make a claim that's different from the initial competition...something unique. But you're tapping into the same desires as the first in the market. Still...there's less skepticism.

Stage 3. They've Heard It All Before.

Several products have entered the market. More products and competitors are on the way. The prospects are extremely skeptical due, in part, to the barrage of advertising. Think diets and ways for men to regrow hair. In this case, you'll have to bring a new mechanism to the party. What's the latest diet promise? What's the latest way to get hair growing again? What's the latest way to bring dates into the world of the dateless? Romance, not the fruit, in case you were confused.

Stage 4. Mechanisms Start Competing With Each Other.

As I write, the diet market is selling ketones as a way to block fat from developing. There's clearly a market for the product and the new mechanism but there are other competing mechanisms. The paleo diet is one. Veganism is another.

Stage 5. Nothing Is Working.

Now you've got a problem. The market is totally skeptical because they've heard everything. The market is saturated.

It's here where you see a lot of headlines that seem angry or totally over-the-top. It's here where some copywriters start to bend the truth a little, or a lot.

Markets Change Over Time

Here's another big lesson from *Breakthrough Advertising*... MARKETS CHANGE OVER TIME.

Let's think about golf.

Around 1995, golf club makers started using titanium in drivers instead of steel. Suddenly, you could get an extra 20 yards off the tee just by switching to titanium. But today, EVERY driver is made of some type of titanium. So if I wrote, "Get a titanium driver" today, golfers would laugh and not buy the driver. So the people who make drivers have to come up with some type of new mechanism every time they release a new driver. And I, as the copywriter, have to be aware that it's a crowded marketplace plus I must address that dominant resident emotion of the golfer...to feel great smashing the ball down the middle of the fairway.

SIXTEEN. Call Center Conversations. If a company is big enough to have a call center, I want to spend a couple of days listening in. It's perfectly legal provided the company says, before each call, something along the lines of: "Your call may be monitored or recorded for quality assurance." The people who answer the phones for a company are right at the front lines of the sales process. I'm especially eager to hear the objections they hear... and how they overcome them.

More Thoughts About Research

It's not always practical to conduct all this research. It can take a lot of time and this can mean a lot of money from my client. But when I get the time to conduct the research, excellent results almost always follow.

As a client, your job is to help the copywriter with the research. You know your products and your market with a deep sense of intimacy. Provide as much detail as you can to your copywriters and you will generate more revenue.

Now let's get into writing the copy. You've most likely seen a lot of branding ads. A typical branding advertisement in print has a photo, a headline, plus some body copy, which is what we call the "blocks" of words, usually in smaller print.

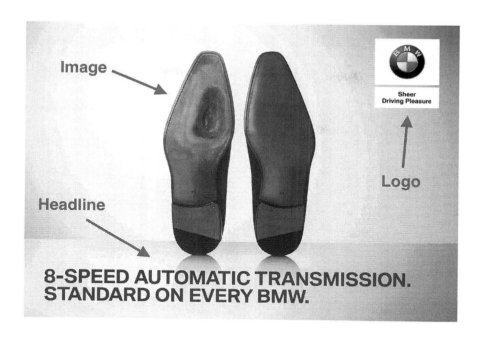

In this example of a "clever" branding ad, there's no body copy. I suppose you're supposed to see this ad and rush over to the BMW dealership and plop down $50,000 for a new car with an 8-speed automatic transmission. The shoes are not included.

When it comes to branding ads on TV, you can see pretty much anything. Soppy. Weepy. Totally over the top. Hyperbolic. Testimonial. Demonstration.

Anything can, and does, happen. Some of the approaches resemble the proof elements we have in direct response copywriting. If you make totally outrageous claims in branding ads, that's perfectly OK because it's just a bit of fun. But make them in direct marketing and the FTC is coming to see you. That's a discussion for another time, another place.

Let me annotate a couple of direct marketing ads. The first is a print ad for David Ogilvy's agency.

How direct response advertising can increase your sales and profits

Even if your company has never used direct response, read what Ogilvy & Mather has learned from half a billion coupons

Ogilvy & Mather has created more than $150,000,000 worth of direct response advertising—in mail and media—for the American Express Company, Burpee Seeds, Cessna Aircraft, Nationwide Insurance; Shell Oil, Sears, Roebuck and other clients.

In the process, we have learned that direct response advertising can help sell $750,000 jet airplanes as well as 25¢ packets of flower seeds.

Here are a few of the ways Ogilvy & Mather uses this most *accountable* form of advertising as part of our clients' marketing programs. Some of them may be useful to you.

1. Direct response can be your "secret weapon" in new product introductions. Cessna Aircraft used direct mail in its introduction of "Citation," a new $750,000 business jet. Ogilvy & Mather began mailings to a list of key corporate executives and their chief pilots long before the first "Citation" was in production.

Sales leads in response to these mailings helped "Citation" become the world's largest selling business jet in just one year.

2. A remarkably efficient way to reach your best prospects. Today Mercedes-Benz diesel-engine cars sell well in America. But ten years ago, it was difficult to identify and reach the limited number of high-potential prospects for diesel cars.

Ogilvy & Mather compiled a list of people who matched the demographic profile of *existing* diesel car owners, then sent them an 8-page letter. As a direct result of the letter, Mercedes-Benz sold 716 diesel cars within eight weeks.

3. How to land your most profitable new customers. Ogilvy & Mather has developed special acquisition programs designed to acquire new credit customers for our clients on a highly selective basis.

These programs combine sophisticated list segmentation techniques with a remarkably precise formula that identifies the profitable customer; establishes his real value; and reveals how much should be spent to acquire him.

PRESENT VALUE FORMULA

$$PV = \int_0^5 (\alpha r \pi \eta e^{-t/\lambda} - \alpha r d e^{-t/\gamma} - \alpha C_b e^{-t/\lambda})\, e^{-\rho t}\, dt - S e^{-\rho L} - M - RC_p$$

This is an example of a "present value" economic model. This model—programmed with test results and appropriate up and downside risks—reveals the true cost of acquiring a new credit customer and predicts the net profit he will return over the next 5 years.

4. How to build a bank of localized leads for your sales force. The pinpoint accuracy of direct mail makes it the ideal medium for obtaining sales leads exactly where you need them most.

Our computerized "Commodity Futures List Bank" supplies *localized* leads to Merrill Lynch representatives from Saskatchewan to San Francisco.

5. Direct response can make television dollars work harder. Television commercials for American Express Credit Cards end with a request for a direct response by phone. This produces tens of thousands of applications for the Card.

Ogilvy & Mather has also improved response to direct mailings by timing mail drops to coincide with television advertising.

6. Direct response is an indispensable element in successful travel advertising. Direct response, in mail as well as other media, has proven to be a key ingredient in marketing travel. The secret is to close the sale by mail—or to obtain a highly qualified lead—instead of wasting a fortune mailing expensive booklets and pamphlets.

Ogilvy & Mather coupon advertisements for Cunard have paid out four times over in immediate ticket sales.

A direct mail offer of free London theater tickets produced response rates as high as 26 percent for the British Tourist Authority.

7. You can now sell high-ticket items direct by mail. Today's ever-increasing distribution of credit cards has revolutionized marketing by mail.

Credit cards now make direct mail practical for selling sewing machines, calculators, color television sets and many other products costing hundreds, even thousands, of dollars.

As sales costs escalate, more and more manufacturers will turn to this new way of selling direct to the consumer.

How to capitalize on new profit opportunities in direct marketing.

Today, more and more major corporations are considering direct marketing in their search for new sources of profit.

It pays to look before you leap into this highly specialized business.

Ogilvy & Mather has found that the odds for success improve if you can use your own customer list and retail packages as an entrée into direct marketing.

One mail marketing business we helped develop now does fifty million dollars in annual sales.

Techniques that work best in direct response advertising

8. Challenge dogma. Ogilvy & Mather has found that it often pays to challenge dogma and test for breakthroughs. Our tests show that:

- An inexpensive offset letter can often outpull far more costly computer letters.
- "On-page coupon-envelopes" can be more cost efficient than expensive preprint inserts.
- An innovative *letter* can be more important to your success than a big, beautiful 4-color brochure.

Note: These examples are not offered to create new dogma but to emphasize that *it pays to test.*

This innovative "personal" letter from Peter Ilich Tchaikovsky—created from hundreds of letters actually written by the great composer—substantially increased response for a new record offer.

9. How to make long copy succeed. Tests show long copy usually, but not always, pulls more orders than short copy in direct response advertising.

Specifics are the key ingredient in successful long copy. Glittering generalities turn readers off. Beware of long copy that is lazy. Supply facts and figures. They impress the reader and help close the sale.

10. The way you position your offer can double your response. We recently split-run three new advertisements against a successful Burpee advertisement that featured a $1 offer in the headline.

All three new advertisements improved response. The one shown below increased results 112 percent.

Old.

Burpee's New
1973 Garden Catalog-Free

New: 112 percent more response.

The reason: The new advertisement offered a free catalog—and clearly positioned Burpee as America's leading breeder of new flower and vegetable varieties for the home gardener.

11. It pays to demonstrate. Product demonstrations are not easy to do in direct mail. But they are worth the effort. They can be exceptionally effective.

Ogilvy & Mather's mailing for Cessna's "Citation" jet enclosed a recording that contrasted the "Citation's" low noise levels with competitive jets—and even an electric blender.

The record proved Cessna's case; words alone could only have made a claim.

12. Asking the reader to quiz himself increases response. Inviting readers to take a quiz involves them with your advertising.

This can pay handsome dividends, as this split-run test shows.

WHICH AD PULLED BEST?

To every woman who would like a career in Interior Design.

"Can you spot these 7 common decorating sins?"

The advertisement on the right invited the reader to quiz herself—as we are doing here by asking you to guess which ad pulled best. (The "quiz," of course, by 230 percent.)

13. The "close" is crucial in direct response. The reader who makes a mental note to "mail the coupon later" usually never does.

One survey showed that less than a third of the readers who *intended* to send in a coupon actually did so.

Ogilvy & Mather uses a four-point checklist to ensure that our copy does all it can to get the reader to tear out the coupon before he turns the page.

14. The position of your advertisement can make the difference between profit and loss. Tests show that the back page of a publication, or the back of one of its sections, can pull 150 percent better than inside pages.

POSC—page opposite third cover in magazines—is another winning position. You can often buy it without paying a premium.

15. New direct mail techniques. The efficiency of mailings can be substantially improved through new techniques.

These techniques—"merge-purge," "hot-line" mailings, timing sequence—produce more response for every dollar invested.

16. Separate the wheat from the chaff. List segmentation concentrates your dollars where they will do the most good.

List segmentation—by both demographic and psychographic factors—becomes critical to profit as direct mail costs go up and up.

Take full advantage of computer technology and sophisticated segmentation procedures—zip code analyses and consumer criteria grids. They now make it practical to single out your best prospects.

Separating the wheat from the chaff is the secret to successful direct mail.

17. Pretesting copy can reduce costs and improve response rates. Ogilvy & Mather's Research Department has developed inexpensive techniques that rank copy promises *before* mail or media testing.

This saves time and money—and increases your chances for success.

COPY PROMISES CAN VARY WIDELY IN APPEAL

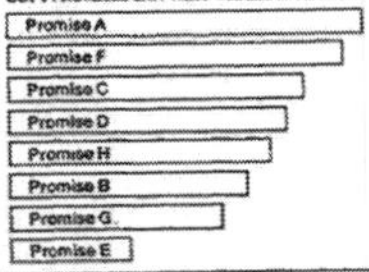
Promise A
Promise F
Promise C
Promise D
Promise H
Promise B
Promise G
Promise E

"Promise Test" research ranks your selling points before mail or media testing. In the above example from an actual test the winning promise proved to be almost three times stronger than the weakest one.

18. Success can be exported. Ogilvy & Mather has found that direct response principles which work in the U.S. are frequently just as effective when applied abroad.

We export these principles to 57 Ogilvy & Mather offices in 30 countries, and coordinate international campaigns through New York.

Example: A series of new direct response advertisements and mailings, initiated in New York and carried out by our Paris office, tripled response for one of the leading book clubs in France.

19. The most accountable form of advertising. Claude Hopkins titled his famous book "Scientific Advertising."

He emphasized that coupon feedback makes direct response the most *accountable* form of advertising. It allows you to measure precisely what every dollar invested returns in sales and profits.

We use coupons and sales conversion rates to evaluate the specific contribution direct response advertising makes to our client's marketing programs. Results show direct response has increased sales and profits in almost every case.

An Invitation

Ogilvy & Mather's Direct Response Division employs three dozen people who specialize in this demanding discipline.

The body of our experience—which can only be hinted at in the space available here—is revealed in a slide presentation: *"What Ogilvy & Mather has learned about direct response advertising and marketing."*

To arrange a presentation, please mail the coupon today.

Ogilvy & Mather

Barry Blau, Managing Director
Ogilvy & Mather, Direct Response Division
2 East 48th Street, New York, New York 10017

I would like to arrange for a special presentation of *"What Ogilvy & Mather has learned about direct response advertising and marketing."*

Name ____________________
Company ____________________
Title ____________________
Address ____________________
City ____________ State ________ Zip ________
Telephone ____________________

An advertisement everyone in advertising should study very closely. I spend this entire book stating what David Ogilvy writes in this advertisement.

Now let's get into more detail.

How direct response advertising can increase your sales and profits

Even if your company has never used direct response, read what Ogilvy & Mather has learned from half a billion coupons

Headline

Subhead

Lead

Body copy

Chart/graph with caption

Formula … direct marketing is a science …

Three images with captions

How many advertising agencies could ever produce advertising like
that? When do advertising agencies ever advertise themselves successfully? Search your local area for advertising agencies and you'll get vacuous
nothingness like this...

EASY IS FOR SOMEONE ELSE

WE GO OUT AND MEET CHALLENGES HEAD ON. IT SHOWS IN OUR WORK.

FIRSTS THAT LAST

ABOUT

has one rule: Craft great work for people we like. We don't see our clients as clients. We see them as partners. And they see us as part of their internal marketing team. Collaborative relationships are fun. And when you're having fun, great ideas happen. After all, we are all working toward the same goal. **Innovative work and incredible results.**

Believe it or not, these web pages are for advertising agencies. Compare the detail in the Ogilvy ad to the vagueness and nothingness of the web pages above. If you're the decision maker at a company and you're eager to work with an excellent advertising agency, which approach will attract your attention?

I bet the coupons flew in for the Ogilvy ad and Ogilvy had to turn clients away. I'd give my back teeth to see the slide presentation. I'd give my front teeth but I lost those in Philadelphia.

You can find the Ogilvy ad online through this search: David Ogilvy direct response ads. Study it closely.

What do I love about this ad?
Lots. This will take a while.

- The simplicity and total clarity of the headline and subhead.
- Instant proof in the lead paragraph.
- Superb direct response copy.
- Lots of copy.
- Three carefully chosen images that provide proof. They also have clear captions.
- A pull-quote...always an excellent away to draw the reader into the body copy.
- Black type on a white background. Always the most readable.
- Ample numerical proof...but not a barrage of numbers.
- Superb typesetting that makes an advertisement that's packed with copy very clear and readable.
- Use of a list...for additional clarity.
- An introduction to the science of direct marketing. Direct marketing is science first, creativity second.
- Proof elements in abundance. A chart. A formula. The names of clients.
- You can get the message simply by reading the subheads—perfect for the scanner.
- Newness... The copy talks about new opportunities in direct response marketing.
- A little bit of boasting about the agency...but backed with proof.

Who wrote all those words? A direct response copywriter. I would wager David Ogilvy had a hand in the copy.

Now let's turn to the Internet. I'm going to point you toward the home page on my website.[4]

My home page ranks #1 or #2 in the organic search engines for "direct response copywriter" and other search terms. The copy on this page, and other pages, has generated over a thousand highly qualified leads in the last six years.

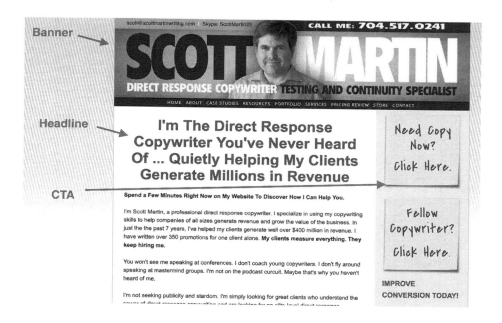

---

4   ScottMartinCopywriter.com

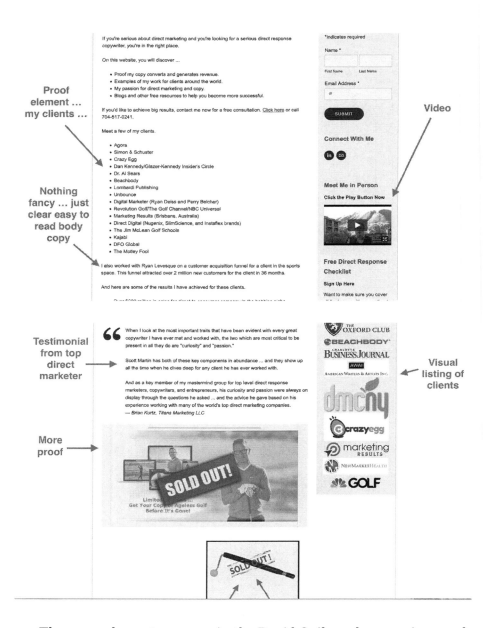

The same elements you see in the David Ogilvy ad appear in my advertisement for my work. The same elements appear in all direct response ads. Why? Because they work: they motivate customers to try products and services.

CHAPTER 10

Headlines and Leads. Grabbing the Attention of Your Prospect.

The headline is the advertisement for the advertisement. The goal is to grab the attention of the reader/viewer/listener and draw this prospect into your advertisement.

You see headlines every day and lots of them. You see them in newspapers and magazines. The title of a book is a headline. Each chapter heading in a book is a headline. Email subject lines are headlines whether the email is an ad or just an email from one friend to another. Even a guitar riff at the beginning of a song is a form of headline, with the goal of gaining and keeping your attention for three to four minutes. You also see headlines on the web, either for international newspapers that are online, or the long sales pages I write for my clients around the world.

At newspapers and magazines, the copy editors typically write the headlines. And many are brilliant at consistently getting your attention. I once heard, although I couldn't verify it, that Cosmopolitan Magazine paid their headline writers over $1 million a year. True? I don't know. But either way, those headlines on the cover of that magazine are superb, whether you like/agree with the magazine's content.

Direct response copywriters have different approaches to writing headlines. But EVERY copywriter can agree...

- With a powerful headline, the advertisement can convert prospects into buyers.
- With a weak headline, there's no chance.

One copywriter I know saves the headline writing process for last. Another spends 60 minutes writing potential headlines before writing the rest of the copy then chooses the one he likes the best. He often uses the "rejects" for subheads. I like to write the headline first then tweak it during my editing/cleaning-up process.

But there's a definite method to my headline writing process. It's not random. I base my process on what's worked for other successful copywriters plus the results of my own testing.

But there's one formula I almost always use and it comes from a copywriter named John Caples, one of the greatest copywriters of all time.

Caples wrote this advertisement.

Right from the beginning of his copywriting career, Caples tested like crazy, studying response rates and applying what he discovered to his copy. He wasn't trying to be creative; he was trying to drive revenue based on data. His book, *Tested Advertising Methods* is a must-read for every copywriter and everyone in marketing and business.

According to an article from one of the main advertising organs, Ad Age...

"Caples began to experiment with split-run ads in the 1940s; by the 1970s, he was running 40-way split-run testing. In a simple split-run, if an advertiser has two different ads, it runs both on the same day in a single publication with each appearing in only half the circulated copies. Coupons in each ad are coded, so the advertiser knows which ad is eliciting more response from consumers. Mr. Caples believed this to be the most scientific means of testing copy. While his methods were at first ridiculed, the concept eventually became an accepted part of ad testing and development."

Copywriter Gary Bencivenga once said, "Not reading and studying John Caples is marketing malpractice." I agree. Caples was a direct marketing expert and famously hated humorous copy, writing, "Clever ads seldom sell anything." Caples was all about sales and revenue...not plaudits for creativity.

Caples had a "base" headline formula, and it's the one I use all the time.

Curiosity + Self-Interest = Compelling Appeal

Let's think about this for a second. You've heard that "the goal of the headline is to get someone's attention," but I also wrote that the goal of a headline is to keep the reader reading. So, the Caples headline formula achieves both...

- The self-interest part is usually a benefit or the promise of a benefit.
- The curiosity part is there to keep a reader moving forward through the copy.

The most important element is **curiosity**. The more I write copy, the more I value and understand the power of curiosity in headlines and subheads.

Here's something else I love about the Caples formula... It can be applied to just about every headline template I use. I list and describe these templates later in this chapter.

Gary Bencivenga has a slightly different way of looking the Caples headline formula.

I = B + C

Interest = Benefit plus Curiosity.

The interest factor gives you the attention of the reader. The reader might have an interest in the product or service you're selling, but remember that predictability kills curiosity. I see so many headlines that give too much away in the headline.

Bencivenga writes...

"When an article promises something of interest and the title leaves me wondering, 'How could this be?'...in other words, when its content is unpredictable...it inflames my curiosity and I have to read it."

My goal is to organize the headline so the copy is easier to read than ignore. Let's look at three headline templates and relate them directly to the Caples formula.

Let me give you some examples.

How to Solve Chronic Back Pain Without Expensive Surgery and Without Anything Crazy Like Sticking Needles in Your Spine

We've got the benefit—an end to back pain; plus, there's an element of intrigue—the reader with back pain will want to know about the alternatives to surgery and needles. It's why I often write headlines with some type of qualifier relating to pain. This gives the headline a bit more oomph plus it's more closely aligned with the Caples formula.

Here's another...

Secrets of The Harvard-Trained Doctor Who Helped 93% of His Patients Solve Back Pain Without Expensive and Harsh Surgery

If you've got back pain, then I challenge you not to keep reading. Notice how I included a number in the headline...always a bonus. Plus there's a proof element: the "Harvard-Trained" doctor. The 93% is a realistic number. It's believable.

Some additional headlines.

Are You Missing Out on Dates with Women...Because of Your Thinning Hair or Bald Spot?

Or more directly...

"Are You Struggling with Constipation? Yes? Then Read About a New Discovery That Worked for 444,340 People Just Last Week."

But there doesn't have to be an instant answer. Here's a total gem/peach of a headline I WISH I had written.

When Doctors Have Headaches, What Do They Do?

Do you need to agonize for several hours over a headline? No. I spend about 20 minutes writing a headline...if that. I credit my headline templates, supplied and explained in just a few pages.

Clayton Makepeace, and copywriters who were fortunate enough to train under him, like a slightly different headline format with a couple of words in big type followed by a sub-head...or incorporated into the headline. Take a look.

Figure 21-2

MARTIN D. WEISS, PH.D. — the analyst who correctly forecast ● The **Great TECH WRECK** of 2000 ... ● The **BLUE CHIP BUST** of 2001-2002 ... ● The **GOLD STOCK BONANZA** of 2002-2003 ... ● and whose best investment recommendations have **SURGED 562%** in this tricky market issues his most disturbing warning to date ...

Retirement
RED ALERT!

READ THIS NOW or KISS YOUR RETIREMENT GOOD-BYE:

These 3 All-New RETIREMENT NIGHTMARES
Are Set to SHRINK Your Stock Portfolio ...
SLASH Your Income ... SMASH Your Bond Holdings ...
and Cause Your Pension, Social Security
and Medicare to Vanish into THIN AIR!

In this eye-opening report:

■ What you MUST do NOW — within the next 10 trading days — to INSULATE your IRA ... your KEOUGH ... your 401(k) ... or your SEP from The Great Retirement Swindle of 2004-2005!

■ PLUS — if you're APPROACHING RETIREMENT: SUPER-GROWTH INVESTMENTS with <u>562% growth potential</u> ...

■ AND, if you're ALREADY RETIRED: 4 SUPER-YIELD INVESTMENTS to lock-in up to 20% INCOME in 2004-2006!

Martin D. Weiss, Ph.D.
Editor, SAFE MONEY REPORT

Dear Fellow Investor,

If you ever hope to retire — and especially if you're ALREADY retired — you'd better hang onto your hat — AND your wallet.

Through no fault of your own, nearly everything you've ever worked for — and virtually everything you've ever wished for in retirement — is now in peril. As you're about to see in this Urgent Alert, your lifestyle, your comfort, your very financial independence are now in danger of being blown away, unless you take action IMMEDIATELY.

(Continued on page 2 ...)

748   *www.makepeacetotalpackage.com*

Glorious copy.

Here's a headline I wrote for a golf product.

> **"How Did Phillis Meti Smash the Ball 406 Yards Right Down the Middle...and in the Heat of Competition?**
> **EASY...**
> **She Used THIS Driver..."**

If you're a golfer, you're going to want to know about the woman who hit that ball 406 yards and you're going to want to know about the driver she used. This promotion sold through the inventory. Quickly. The golf copy I wrote for one client used to shut down their servers.

Before getting into my headline templates, here are the roles of the headline.

- Motivate the reader to keep reading.
- Capture the attention of the prospective client or customer for all the right reasons.
- Stir up curiosity.
- Alert the reader to the primary benefit of the product or service.
- Be totally clear.

I'm sure you can come up with some other roles but the roles above are the most important. The most important role? See #1 above.

Remember to apply the Caples headline formula to my headline templates.

The "How To" Headline

In direct response copy this might be the most prevalent headline. I attended a seminar where a speaker told the assembled the "how to" headline beats other types of headlines 90% of the time they run tests.

The "how to" headline has the significant benefit of built-in curiosity. You don't need use the actual "how to" in your "how-to" headline. Here are two variations.

Golf Instructor to PGA Tour Stars Reveals How to Hit the Ball 20-35 Yards Further off the Tee...

Hit the Ball 20-35 Yards Further off the Tee Thanks to This "Secret Move" All the PGA Tour Stars Are Desperate to Know...

The reader, hopefully, wants to know precisely how to get that extra distance. They will want to know the secret move.

You can also augment the "how to" headline with the "without" clause.

WOMEN: How to Look 10 Years Younger WITHOUT Plastic Surgery or Crazy Chemicals.

Here's the basic formula.

How to get xxxxx (the primary benefit) without xxxx (the pain/hassle/expense).

The "Are You?" Headline

Question headlines are fine, provided the reader already knows the answer.

Have You Tried All the "Typical" Diets? Are You Ready for Something New...That Actually Helps You Lose Weight and Keeps it off for Good?

"Yes" and "Yes" are the answers, if you're eager to lose weight.

The "How I" Headline

It's essentially a variation of the "how to" headline, but it's valuable when the copy is written in the first person.

"How I Increased Revenue 26% in a Week by Learning This Super-Simple Marketing Technique."

The "Secrets of" Headline

Who can resist a secret? The very notion is all about intrigue and curiosity.

Two Secrets of the Long-Drive Champions Revealed

She Hit the Ball 402 Yards in a Long-Drive Tournament. Discover Her Secret Below...

In the latter headline, I was tempted to write, "What's her secret?" but I try to avoid questions in headlines when the reader doesn't know the answer. Notice how I can encourage the reader to "look below" to direct the reader's attention.

"Thousands" Headline

Thousands (hundreds, millions, etc.) now _____, even though they _____.

> **Thousands Have Found Relief from Chronic Gas and Constipation Without Prescription Medications... Thanks to This All-New Solution Created by Harvard-Trained Doctor...**

You can use the "even though they" clause with this headline template provided it makes sense stylistically.

The "Warning" Headline

One of my absolute favorite headlines. It can only be used sparingly, though. You can't just invent some type of event—the "warning" headline needs to connect with some news.

> **WARNING: New Secret Government Agency Is Planning to Steal Your 401(k) Gains Through a Stealth Tax. Here's What You Need to Know. Look Below Now.**

The benefit is protecting the retirement nest egg. The curiosity comes from wanting to know exactly what this agency is up to and how to deal with it.

Here's another "WARNING" headline, targeted at people who work in the hospitality trades.

WARNING: Robots Will Soon Be Taking Almost EVERY Restaurant Job. Discover How to Prepare for This Revolution and Make Even More Money.

The "Give Me" Headline

A favorite of Gary Bencivenga, and thus, a favorite of mine.

Give Me Just 16 Minutes and I'll Show You How to Cut Your Health Insurance Costs by 32%

The "Ways to" Headline

Some copywriters say it's best to focus on one reason and one primary benefit. Others, like me, say it's OK to provide several reasons. Here are two version of the "ways to" headline.

Retired Wall Street CEO Reveals the Shocking Reason She's Staying Away from Medical Stocks for at Least 21 Months.

Doctor Reveals 14 New Ways to Beat Joint Pain WITHOUT Prescription Drugs

I prefer the "several" ways because I see this type of headline in newspapers and magazines. It's often a great idea to imitate excellent headlines from newspapers and magazines.

The "Imagine" Headline

Rarely seen and that's perhaps a shame. I should try this headline more often.

Imagine 'Working' Just 12.5 Hours a Week and Earning Over $100,000 a Year...Right from the Comfort of Your Home. Read Below to Discover How to Transform Your 'Working' Life...

Motivating a prospective customer or client to use their imagination can be powerful.

The "Straight-Talk" Headline

A direct, no nonsense headline. Another I should try more often. This headline can work especially well when the copy comes directly from an authority figure.

Some Straight Talk About Tech Stocks

A photo of a financial specialist could accompany this headline along with a caption saying something like... "Kim Smith Has Tracked Tech Stocks for 15 Years and She's Got Some Bad News." Notice how the "straight talk" phrase provides, with great subtlety, the curiosity factor.

The "Case Against" Headline

Again, it's a headline that can work well with an authority figure. I like its contrarian nature but the headline must go against conventional wisdom.

The Case Against Investing in Google...Despite What the Wall Street Experts Are Saying...

That's a headline certain to get the attention of someone who believes it's a great idea to invest in Google.

The "Mistakes" Headline

A famous headline but not seen much these days.

Do You Make These Mistakes When You Speak English?

But you can apply this headline to just about anything. It's one I've used successfully in golf. Jim McLean, the famous golf instructor, used it in his

"Death Moves" which describe moves you must not make in your golf swing if you want to be consistent.

The "Doctors" Headline

Another famous headline.

When Doctors Have Headaches, Which Aspirin Do They Take?

In the financial space, you can get more specific. "When This Super-Successful Hedge Fund Manager Invests in the Automotive Sector, Here's What She Likes." It seems that Warren Buffett is the favorite of headline writers in this space.

Discover More About the Sector That Warren Buffett Is Looking at Closely FOR THE FIRST TIME.

The "Believe It or Not" Headline

A favorite of Gary Bencivenga.

Believe it or not, I've discovered an investment that's safer than your bank and offers all these advantages...

- **Advantage 1**
- **Advantage 2**
- **Advantage 3**

I like to see a photo of an authority figure with this headline. Again...it's a contrarian headline and these can work well. Notice the curiosity factor, which is strong in this headline.

The Benefit/Offer/Discount Headline

As direct as they come.

Kiss Foot Pain Goodbye in 20 Minutes.

Buy One Banana...Get Two Free!

Save 40% on Prime Rib...but Only Until Tuesday at Midnight.

The "News" Headline

Perfect for advertorials.

New and Powerful Laptops Selling for Just $299

Newspapers may be going the way of the horse and buggy but I know several marketers who are making a killing through newspaper ads. And they're using news-style headlines.

The Testimonial Headline

Super popular, especially in the branding world.

"I always fly Pan Am because they have the best connections and I don't have to spend hours in the airport. I spend more time with my family thanks to Pan Am." —Marcus Smith, Des Moines, Iowa.

I don't use testimonial headlines very often although maybe I should. You need the right testimonial and remember to keep the curiosity and benefits in there when possible.

Headlines With "Free"

FREE FISH AND CHIPS on Wednesday at Sir Ed's Pub in Park Road Shopping Center.

The "Guarantee" Headline

And finally, the guarantee headline. Another one of my absolute favorite headlines on the planet. A couple of examples.

> **I guarantee my direct response copy will generate revenue exceeding the investment in my services or I will rewrite the copy for free. No questions asked.**

Even though there's absolutely no correlation between copywriting and pest control services, the guarantee headline and approach work superbly well in pest control.

A personal guarantee from Robert Jones, owner of Nuclear Cockroach Services:

> **If a cockroach appears in your home up to three months after we provide our special 'Total Deterrent' service, we'll provide the service again absolutely free. AND write you a check for $200 to cover your time.**

The reader should be curious to know about the guarantee. It's important to add a proof element that's directly relevant to the claim.

Decks and Subs

A headline rarely exists in isolation. There's almost always some type of subhead in direct response copy. I like to write a series of subheads directly underneath the headline. These are known as decks. These must provide some additional curiosity along with some benefits.

The subheads and captions throughout a promotion are simply headlines. Again, they must keep the reader reading.
And remember all those "stealth" headlines.

- Subject lines of emails.

- Envelope copy.
- Display ads.
- PPC ads.

Use proven headline techniques for all of the above.

Testing

I could sit in a room with 10 other accomplished copywriters and we'd write 50 different headlines for the same product. They'd all be solid headlines.

Another copywriter, perhaps someone more experienced, could enter the room and rank the headlines. But that's irrelevant. There's only ONE ultimate judge when it comes to the pulling and conversion power of a headline and that's the potential customer.

To discover which headline gets the job done, it's VITAL to test. I talk about testing in a later chapter but here's an important point I'll give you right now.

In direct response, we test everything we can, including headlines. In branding advertising, there's no testing related directly to revenue. Even better, in direct response, once we have a clear winner, we try to beat it as part of the constant quest for improvement.

CHAPTER 11

PROVE IT TO ME!

Anyone who can string a few sentences together can be a copywriter. All you have to write, if, say, you're selling ice cream, is...

SMITH'S ICE CREAM IS THE GREATEST
ICE CREAM ON THE PLANET!!!!

But in direct response, where everything is measured to the penny, we have to be more professional, more cautious. It's the professional direct response copywriter who knows how to provide proof to back up the claims in the copy. I never let a claim become bigger than believable proof.

We have to provide proof. And the proof has to be plentiful plus it must be relevant, complementary, and believable. Proof augments the benefits and buttresses the claims.

Why is proof so vital?

Potential customers and clients provide some curious anomalies. They're...

- Ambitious but afraid.
- Brave but wary.
- Desirous yet not ready to spend money, especially lots of money.
- Happy and unhappy.
- Unhappy and happy.
- Never totally satisfied yet boastful of achievements.
- Wanting to believe but totally skeptical.

Skepticism is the crucial word and concept. People don't buy for a lot of reasons but the main reason is trust, which is closely tied to skepticism.

Once you overcome the skepticism, then you can start selling more products, more often. You can motivate potential customers to try a product or service when you have plenty of proof.

PROOF OVERCOMES SKEPTICISM.

Let me write that again because it's so vital for every business and their marketing.

PROOF OVERCOMES SKEPTICISM.

The amateur copywriter ignores proof. Branding copywriters usually ignore proof or briefly include it. The professional direct response copywriter with a long track record of generating revenue for their clients understands the prudent application of proof and how to harness its power. To most copywriters, proof is boring and finding it can be a pain. But proof increases response and revenue.

It's a lot like sitting at a bar, listening to someone talk about themselves.

I've visited the occasional bar and I vividly remember someone who shall remain nameless telling me about his time as an adjunct professor at a local university.

This might seem a tad impolite but I wasn't the one at the bar telling the story so I feel it's acceptable here.

The former adjunct professor started describing various antics that various young ladies, in the front row of the lecture hall, would engage in during classes. The goal of said antics was to get the attention of the adjunct professor, who, incidentally, is one of the uglier human beings you will ever meet. The attention would lead to higher grades, at least in theory.

After hearing this absurd story, I resorted to some wonderful Scottish slang.

"I know what happened next," I said.

"What?" asked the former adjunct professor.

"Don't tell me...and then your 'erse fell 'aff."

Translation: the next thing that happened was that your buttocks both fell off your body at the same time.

That's how the Scots express skepticism. I'm not Scottish but I adore Scottish slang.

In my own way, I was asking the adjunct professor to provide some proof to back up his raw absurdity. Not surprisingly, he failed, and I remain totally skeptical to this day.

None of the female participants in his classes were "showing off" in the front row in order to gain better grades. It never happened.

Your prospective and even your current clients and customers are exactly the same when it comes to skepticism. So you have to provide PROOF to back up even the most believable statements. It's the serious direct response copywriter who can always back up claims with believable proof.

Here's what Gary Bencivenga writes about proof.

"Never make your claim bigger than your proof. And always join your claim and your proof at the hip in your headlines, so that you never trumpet one without the other."

In fact, the welding, in the headline, and throughout the copy, of believable claims with believable proof, is, in my opinion, Gary Bencivenga's great secret. I strive to achieve this level of "welding" in my copy and I'm always looking to find ways to provide even more proof.

One of the many reasons that long-form copy from direct response copywriters beats short form from branding advertisers? Easy. You can include more proof elements in the former.

Here's a list of proof elements. These come from Will Swayne, a client who runs a marketing agency in Brisbane, Australia called Marketing Results. Will is an elite-level direct marketer.

A few years ago, Will decided to provide the marketing world with a free poster called "Monster Cheat Sheet of Marketing Proof Elements." Google it. You'll get 42 proof elements in the next 10 seconds.

I had a local company print a big version of this poster. All the proof elements in this chapter come from that poster. Will and his team at Marketing Results deserve all the credit.

OK…let's get into the proof elements. These are in no particular order.

Quote an Authority

You've made a claim. Now you have to back it up with proof from some type of authority.

Struggling to find an authority figure in the financial space? Dig around The Wall Street Journal site or The Financial Times site and you'll find something you can legally quote. How many financial promotions quote Warren Buffet? A ton. Does he give them permission? No.

What about the health space? I've quoted The Mayo Clinic site and Harvard Medical School and other health-related authorities. Golf? I'll find a quote from a famous golfer or something from one of the many golf magazines.

Awards

Won some awards? Put them in the copy. Use photos of grinning recipients if you can but make sure you include that caption. But be careful with the use of awards. I'm impressed with some awards but I'm not impressed when a branding agency says they won some award for creativity. So what? Show me the revenue the ad actually generated. Elucidate and don't assume the prospect knows what the award is. I was a Morehead-Cain scholar at The University of North Carolina. People know what that is in North Carolina and in certain other areas but I'd have to explain that to 98 percent of the American population. Explain the award and provide details. And never write something as vapid as "most awarded" because nobody will ever care and even fewer people will know what "most awarded" even means.

Founder or Team Photo

Potential clients and customers LOVE to know more about the people behind the company or a product. We all love personality in copy so I like to include that founder photo along with others involved in the product. I write a caption so it's not just a photo of some person nobody knows.

Celebrities

A controversial subject. My brothers and sisters in the branding world believe this: hire a celebrity and watch revenue soar. Of course, that's total rubbish. There are three problems.

- First, revenue doesn't always soar. In fact, it rarely increases that much.
- Second, when media and celebrity fees are factored in, the ROI is rarely worth it.
- Third, what happens when the celebrity goes on a five-day bender, crashes the Ferrari into a Dairy Queen in Iowa, and stumbles around naked with a female, who is also naked and mega high on something and is not his wife?

I like to include celebrities in copy but only as a proof element. For example, I was writing copy to sell DVDs that included advice from a golf instructor. Turns out that Jack Nicklaus sent his children to said golf instructor. I built much of the promotion around this fact. Just remember that the customer doesn't care about the celebrity; they care about themselves. The celebrity brings attention. That's good. But the celebrity is NOT the reason someone buys a product or service. Mega-brands like to use celebrities but it's a poor tactic for all but the world's biggest companies.

Guarantee

A guarantee, along with a seal, is vital in direct response copy. It's proof there's a solid company behind the product.

But AMP UP that guarantee.

I could write...

"Your satisfaction is extremely important to us here at Acme Halitosis. If you're not totally satisfied, you get your money back. No questions asked."

Not too exciting or enticing. Anyone could write that.

A direct response copywriter would write...

PUREBREATH 365-Day Rock-Solid Guarantee: Money Back, Plus $10 Just for Trying PUREBEATH if You're Not TOTALLY DELIGHTED

PUREBREATH from Acme MUST end your bad breath forever. Your significant other must look forward to kissing you and notice the difference in your breath. You will never again see people recoil and run away because of bad breath. You will enter every conversation with total confidence. You will have fresh and agreeable breath even if you have been smoking, have been eating onions doused in a rich garlic sauce, and have been glugging down black coffee.

In short, PUREBREATH from Acme must transform your life and end the social leprosy that often comes with bad breath.

If PUREBREATH from Acme fails to fulfill the promises we've made, you can receive a full, prompt, and courteous refund. If, for any reason, or no particular reason, you're not totally delighted, call our customer support team at 800-800-8000 and we'll dispatch your refund PLUS we'll send you a $10 check as our sincere "thank you" for trying PUREBREATH from Acme. And, of course, you can keep all the bonus items as an extra "thank you" for trying PUREBREATH from Acme.

Once again...your satisfaction is VITAL to us. We want you to be totally delighted. We want to end all the social, sexual, and business hassles that come with halitosis and bad breath. We want you to join the community of people who trust PUREBREATH from Acme.

● ● ● ●

Now THAT'S a guarantee a potential customer can believe. The selling of the product continues even in the guarantee.

Admitting a Fault or Limitation

It's not the biggest or most prominent proof element but it's one I like to include when possible. You can say, in the financial space for a stock picking service, that there have been some stock picks that didn't work out from the stock picker. In the medical space, you can say that a very small number of people who try the product find it doesn't work...then stress the guarantee. You can write...

Look...this product isn't for everyone. It's only for the select few who genuinely value the finest cigars on the planet...and want that level of quality for themselves and their friends.

Admitting a fault or limitation brings out your humanity and decreases the hype factor. It helps to overcome skepticism.

Metaphor

The well-chosen metaphor is the hallmark of a top copywriter. However, if you can't find that metaphor, avoid using this proof element. You can quickly get into the realm of the cliché when you write, "It will make your shirts as white as snow" or "It's like motor oil for your joints."

A metaphor can become the "big idea" that is the foundation of a successful promotion. But I'm careful with metaphors and similes. I use them sparingly as it's easy to mix metaphors and this can confuse the reader.

Take a look at this for a financial promotion...

Subscribing to Profits Down Under is like having your very own 10-person stock research team in Australia and New Zealand—letting you know about exceptional opportunities in these countries...before other investors—for a fraction of the cost of hiring that team.

That's copy from a promotion I wrote that generated over $1 million in revenue for a client.

Don't Exaggerate

Veracity is a built-in proof element. If I write that an SUV can carry an elephant, I've lost the reader. But if I organize a photo showing how it can carry a ton of "normal" stuff plus a couple of bicycles, that's realistic and totally believable.

I've been watching quite a few branding ads in the last few weeks, just to see how they're put together. Exaggeration, often somewhat humorous, is a technique in branding advertising. I guess that's OK when there's no accountability. You can get away with making stuff up all day in the branding world and nobody really cares.

Scarcity

It's not necessarily a "pure" proof element but real scarcity can prove a statement like: "We only have a limited number of these knives at this price." And if you set a deadline, stick to that deadline. I was interested in a product the other day. The offer was $99 for all the information, for a limited time. I missed the deadline and when I returned to the web page, the price had increased to $999.

Thousands of legitimate and successful products have some scarcity built in. Readers almost expect it.

Human Stories

Stories can provide a positive impact on copy and I've built many promotions around great stories. But note...the story has to be a jaw-dropping one, often with a lot of intrigue and mystery.

Simply saying, "Donna bought this product, and it changed her life forever!" is a story, technically, but it's a pretty mediocre story plus it's raw exaggeration.

But I recently wrote about a doctor whose husband started showing signs of dementia. I included the story of what she started feeding her husband, based on her research, and what happened after the change in diet. The VSL that included that story helped to generate $1.5 million a month for a $19 book.

Before and After

You've probably seen the power of this format when it's visual, but it can be just as effective in copy. The before and after proof element works extremely well in the infomercial format.

In copy, I describe life before the product, with all its problems. Then I describe life fully transformed by the product. I keep it believable because the story is based on the truth.

Test Data

Test data is especially important with health-related products. But I have also used test data in golf-related copy. Sometimes you can use test data from extensive tests and trials. Sometimes I'm a big fan of data from surveys but sometimes I'm not: it depends on the data.

Charts and Graphs

Charts and graphs are always valuable...but with these caveats.

- A chart or graph must be super clear.
- There should be a copy doodle and caption saying "here's what this graph proves" along with some type of benefit.
- The chart or graph should be relevant.

Dan Kennedy says, and I agree, that a copywriter must be totally involved with the graphical presentation of the copy. I'm not a web developer and I'm not a graphic designer but I always want to provide graphical direction to the people who are putting together the final piece, online or off.

Specificity

It's pretty simple: instead of writing, "You'll hit the ball further with the Max Cannon Driver," I write, "Gain an Extra 14-25 Yards off the Tee With The All-New Max Cannon Driver."

Specificity is so important; you'll find a chapter about it in *Scientific Advertising*.

But you have to be extremely careful with this weapon...and specificity is more than just numbers. Specificity can be about individual success stories, geographic examples, relevant studies, testimonials from experts, and more.

Let's talk about numbers for a minute.

- I choose the numbers extremely carefully and find the ones that have the most impact...plus are most relevant to the most important benefits of the product or service.
- You can quickly and easily overwhelm the reader/viewer/listener with too many numbers. The prospect's head can be spinning thanks to the surfeit of numbers and there won't be a sale.
- Specificity is obviously vital and must replace vagueness wherever and whenever vagueness appears in copy. But I'm careful...especially with numbers. Copy that's just a sea of numbers will drown the reader.

Comparisons

I'm quite a big fan of Car and Driver Magazine, a publication that routinely runs comparison articles. They'll test between two and five different cars and tell you which car they liked the best...and then rank all the contestants. It's fun reading plus it motivates car lovers to open the magazine to see which car won.

In direct response copy, comparisons can be a proof element, usually in some type of table that compares your product to others in the market. You have to be careful and I'm NEVER in favor of bashing the competition, even if the competition is totally bashable. In fact, I'm working on copy where the control bashes doctors, drug companies, and pretty much everyone. My new copy doesn't bash anyone.

The comparison I prefer is what I call the "self-comparison" where I provide two offers for the product, each with different levels of features. It's the old, GOOD-BETTER-BEST self-comparison.

Scientific Findings/Research Findings

I'm going to group these together because they're very similar…and mostly self-explanatory. It's not hugely difficult, although it takes a lot of time to come up with research to back up claims. Many times, the client will have this research ready to go.

And it's not hugely difficult to pump a ton of research and related content into a promotion. But you have to be careful.

Just above, I wrote how it's really important to be careful with specificity. I can include a lot of numbers and specificity but I can end up bombarding the reader with too much information and the surfeit of specificity can confuse everyone and negate the all-important clarity. And confused prospects don't buy.

So…with scientific and research findings, I choose wisely and only include the most salient findings that buttress the claims in the copy.

If I have a lot of "leftover" research that I really like, I can create a Johnson Box with a subhead saying, "Here's Additional Research About Product X," or I can include it after the P.S. in a Q&A.

Unique Mechanism

I could write a book about this proof element.

The unique mechanism is not just a proof element. It can be a core element of profitable copy. Over the next couple of days, pay close attention to the advertising you see and hear and you'll see the "unique mechanism" tactic used over and over. It's such a vital way to differentiate a product or service.

In the automotive space, you see unique mechanisms all the time. It could be a new type of engine. It could be a new safety feature. It could be a new way to communicate.

But you can't just plop down the unique mechanism and say, "Here's a unique mechanism so that's why you have to buy." The prospective client will say, "Yeah, right."

I have to explain the basis behind the unique mechanism plus I have to prove that the unique mechanism actually works and makes the product better than other similar products.

If I'm writing about a dietary supplement, then I can highlight a new ingredient. Then I have to prove the new ingredient performs as advertised.

Let's say I'm selling a ski with a new technology that makes it easier to turn the ski and thus have more fun skiing...with less effort. I have to explain the new technology with video plus images and copy. Then I have to show it actually works. I can use before and after images, testimonials, and celebrity skier endorsements.

Here's an important point about proof elements. They don't work independently. They are totally connected.

Reasons Why

Look at my copy and you'll ALWAYS see a section titled, "33 reasons to get (insert product/service)." The number of reasons varies but I always strive to include as many salient and relevant reasons as I can. I aim to include every conceivable reason without getting contrived. It's here that I stress all the benefits. This section can really motivate the prospect to try the product or service. In a perfect world, I have an odd number of reasons, say 27 instead of 20. I can't prove it but the odd number makes the subhead stand out more.

Logical Argument

I rarely see direct response copy with a strong logical argument to try a product or service. Yet it's vital in any type of direct response copy. The classic example of the logical argument is the problem/solution approach to copy. Here's your problem... I understand the problem... Here's the solution... Here's proof the solution works... You can try the solution with no risk.

Specialization

I write quite a bit of copy in the golf niche. I often write the copy in the voice of a golf teacher who has taught many of the world's top golfers. The specialization here is definitely a proof element.

The message to the potential buyer is: "Look... I'm a specialist with tons of experience and success. Due to my expertise, I've got what you need to get you where you want to go."

Do not confuse this proof element with a celebrity endorsement. The two are very different.

Third-Party Verifications

These are primarily endorsements from media. So...if The Wall Street Journal reviewed your product, favorably, of course, then I'll include that review or a portion of the review. I include the logo in the sales page.

Trust Seals

Let's say you have a partnership with an organization like the AAA here in America. Include that logo.

Let's say you're a member of the local chamber of commerce where you live. Include that logo.

Let's say you sell dietary supplements and you follow GMP practices. Include the GMP logo.

Infographics

When I'm working on copy, part of my job is helping to organize graphs, illustrations, and photos.

Another part of the equation is making sure they complement and augment the copy.

Infographics can summarize the entire theme of the promotion but should encourage more reading and more time spent with the promotion. ALWAYS include a caption and always include a benefit in the caption.

Testimonials

Three things. First...it's OK to edit testimonials for grammar and clarity. Second...I put a headline on every testimonial and base this headline on a benefit. This headline should be three words, when possible. Third...testimonials are like snow at a ski resort. You can never have enough testimonials, even if people don't read all of them.

Demonstrations

Can't do a demonstration in direct mail? Can't do a demonstration on a sales page? You can certainly organize them on TV because it's the perfect medium for demonstrations. You could include a thumb drive with direct mail. You can certainly organize a demonstration on your webpage, using a simple video. Your copy will convert better if you can provide this proof element.

Client List

Big in the B2B space, not so much in the B2C space. I've had potential clients tell me they have contacted me specifically because of my client list. Are you listing your clients on your site? It's especially important in the B2B space.

Social Media Proof. Reviews. PR and Media Exposure.

I'm going to group these three together because they're closely related.

Social media proof can be screenshots of positive activity from all your favorite social media sites.

Reviews are from actual customers/clients and are a lot like testimonials.

PR and media exposure can be extremely valuable and I've even built entire promotions around a great piece from a big outlet. You can also put the logos of media outlets on promotions.

Valuable Content

Many of my clients are superb at organizing regular content that's fun and valuable to their current and prospective clients and customers. This content builds trust and makes my job as a copywriter a lot easier. I have two folders full of successful Boardroom promotion and each one provides a ton of useful information...for free. You can and should build as many promotions as possible around valuable content. The content sends a clear message to your prospects: "We're on your side. We know what you want. We're the company that's going to help you."

Credible Photos

A picture is worth a thousand words, right?

Wrong.

Wrong.

Wrong.

Wrong.

Wrong.

If that statement was correct, direct response ads would be all photos with no copy.

But photos in direct marketing can be valuable. They must be chosen carefully and, most importantly, there MUST be a caption right on the photo or underneath. The goal of the caption/photo is to illustrate a benefit or draw the reader deeper into the copy.

I was recently at a photography exhibition in Manhattan. Under each photo was a long description of the background behind the photo. The photo got my attention and drew me into the copy. A photography museum needs copy under its photos. The same applies to your ads.

Final Thoughts About Proof Elements

In a bar, you'll hear a lot of crazy statements. You'll hear people say, usually using bad language, "That's not true." And you'll hear the originator of the crazy statement say something they believe will prove the statement. Many times, they will pick up their phone and find a video on YouTube or a website. Why? To prove what they just said. They're being copywriters.

Proof is your friend, my friends. Find it. Use it. Prove every statement.

The Biggest Enemy of the Direct Response Copywriter

I have a lot of enemies as a direct response copywriter but the biggest enemy is skepticism.

Nobody believes anyone.

Let me write that again.

Nobody believes anyone.

OK... Let me modify that a little. Nobody believes anyone at first.

Why the skepticism?

- People are naturally skeptical. It's how we're built and it's part of our chemistry.
- The direct marketing business is known for scamming and scammers. It's not the only business with scamming and scammers but people associate advertising with scams. They don't always associate banking with scams although there are plenty of scammers in the financial world. Most people I know in direct marketing are not scammers. But the public's perception is otherwise.
- The price seems wrong...either too high or too low.
- They've been burned before, possibly in the same product category.
- There's a lot of hype in the copy with very little proof. Just a lot of exclamation marks!!!!!!!!!!!!!
- There's something wrong with the product.
- They don't know the company.
- They know the company but they don't like the company.
- They are looking for proof but they're not finding any. Hype = Outlandish statements that go beyond the ability to be proven.
- They don't feel like they're getting value for their money.
- They're worried about credit card information and data getting compromised. Privacy.
- The benefits have not been fully and completely presented.
- Lack of guarantee.
- Lack of personality.
- Lack of relevance.

The world's top direct response copywriters understand the ogre of skepticism and how to beat it. The higher the number of salient proof elements I can include, the stronger the response. Why? Because I'm overcoming skepticism.

CHAPTER 12

Mastering Body Copy

In the body copy, I provide details about the product or service I'm selling. The body copy flows from the headlines, the sub-heads, the captions, the graphics, and the other elements of the copy.

Think about an article you may have seen in a magazine like Time. Or think about an article you saw online from a site like The Denver Post. The body copy provides the bulk of the article. It's the same in direct response copy. I provide the majority of the information about the product or service in the body copy.

I Never Really Knew These People Existed ... Until I Met Chris Como ...

Subhead

Turns out there are highly trained specialists ... from around the world ... who specialize in generating power from certain movements and parts of the body.

- There's someone who specializes in power from the core.
- There's someone who specializes in hip rotation.
- There's someone who specializes in understanding the back and its role in athletics.
- There's someone who knows how to generate additional power from the ground up.
- There's even someone who knows how to generate more power from the upper torso.

Did you know these people existed? No ... I didn't either.

But these specialists are working with professional athletes, including tour pros, and you can see the results above.

One teaching professional has paid close attention to these specialists. In fact, he's incorporated ALL their ideas into HIS teaching.

His name is Chris Como.

Body Copy

Here's what I'm thinking when it comes to body copy.

- I keep sentences short with 10 words max.
- The first word of the next paragraph is always different. This brings syntactical balance to the copy.
- I personally like to use a lot of ellipses to break up copy and make it more readable... Some copywriters avoid the ellipses... I'm not one of them.
- Copy must never be too dense. Want to see an example of dense copy? Read a novel by Charles Dickens. Break up dense copy.
- To make the copy readable, it must be set in black type on a white background. A serif font, like Times New Roman, for printed material and a sans-serif font, like Helvetica or Arial, for the web. Copy should be double-spaced or set in 12-point type with 16-point leading.
- A block of body copy between the sub-heads should be five to seven sentences long.
- I like to bold certain words or italicize or underline some words, phrases, and sentences.
- In body copy for direct response copy, I like to write in 7th-grade English that's super-clear. I check the copy using the Flesch-Kinkaid readability scale. No big words. *Just total clarity at all times.*

Some people will read all the body copy three times before making the decision to buy. Others will scan it and still buy. The body copy has to be motivational because it's where I motivate people who are on the fence to try the product or service I'm selling.

I tell stories in the body copy. I provide additional proof. I give details about the background behind the product or service. I take what I discovered during the research phase and pack it into the body copy. I build an argument for what the company is offering and why you should try it.

But perhaps most importantly, I'm always thinking about the crucial question the reader is asking: "What's in it for me?"

CHAPTER 13

Sub-Heads, Pull Quotes, and Captions.

The vast majority of readers read the headline first, perhaps the first paragraph of the copy, then start scanning the rest of my copy. It's how I read copy. And it's how you most likely read copy.

That's why I pay super-close attention to my sub-heads, pull quotes, and captions.

- A sub-head is simply a headline placed between blocks of body copy.
- The pull-quote is a few words of copy placed in a slightly larger font somewhere in the copy. The pull quote can be from the body copy or it can be different. It should emphasize a key benefit.
- A caption is a couple of lines of copy placed directly on a photo or underneath a photo.

Cut Golf has introduced several new golf balls ... let's meet one of them ... the CUT GREY ... a 3-piece super-premium golf ball WITHOUT the super-premium price.

The Cut Grey. Tour-Level construction and materials for under $20 a dozen.

Photo with caption

Many golfers report using just one ball for at least 36 holes.

- 3-piece construction ... distance off the tee plus control around the greens.

With all three, I use precisely the same headline formulas I just detailed in the chapter about headlines. The goal is to keep the reader engaged and reading more of the copy. I include some intrigue.

CHAPTER 14

The Surprising Way People Read Copy.

In a video, TV ad, or radio ad, the viewer/listener gets the entire ad...unless they change channels. But in print and online direct response copy, things are very different.

Thanks to the list-buying and list-building brilliance of my clients, the people who read my copy have a genuine interest in what I'm selling.

For example, when I write about a golf product or service, the people who are reading my copy have a genuine interest in getting a lot better at golf. When I'm writing about a dietary supplement that will help with arthritis pain, I know I'm talking to an audience that's suffering from joint discomfort and all the related problems. And with my website, I know I'm speaking to people who want an experienced direct response copywriter with a track record of success.

Still...the readers are easily distracted and are often looking for a reason to stop reading. That's why I have to understand how people read copy.

You can find exceptions but it generally works this way.

- People read the headline, deck, and sub-heads first.
- They will head to the bottom of the letter or sales page and read the P.S.
- If they're immediately interested, they'll look at the price.
- If they can afford the price they will scan the sub-heads and pull quotes, then look at the photos and captions.
- Then the reader, if they're still interested, will start to dive deeper into the copy based on what's important to them. For example, I'm always interested in the guarantee. "What happens if I'm not totally

happy with the product or service?" I ask. "Will I get my money back?" "How much time do I get to try the product or service?"

- If the prospect is still on the fence, they will read the body copy, often many times.

I write for a variety of clients but I also write to sell my own products and services. My copywriting website motivates people to contact me. I also provide access to a series of copywriting training videos.[5]

Here's what I've heard about the copy for the latter...and this from people who have actually bought access to the videos.

"I was really thinking about the product for several days and I read all the copy three times."

When I'm shopping for a product, and especially when it's expensive, I spend a lot of time reading every word. But, like most everyone else, it's the headlines, sub-heads, and other elements that draw me into the copy. I build/write the copy around how most people read copy.

With online copy, advanced direct marketers use a variety of tools to test precisely how the reader is looking at the copy when it's online. Two of the more popular tools are heat map software and eye tracking software.

When people read a book, they start at the beginning and read until the end in a linear process. When they read a newspaper or magazine, they scan, looking at the headlines, sub-heads, photos, captions, and pull-quotes... Then they read the body copy.

But with advertising, online or off, they're also trying NOT to pay attention even if they're interested in the product or service. The successful direct response copywriter knows how to keep the attention of the reader and keep the prospect reading the copy to the point where the prospect becomes a customer. That's an extremely rare skill and the paucity of this skill explains, in part, why companies pay so much to direct response copywriters.

It's also NOT a skill that's easy to acquire. It takes at least seven years for a direct response copywriter to get to the point where they can consistently generate significant revenue for their clients. Plus the direct response copywriter needs to come to the profession through an extensive background in either sales, writing, publishing, or some type of related trade.

---

[5]   www.AspenSchoolofCopywriting.com

I understand how people read copy because I have a lot of experience in magazine publishing. Plus I've written copy for 32 years and closely studied reading habits. I also know how people read copy because I buy products myself and, like most people, have a short attention span. People read copy like I read copy...and like you read copy.

CHAPTER 15

Guarantees

It's extremely rare to see a direct response advertisement WITHOUT a guarantee. It's something I point out when people think that direct marketing is not exactly above board. But how often do I see a full-on guarantee in a branding ad? Almost never. I can flip through the pages of a fancy-schmancy magazine like Vanity Fair and see all these beautiful ads for clothes and handbags. How many times will I see a guarantee? NEVER.

Let's say you buy a $5,000 handbag from one of the companies that sells $5,000 handbags. Let's say you're not totally and complete satisfied in every possible way. Let's say you march into the store demanding your money back. What's going to happen? They're going to call the police.

My clients offer a money-back guarantee and I've had some clients who go a step further and offer a double money-back guarantee. You get your money back plus even more money. My clients stand behind their claims and their products. One of my clients provides a 365-day guarantee and stands by it.

The elite-level direct response copywriter writes a guarantee with more impact. It's not especially difficult to write a guarantee. In fact, I'm going to write a "basic" guarantee right now.

100% satisfaction or your money back.

There. How hard was that? A 10 year old could write that guarantee.

Here's the problem with guarantees: they're everywhere.

Name me a company today that doesn't provide some type of guarantee. I can walk into a Wendy's and find a guarantee. I'm sitting in a Starbucks as I write this and I can't see a guarantee but I'm confident that if I go back to the counter with some type of complaint, the hyper-happy barista will find a way to satisfy me.

You've heard this copy, I'm certain... YOUR SATISFACTION IS GUARANTEED.

The quality of the writing in a guarantee can sway a hesitant prospect. A poor guarantee has kept me from buying. A solid guarantee has motivated me to try a product or service, even if it's an expensive product or service and I was on the fence.

I rarely complain and I rarely return products but when a product fails to live up the promises in the copy, I ask for my money back.

You can see an example of a powerful guarantee in the chapter about proof.

CHAPTER 16

The Offer

There's a semantic issue here. You might think "the offer" is something like "50% off everything on Tuesdays," but in direct response, we define "the offer" as...

In return for your money and/or information, here's precisely what you're going to get.

A discount or other incentive is part of the offer but it's not THE offer.

Part of my work as a direct response copywriter is helping my clients create and refine the offer. I also help them include incentives and freebies to make the offer even more attractive.

More advanced direct marketers are constantly testing offers to see which one generates the most revenue. Testing often yields surprising results. For example, a higher price can generate more response and more revenue than a lower price. More about pricing later. Pricing is one of my favorite subjects.

Upsells, Downsells, and Cross-Sells

When a customer has decided to buy a product, my work isn't over. I want them to buy another product, or several other products, while they're in the buying mood. The upsell can be more of the same product or a complementary product. A cross-sell is a totally different product that will likely be of interest to the customer.

The more advanced direct marketers have the ability, with the help of technology, to offer a different and less expensive product to a customer who didn't want the original product. Let's say I'm writing copy for a magnificent set of knives priced at $100. When the potential customer clicks away from the page, an offer for a smaller set of knives might pop up…at a lower price point.

I keep selling until the customers says, "OK, I've got enough." I'm regularly surprised at how much some people will buy in one transaction.

Broccoli or Carrots?

I have a lot more success with copy when there are two or even three versions of the offer. These too must be carefully written and crafted. I work closely with the client and their financial goals for the promotion.

For example, let's say I'm selling golf balls.

- Offer A could be one box for $30.
- Offer B could be two boxes for $55.
- Offer C could be five boxes for $99 plus a free Donald Duck golf towel.

The option NOT to buy isn't even an option.

Testing will show which offer produces the best financial results.

I have to be extremely careful to ensure the offers are totally clear. I regularly see offers that are not clear. That's a shocking mistake.

Next time you're buying a product or service based on the advertising, take a close look at how the copywriter presents the offer.

CHAPTER 17

Videos. And the Direct Marketing Maverick.

I love the marriage of videos and direct response copy. Why? Because videos present the reader with a powerful proof element. Videos also bring an extra dimension to copy. Most importantly, videos bring my clients more customers and more revenue.

In this chapter, I'll explain how to use videos in copy for the digital environment. But you can also use videos with direct mail.

Videos on YouTube and other platforms can be productive. Then I'll introduce "the maverick"...the video sales letter, usually called a VSL in my profession.

I was having success with one of my clients in the hobbies niche. The client has an outstanding list (database of prospects) plus excellent offers. Remember this direct marketing formula.

Right list + right copy + right offer = tons of money.

The sales pages were fairly standard web-based sales pages. And they were working.

Then we decided to insert a four- to five-minute video just below the headline. It was a test. Conversion increased dramatically and we still use this approach today.

For this client, and for others, I strive to insert two to three additional videos deeper in the copy. I usually write the copy for the videos and they follow the standard direct response copy formula. Let me detail what should be in these videos and then detail why they work.

In the four- to five-minute videos, here's the basic format.

- Introduction of "host" and the "guest." The guest is usually the person behind the product we're selling.
- Statement of the problem.
- Introduction of the solution.
- Demonstration.
- Next steps... And the next step is typically scrolling through the web page.
- Mention we've got the lowest price, a guarantee, and that quantities are limited.
- Restate next step—reading the copy below.

The video warms up the prospect for the copy. That's why the video is important. This client has tested just videos alone. They have also tried shorter copy. But the combination of the videos with long-form copy works the best, by far.

When I put a video in the body of the promotion, it's to provide proof, usually in the form of a demonstration. These videos should be two to four minutes long.

A video is part of the mix when it comes to selling products and services through copy. You can include a video with a sales letter sent in the mail by including a thumb drive. It can be expensive but it can work, especially for high-ticket items.

But the video is there to complement and augment the copy... UNLESS... it's a VIDEO SALES LETTER.

● ● ● ●

A Quiet Revolution in Direct Response Copywriting... The VSL...

Around 2010, a couple of direct marketers started experimenting with video-only promotions. They knew that long web-based sales pages could work but they wanted to see if they could boost response and revenue.

So they tried what's now known as a video sales letter, usually abbreviated to VSL. It's essentially a narrated PowerPoint presentation that lasts anywhere from 15 to 60 minutes. You might find a few photos in some VSLs, but the format is extraordinarily simple...an expert talking about his/her chosen subject. The narrator is simply reading the PowerPoint presentation.

It's definitely an exercise in direct response copywriting. The format is slightly different from writing for direct mail or the web but I've adapted to this format and produced staggering results for my clients. One of my VSLs was selling $1.5 million worth of $19 books every 30 days. If this result fails to impress you then you should stop reading right now.

Here's the basic VSL format.

- What's going to be in the video.
- Who the video is for.
- Who the video is from/qualifications of the narrator.
- Statement of the problem. This can be quite long and is often pretty terrifying.
- The solution. Usually some type of free information in return for trying a product or service.
- What's in the information and why it's worth getting.
- Guarantee and call to action.
- Summary.

Many direct marketers sell more directly through VSLs. Others simply gather information to build a database of prospects.

But the VSL definitely works and it's still working today. The top direct marketers test them extensively against copy-only promotions. There's only one drawback with the VSL: it's harder to test. You can still test them but it takes more time plus production costs can increase. Some direct marketers like to run a VSL in a bare-bones format then add additional graphics and sizzle. Sometimes this increases response. Sometimes it fails.

I'm a huge fan of videos. They help my clients generate more revenue, more often. But you must have a direct response copywriter write them and they must always have a direct response structure.

CHAPTER 18

Testimonials

You've seen plenty of testimonials in ads. They've been a long-time staple of advertising for decades and they'll continue to be around for further decades.

What's a testimonial?

Somebody gushes about a product or service they love. I was just writing copy for a company that sells a new form of laundry detergent. Customers were saying amazing things about that laundry detergent.

Many companies even base entire campaigns around testimonials. They fill entire ads with testimonials. It's not an especially difficult tactic to execute but the advanced-level direct response copywriter takes testimonials to the next level.

Testimonials are a proof element, as I discussed previously, but I'd like to dig a little deeper.

Testimonials should be all about the benefits of the product or service.

I like to write a short intro to each testimonial...again, focused on a key benefit. Here's an example...from the golf world.

● ● ● ●

Longer. Much Longer.

"After buying the MAX CANNON driver, I can definitely say I'm longer off the tee. Much longer." —Pete B., Miami, Florida.

● ● ● ●

- You can't have too many testimonials. OK...a prospective customer might not read every single one in the copy but the sheer volume of testimonials can be an impressive proof element.
- Some copywriters, myself included, like to use a headline for each testimonial. Nothing wrong with that, provided it stresses a benefit.
- It's perfectly acceptable, legally, to edit testimonials for clarity and grammar. A lawyer who specializes in direct marketing told me this. It's not acceptable to make them up or change the meaning.
- If you can get photos of the testimonial providers...all the better. Some clients use stock shots although actual shots are preferable.
- I'm a big fan of the video testimonial...if you can get one or two.
- Sometimes, as a copywriter, it will be your job to harvest the testimonials. But the client should have plenty.
- Dan Kennedy says that testimonials should focus on benefits, especially in the synopsis above the actual testimonial. I agree.
- As a copywriter, testimonials can give you excellent insight into what people really like about the product or service. It's part of the research.
- Some testimonials may seem over the top. Leave these out.
- I can tell when a serious copywriter has written the copy. The testimonials are well-organized, clear, and benefit-driven.

Testimonials are like snow at a ski resort. You can never have enough snow at a ski resort especially in the winter.

CHAPTER 19

AIDA and the Correct Structure of Copy for Maximum Revenue...

A IDA. No...it's not the opera by Verdi. It's the most basic formula for direct response copy.

A = Attention
I = Interest
D = Desire
A = Action

There's another version I like, created by direct response copywriter Michael Fortin: QUEST.

- Qualify
- Understand
- Educate
- Stimulate
- Transition

Here's how I like to structure copy...for TOTAL clarity plus maximum revenue and conversion for my clients.

- Tell them what you're going to tell them.
- Tell them.
- Tell them what you told them.

Not exactly complicated in theory. But extremely difficult to execute in reality.

Let me go into more detail about the structure as the above is a touch too simplistic.

- Pre-head
- Headline
- Deck
- Relevant and interesting information (could be description of a problem)
- Description of the product/service
- Proof it works
- Benefits of the product/service
- Testimonials
- Presentation of the offer and invitation to buy
- Price justification
- Scarcity
- Guarantee
- Close
- P.S.
- Q and A

Yes...there are variations on this structure but it's the standard structure I use pretty much every day. Why? Because it's proven to generate money.

CHAPTER 20

Bullets, Benefits, Fascinations, and Features

In direct response copy, from a graphical perspective, bullets break up dense copy and improve readability. But there's much, much more to the bullet. In case you're asking, "What's a bullet?" here's an example...or four.

- Keeps migraines from ruining your day.
- Restful sleep.
- No prescription necessary.
- Fully guaranteed—see below.

You can have bulleted bullets, as above. You can have bullets with slightly funky graphics like check marks.

- ✓ Strongest titanium currently available for maximum ball speed and distance.
- ✓ Large sweet spot for maximum forgiveness.
- ✓ Pro-grade shaft...which usually costs $100...included.
- ✓ Deep face design preferred by better players.

Or you can have numbered bullets.

1. Stock research not available anywhere else...only through this newsletter.
2. Dan Dickinson spent 25 years on Wall Street as a top researcher. Now he's available to you.
3. Recommendations sent via email when there's a major news item.

4. Specific focus on stocks where companies generate repeat revenue.

You can use bullets for lists of features. But I like to use bullets to emphasize benefits. I also use them for what we in direct response copywriting call fascinations. I'll get to fascinations in a minute but let's start with the art and science of turning features into benefits.

Features and Benefits

It's extremely easy to list the features of a product or service. The elite-level direct response copywriter then turns the features into benefits that directly appeal to the reader and what they want. Let me give you some examples, bulleted, of course.

- The all-new BIG MAX driver has a 460cc titanium head for maximum forgiveness if you don't hit the sweet spot.
- Our newest lawnmower, The Legend, has power-driven back wheels so it's easy to mow even the hilliest yard.
- Once you take home your Friendly 22 Gas Grill, you'll love the improved thermostat which keeps poultry, meat, and fish at the perfect cooking temperature...for results that will make you a rock star griller and main attraction of your cookout every time.
- Our DialDD Water Purifier has a special filter which is the only one currently available that filters out the AlphaG bacteria, which has been shown to lead to numerous diseases.
- At Vega's supermarkets, we only stock certified organic produce so you can avoid all the risks associated with pesticides and other chemicals.

In direct response copy, my job is to list the features but then go several steps further by adding benefits. And then I try to give the benefits some color and dimension.

It's a place to be careful. Some direct response copywriters go over the top, make things up, and risk losing the reader. I tend to be more straightforward, less colorful, and thus more believable. My goal is clarity above all else.

For example, I will write...

Get the GreenMax lawnmower and you'll delight your spouse and family with a glorious and perfectly manicured lawn that will make everyone super proud every time they pass by.

Another copywriter might say...

Start using the GreenMax lawnmower and your lawn will look so friggin' perfect all the time that your wife will want to jump in bed with you after months of saying "no" to your advances.

I'm not joking here. There are direct response copywriters who will go totally over the top and blatantly lie in order to get a response. I'm not one of them.

The readers/listeners/viewers have imaginations. I keep the copy mostly tame for several reasons...

- Clarity. Copy that's simple is clear...and clarity is VITAL in direct response copy. Benefits...features...everything...must be totally clear at all times.
- With relatively simple and straightforward copy, the truth comes out and people generally prefer the truth to lies. Shocking, right?
- I've had a huge amount of success with copy that's straightforward with the features and benefits clearly explained. Why should I change? And when I'm talking about success, I'm talking about revenue.

Bullets help me emphasize key features and benefits I believe will most appeal to the prospective clients and customers.

FASCINATIONS

Remember what I wrote about creating a sense of intrigue with headlines?

A truly intriguing headline keeps the reader moving into the copy. Fascinations are the same way. I could use the word "tease" but that's not totally semantically correct. I prefer to "fascinate" the reader so the reader keeps reading and becomes extremely interested in trying the product I'm selling.

Let me explain.

Fascinations are short sentences I create to motivate the reader to try the product or service. They only really work when I'm selling an information product.

For example, I have helped clients in the golf space sell videos about how to become a better golfer. Many of the teachers in the video are well known in their own right. They're also famous for teaching the world's most famous golfers. Two instructors I've worked with taught Tiger Woods.[6]

Let's say I'm writing the copy to sell a video series featuring the teacher who used to teach Woods.

I could write...

In the first video, you'll discover the backswing advice that turned Tiger's career around. The teacher told Tiger to keep the clubface slightly shut for the first 12 inches of the backswing.

Not much in the way of intrigue there. In fact, I'm giving away too much.

So, instead, I'll write...

Discover the one simple change that totally transformed Tiger's ball striking and consistency. You can take it straight to YOUR game and start hitting crisp irons and fairway woods every time you're out there on the course.

In theory, at least, the reader is asking, "What's that one simple change?"

I can't write fascinations when selling a lawnmower. But I can certainly use fascinations when selling an information-based product. The product could be a book, a DVD, a conference, or a subscription to a newsletter or magazine.

Fascinations are very closely related to headlines. In fact, I have templates for fascinations, just like I have them for headlines.

Let's look at some bullet-writing techniques...with examples. Instead of writing "bullet" I could write "fascination." The two words are essentially interchangeable.

---

[6]   Blatant name dropping.

The "How To" Bullet

How to make yourself safer than 89% of other car passengers. Page 389.

How to hit a power-draw that keeps your ball in the fairway and gives you an extra 15-35 yards off the tee.

The "Secret To" Bullet

The secrets of "Single Finger" takedowns...using a move that is indefensible even by a larger and more experienced opponent.

The secret of "that supermodel complexion" revealed!

The "Why" Bullet

Why up to 65% of all poisonings happen to children under 5... We reveal the way to prevent poisoning from taking the life of your child.

The surprising reason you can't always trust your doctor when it comes to prescription drugs—especially for cholesterol control.

The "What" Bullet

What your doctor won't tell you about fish oil and other heart healthy dietary supplements.

What you must do when negotiating royalties with a client...and what they don't want you to know.

The "What NEVER" Bullet

What never to eat on an airplane.

What never to do on the Internet—especially if you're on a plane or in a coffee shop on public-access WiFi.

The "Plus" Bullet

PLUS...my powerful method to keep the body synchronized with the hands for perfect pitches every time.

PLUS...my complete database of over 2,000 decision makers who are DESPERATE for good copywriters.

The "Number" Bullet

4 ways to get your body to release its own natural painkillers.

7 little-know signs you might be at risk for a stroke or heart attack.

3 often overlooked investment vehicles that have popped up in the last 24 months thanks to new laws...and subtle changes to old laws.

The "Right...Wrong" Bullet

The right way to move the forward knee...and the wrong way to move your lower body in the golf swing.

The CORRECT way to begin your turn in the moguls...and the WRONG way.

Coughing into your elbow prevents spreading a cold, right? WRONG—as you'll see on page 3.

"Car dealers make money on your used car." WRONG...so long as you take these 3 steps before you set foot in the dealership.

The "Warning" Bullet

WARNING! Your #1 asset is now in extreme danger! That's right...the equity in your property might be going away in the next 45 days...unless you take immediate action as detailed in the special report.

WARNING! The FDA is about to approve several new blood pressure medications with potentially dire side effects. Your doctor will prescribe these under duress from the greedy drug companies. We reveal which blood pressure medications you might want to avoid...PLUS give you an all-natural plant-based solution.

The "Are You?" Bullet

"Do you?"

"Does your?"

"Is your?"

Are you fighting high blood pressure? Yes? Then we show you the natural options that work for 98% of people.

Does your stockbroker have a rap sheet with the SEC or NASD? Here's how to find out...in less than 3 minutes.

Is your doctor making this common mistake when treating gout? It's not their fault... New research released in the last 30 days is taking the health world by storm and we reveal this to you.

The Gimmick Bullet

Combines a benefit with something extremely specific—plus a mechanism.

The amazing technique that will help you hit the longest and straightest drives of your life.

An investing technique called "bad news investing" that helps you gain 20% on one stock in just 7 days by focusing on BAD news... That's right...BAD news.

The "Sneaky" Bullet

The sneaky way professional "cage" fighters use the element of surprise to turn around dangerous situations...even when they get "jumped."

Sneaky insurance tricks the big insurance companies might be playing on you. We'll help you avoid these tricks.

The "Statement of Interest Plus Benefit" Bullet

Gold prices are up 20% in just 30 days... Here's how to profit the next time this happens.

Someone gets mugged every 25 seconds in the United States. Here's a way to fight back legally—and without knowing any martial arts techniques.

The "Direct Benefit" Bullet

Create powerful websites that bring you tons of new business... without being a web developer. Thousands are using this new web development tool.

Meet lots of new potential partners without spending hours online on "crazy" dating sites. All you need? The right shoes.

Recover from surgery 35% faster—even if it was serious surgery.

The "Specific Question" Bullet

What time of the day are you most likely to get a heart attack? The surprising answer is on page 54.

Have you wondered how long a pilot has been on the clock when you fly late at night? Get the answer on page 45. You might change your schedule... or you might not, depending on the airline.

The "If...Then" Bullet

If you regularly get migraine headaches, then you should focus on a simple exercise instead of taking medication.

If you've got 20 minutes a day, I will show you how to make money in the gold and silver markets.

If you're a black belt in karate, then I can show you how to teach karate... so you earn great money doing what you love.

The "When" Bullet

The best time to buy options? It's not what your broker has told you.

When is the most effective time to take fish oil? It's not when you think.

When you'll get the best deals from a car dealer. It's not at the end of the month as you've likely been told.

The "Quickest, Easiest" Bullet

The fastest way to get to the top of the hair dressing profession. Hundreds of hairdressers have developed mastery in just 10 months...when it normally takes 10 years.

The easiest way to hammer the competition in your marketplace...legally.

A super-quick way to deal with gout pain and inflammation. Hint: your doctor probably doesn't know about this.

The "Truth" Bullet

THE TRUTH about who really runs your mutual fund.

THE TRUTH about fish oils and which ones provide real purity—and which ones are total junk.

THE TRUTH about hidden airline fees...and how to avoid them.

The "Better" Bullet

BETTER THAN SQUATS... A new "core" exercise that's better for your back and builds key muscles faster.

BETTER THAN BLUE CHIP STOCKS... 5 stocks I love that provide stronger returns than boring old blue chips but also give you that all-important sense of security.

The "Single" Bullet

The single most important nutrient for heart health. It's not expensive but it's hard to find and very few doctors know anything about this.

The single most important economic indicator for bank stocks. And no...it's not interest rates. It's something 99.9 percent of economists completely miss time and time again. Pay attention to this key indicator and you can finally profit from trading bank stocks.

● ● ● ●

As I write, I was just at lunch with a marketing specialist and former CEO who worked with some of the world's greatest copywriters, specifically Eugene Schwartz and Gary Bencivenga.

This person told me that Schwartz used to spend days going through the book or info-product being sold and he would make meticulous notes. These notes became fascinations.

Reasons Why Bullets

I like to go one step further with my bullets. I create what I call "reasons why" bullets. I rarely see these in the work of other copywriters, but they're effective.

Basically, I give the prospect a number of reasons to try the product or service I'm selling. Here's an example.

● ● ● ●

26 Ways FOLEY FACTOR – SHORT GAME Will Help Your Chipping, Pitching, and Bunker Play...Even if You DON'T Have a Lot of Time to Practice Your Short Game

1. **No need to spend hours at the practice facility every week**... That's because I've simplified short game technique for you.
2. **Save 4-8 shots a round**...at least...and even under pressure.
3. **Short game CLARITY** instead of confusion so you improve faster.
4. **An easy-to-understand plan/blueprint** for short game practice and success on the golf course.
5. **More fun on the golf course** because it's a TON of fun to get up and down consistently.
6. **The end of big numbers**... No more "look-away awful" short game shots.
7. **Fix short game problems** if they happen on the golf course...but also avoid them in the first place.
8. **Discover short game "secrets"** from many of the world's top golfers.

9. Turn 3 shots into 2 around the green—key to shooting lower scores.

10. **Short game gems for every golfer**...from beginner to accomplished club player.

11. **FINALLY...move forward** with your short game instead of not improving.

12. **NO MORE SHORT GAME HEADACHES**... End whatever short game issue is ailing you.

13. **Bunker mastery**... Escape any lie from any bunker on any course.

14. **VERSATILITY**... Enjoy solid pitches and chips from any lie on the golf course.

15. **Get it right BEFORE you hit the shot**... How to create a bulletproof setup and pre-shot routine for every short game shot.

16. **Hit more accurate short game shots**...with dramatically improved distance control.

17. Get your club selection correct...a key to short game success.

18. **Have a lot more fun** with your short game.

19. **Discover how to spin the ball with your pitch shots**...so you gain superior control with every short game shot.

20. **No technical mumbo-jumbo**...just clear, simple, and proven advice to help you shoot lower scores.

21. **Helps your full swing...** Many of the fundamentals from the short game translate directly to your full swing.

22. **CONFIDENCE...** Because you approach every short game shot with a plan...and get results.

23. Discover how to deal with those "wacky" situations...like weird lies, deep rough, and more.

24. **CONSISTENCY...** Be consistent with your short game EVERY TIME you play.

25. **Lower scores...** Because you understand the different short game challenges you face on the golf course...and how to overcome them.

26. TOTALLY FREE when you try GOLFPASS. <u>Click here now</u>.

● ● ● ●

The reader is likely already creating their own reasons to try the product or service. The "reasons why" provide an extra nudge in the right direction.

Here are some additional examples of bullets and fascinations, from copy that produced significant revenue for one of my clients.

● ● ● ●

SECTION ONE

- Gary Player's proven strategy for turning 3 shots into 2 on every hole. This alone will save you 10 shots a round THIS WEEK.
- 2 simple steps to hitting a perfect and powerful draw... Yes...it's much easier than you think.
- How to generate colossal torque and power in your full swing—even if you've been sitting at a desk for years and you're not that flexible.
- The TRUTH about the perfect setup for the ideal swing. Hint: it all starts with your toes!
- Go from hating windy days to LOVING windy days...with advice from the man who won his first Open Championship at age 23 at blustery Muirfield.
- Why higher-handicap golfers should instantly trash or sell their 3, 4, and 5 irons. There's a much better way to hit super-accurate shots in the 170–220-yard range.
- The real reason Mr. Player invented his famous "walk through swing" and why YOU should try it.
- It may sound crazy, but the morning newspaper will help you play better golf. Mr. Player reveals how.
- A 30-second exercise you complete before bedtime that will improve your game more than any $400 driver.
- Bad back? Try this simple exercise that's worked for Mr. Player and several champion golfers.
- The surprising truth about the "flying elbow" and why it will actually help your swing...despite what "big name" golf teaching gurus might say.
- How to go "low and through" and why this might be the best swing tip you'll ever hear.
- FINALLY...an easy way to hit great shots out of fairway bunkers... so you WANT to hit fairway bunker shots!

- The secret to developing and creating feel...which is vital to playing awesome golf.
- Are you ready to make the most of your valuable practice time? Mr. Player shows you how.
- The truth about how to swing the club...based on what Mr. Player learned playing with Trevino, Watson, Palmer, Hogan, Nicklaus... and countless champions.
- A surprising and even controversial analysis of how Tiger Woods swings...and what every golfer can learn from Woods...
- The secret technique Gary Player wishes he had known in his 20s...a technique he can now share.
- Why learning how to Waltz (that's right...WALTZ!) will improve your tempo.
- How a little "gardening" will transform your bunker play.
- The 4 secrets to championship-level bunker play so you ALWAYS escape any bunker—from any lie.
- One final thought that guarantees excellent bunker shots. Hint: it has something to do with lighting a cigar.
- Why you need to "read" a bunker just like you "read" a green—if you want to hit jaw-dropping bunker shots.
- Using your "driver" grip and stance for bunker shots? Wrong! Gary Player explains the full set up for correct bunker shots.
- The 3 characteristics of every great champion... Apply these to your game and watch your scores plummet.

SECTION TWO

- Why improvement does NOT always happen on the practice range... and what you can do about it!
- How to attack the flag by learning how to hit some advanced-level iron shots any golfer can master.
- FACT: Modern chipping methods are all wrong... Mr. Player shows you a much more effective way to hit "stone dead" chips.
- The slight change in stance that will help you spin your pitches and chips like a pro.
- 2 simple pre-shot adjustments you can make to help you hit high pitches that land like a sack of feathers right next to the hole.

- A simple "champion's secret" to super-accurate chipping so your chips always look like they're going in the hole.
- Never hit "fat" chips or pitches again—with the help of a simple tip.
- Take divots on chip shots? What Mr. Player says will shock you!
- The formerly secret "Chop Shot" and how it can change almost every part of your short game.
- "Keep it low...to make the dough." Mr. Player reveals how he used this technique to win 165 tournaments and well over $14 million in global earnings.
- One tip that will help you turn 3 shots into 2, even if you don't have much time to practice your short game.
- How to use your hybrids around the greens...for spectacular results from bad lies.
- Ben Hogan's chipping technique...the technique Hogan secretly revealed to Gary Player.
- Why "touch and feel" always trumps "technique" and how to develop your personal touch and feel.
- The real reason you should ignore the old golf saying: "Never up, never in."
- How a simple tip Mr. Player received decades ago on a sand green in South Africa helped him become a deadly putter—in any conditions and on any putting surface.
- FINALLY...a simple way to read the grain on greens and use it to your advantage.
- The ONE surprising characteristic of every great putter.
- The bizarre yet highly effective technique of perhaps the greatest putter who has ever lived: Bobby Locke (4-time winner of The Open Championship).
- Why great vision is overrated when it comes to putting... Mr. Player reveals what's really important.
- A super-surprising and incredibly easy way to determine how a short putt will break.
- How to cure the yips in 3 seconds flat.
- A simple way to develop your own super-effective putting style and why it's so important to "be yourself" when you putt.

SECTION THREE

- It may sound crazy but for ultimate golf power, you need a body like Popeye's. Got your spinach?
- How to develop specific golf strength to help you hit the ball at least 30 yards further in the next 90 days.
- Why FAST muscles are more important than powerful muscles. Mr. Player, from his personal gym, shows you how to develop those fast muscles.
- The secret to maintaining your fitness and motivation...day after day...
- Powerful ways to overcome even the worst adversity, including the one tactic that always works for Mr. Player. On the course. Off the course.
- How to achieve everything you want to achieve...especially after the age of 50...by taking a simple approach to being totally and thoroughly prepared.
- Why it's vital to shed excess weight...for great golf and a long, healthy life. Yes...we even reveal Mr. Player's diet secrets.

Here's an ad written by Gary Bencivenga, one of the greatest copywriters ever. Notice how Bencivenga writes his bullets/fascinations.

I asked Bencivenga how this advertisement performed and he said it performed very well.

I consider the advertisement above to provide the most perfect example of direct response copywriting I've seen. I found that book that Bencivenga was selling on eBay just to reverse engineer the copy. Bencivenga's copy is crystal clear and the copy also provides a superb example of how to write bullets and fascinations.

I have transcribed the ad below.

● ● ● ●

How to launch your own business for under $1,000 and make $25,000 - $50,000 a year!

Management consultant David D. Seitz is one of the nation's foremost authorities on small businesses. He has written 12 books on the subject and more than 2,000 articles in such publications as Nation's Business, Dun's Review, Business Management, etc.

He has spent 14 months researching 18,292 small business opportunities to compile the first complete directory of the most profitable small businesses you can start in your spare time for under $1,000 (many for under $500).

He has published his findings in a book called, "A Treasury of Business Opportunities" published for anyone who's dreamt of opening a business.

In its fascinating pages, you'll learn...

- How Michael S. makes $50,000 a year in a small community by providing a little-known, simple service needed by the graduating class of every high school and college. His student customers are easy sales and his work consists mainly of placing phone calls.
- How John H. runs a weekend business that uses other people's vacant land to rake in as much as $10,000 profit per weekend. No equipment, no investment, no employees needed!
- How James P. charges $2,000 for a simple service most businesses need, but few people are aware of. He has so much business, he doesn't even advertise.
- How Ronald P. earns $100 per week on a $200 investment supplying a service needed by most storefront merchants.

You'll learn about a unique new product that's selling like wildfire to religious people and gives you a 500% markup. You'll discover an easy-to-start business that nets about $25,000 profit in the summer months alone. You'll be given the amazing inside story of a business that requires so little of anything, you could run it out of a phone book. Yet it's quietly making better than $50,000 a year for scores of men and women.

And this is just the beginning. You'll learn how to take in enormous finder's fees for putting two types of common business clients in touch with each other. You'll discover why certain national manufacturers will pay you upwards of $40,000 a year for making local contacts for them. You'll see how to start a business in which moonlighters work their tails off to earn your $50,000 a year.

You'll learn where to haul away crates of what some businesses consider "junk" – but which other businesses need desperately and will pay as much as $50,000 a year for. You'll discover a product that costs pennies to make, sells for $5, and is wanted by thousands in just about every community. And you'll be shown how to start an exclusive kind of club which can bring you more than $50,000 a year from people who'll feel privileged to pay you a hefty membership fee just for the right to belong!

You'll see how to sell a few sheets of paper for as much as $2,000 to businesses all over your home town. You'll read about the "dead flower" strategy that requires only one visit per customer per month yet gives back up to $25,000 per year in return.

You'll discover how to get people all over your community to lend you their cars and then just as gladly pay you up to $50,000 a year to perform one simple, non-mechanical act with these cars.

You'll discover the remarkable story behind one little-known business that is not only recession-proof, but actually does fantastically well when the economy grows worse. Not only are the profits potentially enormous in this business, but there is this unexpected advantage: simply issuing your own business card as a dealer enables you at once to buy men's suits for $22, metal tennis rackets for $8, electric typewriters for $85, and dozens of other items far below wholesale.

If you or your spouse like to "putter" about the kitchen, just turn to page 68 of this book and see how you can make that puttering yield you a spare-time income of $25,000 a year.

And if that's not enough to get you started in your own little "goldmine" business, wait till you discover...

The instant travel business that gives you up to 50% discounts when you wish you go on a trip.

The simple idea that lets you run your own sweepstakes—with someone else putting up the prizes!

The method for earning thousands of dollars on other people's inventions.

23 different ways your car or truck can help produce profits every day.

The way to turn each of your handy-man friends into a spare-time income of $25,000 a year for you.

The technique for having your products displayed and sold in the finest homes in your area – with sales as a high as $500 per home. This cost strategy alone may be worth 100 times the cost of the book—and it's all yours on page 217.

30-DAY NO-RISK GUARANTEE

The "Treasury" is so crammed full of ingenious, proven money-making ideas, that we feel certain you will find the key to make your dreams of financial independence come true. Send today for your 30-day trial copy of "A Treasury of Business Opportunities" by Donald D. Seitz. If, for any reason, you should be dissatisfied with the book, just return it and every penny of your money will be refunded immediately.

● ● ● ●

Perfect examples of bullets and fascinations from one of the greatest copywriters of all time.

● ● ● ●

Some Notes About Bullets and Fascinations

- They provide a useful summary of the benefits.
- Bullets and fascinations break up dense copy and make the copy more readable. They're also perfect for the scanner.
- There's the "tease" element that motivates people to try the product or service.
- It can be a super-powerful way to hammer home the benefits.

- The copy before the bullets and fascinations is there to get attention and introduce problems that need to be solved but it's the bullets and fascinations that really motivate the potential buyer to take the action you want them to take.
- There should be bullets and fascinations woven through all the copy.
- Go through all the features of a product or service to produce bullets.
- Just one bullet in copy has often made me buy something expensive...that one feature/benefit I've been looking for.
- Bullets and fascinations...and headlines...are closely related.
- The more the merrier...but don't write bullets just to write bullets.
- Study bullets when you see copy. How strong are these bullets?
- The design of the bullets can provide additional impact...so work with the graphic designer or developer to make the bullets pop. Try check marks instead of typical bullet points...or stars. Variation in the presentation of bullets and fascinations can help.
- Keep bullets tight. Use sub-bullets if necessary.
- Use "stealth" bullets...in photo captions, subheads, pull quotes, sidebars, and underneath the main headline.

Why pay attention to bullets?

- ✓ That one single benefit...can lead to the sale. Hitting a "power draw" in golf might be the benefit a reader really wants from a golf video.
- ✓ It's a strong way to convey benefits of the product or service.
- ✓ Create intrigue and stimulate curiosity.
- ✓ Keep the reader reading.
- ✓ Build desire for the product or service—slowly, subtly, and powerfully.
- ✓ The reader will know there's something serious about the product or service when there are lots of bullets.
- ✓ They get the attention of the reader.
- ✓ They make the copy more readable and draw the reader into the copy.
- ✓ They provide important variety in the copy.
- ✓ Bullets and fascinations can overcome objections and misconceptions.

Bullets and fascinations will never get the initial attention of the reader. Once I have the attention of the reader through headlines, sub-heads, and photos (with captions), the bullets and fascinations do the "heavy lifting" and really motivate the reader to take the next step in the sales process.

The sense of intrigue is crucial. I was listening to an interview with a top copywriter recently and the copywriter said he had an approach to copy that made him unbeatable and generated big-time revenue for him and for his clients. Needless to say, I was bouncing off the walls in my apartment wanting to know precise details about that approach. That's the power of curiosity. I ended up asking that copywriter about his approach and he told me. I use the techniques in all my copy.

CHAPTER 21

Telling the Prospect What to Do.

You've heard or read these phrases many times.

"Call the toll-free number right now."

"Click the button below immediately."

"Take these steps to try the ACME dust cleaner."

Here's another huge difference between branding advertising and direct response marketing.

It's extremely rare to see a direct call to action in branding advertising. But in direct marketing, we give the prospect extremely specific instructions. Why? So they know precisely how to try the product or service. Here's what I specifically say.

● ● ● ●

Want More Distance with the BIG MAX Driver? Take These Easy Steps Right Now.

STEP 1. <u>Click here</u> or click the button now. You'll get the lowest price we've seen.

STEP 2. Enter your information in the checkout. It takes about 60 seconds.

STEP 3. You'll receive your BIG MAX straight to your home or office.

STEP 4. Start using the BIG MAX and enjoy an extra 15-30 yards off the tee.

The prospect wants and needs clear instructions when it comes to the buying process.

CHAPTER 22

The Close and Scarcity

I f you have recently bought a product with the help of a salesperson, and if the salesperson was a good one, you would have heard some type of close. Something along the lines of...

"Would you like to drive this car off the lot today?"

"I can take you to the checkout right now."

"You can have the blue one or the red one. Which one is going to be?"

"Take this home today. If it doesn't work or you don't like it, bring it back and we'll refund your money."

And so on.

It's the same in direct response copy. There's an opening to the copy, usually in the form of a headline. Then there's a close. I almost always use what's called the "crossroads close."

Here's the basic premise. There's a decision coming up.

You can either continue to endure your pain/agony/inconvenience... or you can try the product/service. I know you're going to make the right decision.

I even like to use the crossroads close as an open, especially in a video sales letter. There are lots of different ways to close the sale. But I like the crossroads close the most.

SCARCITY

Another powerful sales tactic. Watch QVC and you'll almost always see a counter on the bottom of the screen telling everyone how many units they have sold of a particular item. The announcer will say something like...

"Looks like we've sold 355 of these beautiful watches... You need to hurry because we've only got 600 for this offer at this price."

I'm sure some people are tempted to create scarcity, which is essentially lying. I never lie in copy. But when there's scarcity, I always include this frequently in the copy.

Scarcity can apply to a deadline. For example, someone might say, "This offer will only be available until Wednesday at midnight."

Or I might say...

"Tens of thousands of people are seeing this offer, but we only have 300 drivers for this promotion... Click away from this page or come back later and it's extremely likely we'll have sold out. So click here right now."

Again...it's extremely rare to see scarcity in branding advertising.

CHAPTER 23

Why Long Copy Beats Short Copy. Always.

As I write this chapter, there's a change in personnel happening at one of my clients. I'm about to get a new "gaffer" which is UK slang for the boss. I just received an email from the new gaffer saying, "We'd like to try shorter copy."

Quite frankly, it's the type of email that makes me want to fire the client immediately. Why? Because EVERYONE in direct marketing knows...

THE MORE YOU TELL...THE MORE YOU SELL...

And...

Long copy, provided it's thoroughly salient and written by a professional direct response copywriter, ALWAYS outperforms short copy. We base the above on decades of actual sales data.

In the world of branding advertising, copywriters believe that a couple of photos with a few words of copy will create a flood of new customers. They're wrong. We know that longer copy will always outperform short copy.

Let me explain why...

- When a prospect is reading copy and they're genuinely interested in the product or service, they're often looking for that one benefit or feature they really, *really* want. Long copy gives me the opportunity to include EVERYTHING about the product or service...

including that one sentence with that one benefit that will motivate the reader to buy.

- For each promotion, I like to try to include 40 proof elements. Longer copy provides room for as many proof elements as possible.
- When a prospect sees long copy, they subconsciously think, *"There must be something to this."* But when they see short copy, they quickly move to the next product or service.
- For each promotion, here's how readership works.

  ○ One third will glance at the copy and make a decision.
  ○ One third will look at the headline, the subheads, the photos, the captions, and some of the body copy...then buy.
  ○ One third will read every word three times...then buy.

- So...with long copy, you gain sales from all three types of reader. With short copy, you lose the two-thirds of prospects who are looking for more information.
- When someone is genuinely interested in the product or service, you cannot provide them with enough information. It's especially true when the product or service is expensive. With short copy, the reader will soon leave your message and start to find information elsewhere. Who knows what they will find. There could be a lot of negative reviews on nefarious websites. But with long-form copy, it's much, much easier to control the message and keep the prospect from wandering off.
- If you're competing against another company and you have more information than your competitors, you're ALWAYS going to win.
- Long-form copy gives you the ability to charge higher prices more often and get out of the "race-to-the-bottom" price battle. It's because long-form copy means you can justify the higher price for the superior product you're offering.
- You can overcome objections and this instantly means you will generate more revenue.
- I can overcome skepticism in long-form copy. I can't in short copy.

People who believe copy is too long forget two things.

- People still read...a lot...when they're genuinely interested in something.
- The only metric that really counts—revenue—shows that long-form copy generates more MONEY than short-form copy.

The most successful companies in direct response use long-form copy. It's a huge part of their success.

Famous copywriter Gary Bencivenga sells a series of DVDs from his retirement seminar. The cost? $5,000 for 3 DVDs and a book. The length of the copy? 30,000 words. When Boardroom sold subscriptions to a newsletter for $39 a year, the copy was 36 pages long. When I sell a golf training aid that costs around $50, I write at least four thousand words of copy and the copy generates tens of thousands of dollars...out of thin air. The client tried shorter copy. They tried just video. They tried all sorts of "innovative" things but the tactic that always worked the best was...long-form copy written by an experienced direct response copywriter. I just finished writing the copy for the re-launch of my copywriting course: The Aspen School of Copywriting. I wrote 15,000 words.

How Long is Long Enough?

Famous copywriter Clayton Makepeace says, "The copy needs to be long enough to sell the product."

In some cases, short copy can get the job done. But in most cases, long copy is going to smash short copy when it comes to actual money generated, short term and long term.

When someone says to you, "This copy is too long" or "Nobody will ever read this"...then politely ignore them. When someone tells me the copy needs to be shorter, I want to weep. I want my copy to be longer.

In a perfect world, you can test enough to the point where you can determine the perfect length to sell what you're trying to sell. In almost all cases, the copy that will give you the most revenue will be longer.

When There Isn't Much Space

There's only so much I can write in a two-page letter. There's only so much I can write on a postcard. There's only so much I can write on a Facebook ad.

So there are plenty of times when I have to write short copy. The fundamentals of direct response copywriting apply. It's actually more difficult to write short copy because I have to choose what to leave out. In longer copy on a web page, which has no length limit, I can include everything I believe is relevant...everything that will motivate the prospect to try your product or service.

I've had plenty of success with shorter copy but when I can write a ton, I'm always the happiest. Why? Because my client is on the road to being very wealthy.

● ● ● ●

In the chapters above, I revealed the core elements of successful direct response copy. Remember...it's the type of copy that motivates people to try products and services. Only a small number of copywriters really know how to write this type of copy effectively. In this case, "effectively" means actually write the copy so it generates lots of revenue.

Part 4

VARIOUS THOUGHTS ABOUT DIRECT RESPONSE COPYWRITING.

CHAPTER 24

How to Know When Your Copy Is Really Working.

When is direct response copy really working? The answer might seem obvious...when the money is coming in. But there's another level. Unfortunately, it's not something we can measure.

Let me explain.

Perhaps recently you have thought about buying something. Perhaps it's a product or service that's expensive, like a car. Or perhaps it's something less costly, like a fishing rod.

When the product is a big deal to you, you end up thinking about the product several times during the day. I can remember thinking about a product several years ago. The product cost $1,500 and it occupied my thoughts for about two weeks before I hit the "Buy now" button. Here's another example. I have those copywriting training videos that I sell and one day, I received an email from someone who purchased access. She said, "I spent several days thinking about buying your videos after reading the copy."

Copy really starts working when the message starts burrowing into your soul and your thoughts. Again, there's no way to measure this. I must, ultimately, measure the impact based on short-term and long-term revenue but I know the copy is really working when it finds a spot in the consciousness of the prospect. In this case, I'm attaching the product or service to the ultimate desires of the customer.

What also happens? The prospect starts to justify the purchase to themselves. People will justify almost anything. They'll justify a $5,000 vacation when they have $300 in the bank. They'll justify buying a four-wheel drive car because they might go off road two days a year. People will justify all sorts of activities, some good and some bad, based on their own logic.

I don't want to motivate the person with $300 in the bank to take that $5,000 vacation. I don't want to be part of bad decisions. But I want my copy to start a chain of thinking that leads to a sale.

Here's the challenge I have. The customer's exact desire is a mystery. For example, someone, when asked what they want, might say "financial independence and security in my retirement," but what they really want is to spend three hundred days a year sailing their boat. Maybe they have the ultimate goal of sailing around the world.

Data might tell me I'm writing to a list of people who want "financial independence and security in my retirement," but I can't possibly know that my prospect really wants all that sailing.

My copy really works when I bridge the gap between the obvious desires and the real desires. This means I've captured the imagination of the prospect and the prospect is relating their true desires to the product or service. Building that particular bridge is a rare skill that you'll only get from a serious direct response copywriter.

CHAPTER 25

I TELL THE TRUTH.

In the world of branding advertising, pretty much anything goes. Remember those "Most Interesting Man in the World" ads for Dos Equis beer? They featured a guy in his late 50s or early 60s playing cricket, chasing elephants, and being surrounded by vixens in their 30s.

Watch TV for a day and you'll see similar hyperbole. The goal is to be "creative"...whatever that means...and entertain and thus gain the attention of the prospect for 30 seconds. Certain government agencies, like the SEC, have some guidelines about what you can and cannot say in ads, but, overall, it's wide open. You can gleefully make stuff up in branding advertising.

Is it lying? You be the judge.

In direct marketing and direct response copywriting, there are two schools. One group thinks it's perfectly OK to go totally over the top and "bend" the truth. The other school says, "Find the truth and stick to it." There are some famous and big names in the former school. I won't name names because I'm generally way too nice. But there's a significant amount of respect for some of these copywriters. One of them is referred to as a "legend," yet ask me what I think about his copy and I'll happily start with the word shoddy.

The latter school, the truth school, includes copywriters who genuinely deserve the title "legendary."

- John Caples
- Gary Bencivenga
- David Ogilvy

What are the characteristics of their copy?

- Deep research.
- Testing.
- Straightforward and clear arguments and logic.
- Truthful, realistic claims.
- Proof...and lots of it.
- Positivity over bashing others needlessly.

But most importantly, they TELL THE TRUTH. Everything is believable. Why? Because it's true and it's much easier to believe the truth than something crazy.

There are times when a remarkable fact will emerge during my research. For example, I was working with a golf teacher on a series of training videos and he told me about a student who made some changes and gained 51 extra yards off the tee. That's a remarkable result and the teacher had proof from launch monitor data. So I used that in the copy. If the teacher had lacked proof then I would not have used the claim. Other copywriters, from that certain school of thinking, would have used the claim; however, Gary Bencivenga says, "Never make a claim you can't prove." Proof buttresses and augments the truth.

In direct marketing, or any marketing, there's no need to lie to be successful. Customers are intelligent and they quickly see through any syntactical malfeasance. They want and need the truth and they want and need proof. I always write copy with this thought in the back of my mind... The customers really want what this product or service is going to provide. Why? Because the product or service will dramatically improve their life and/or the lives of those people they care about.

Why should I tell stupid fibs in this scenario? I'm going to find the truth during the research and I'm going to present the truth in a logical fashion so the prospective customer will try the product or service.

Verisimilitude

It's an awkward word to spell. It's an awkward word to say. Try saying it five times quickly.

What's the meaning?

You'll find quite a few definitions.

"Similarity to the truth" is one.
"The appearance of being true or real" is another.

Here's my definition.

"Putting the truth in the best possible light."

Let me provide some examples.

- I have written copy for a famous direct marketing company. Sadly, every time I have written copy for them, it's been a disaster. I'm not certain it's my fault. In fact, the head of this company said it's difficult for freelancers to work for his group. Either way, who really cares? I can legitimately list this company as a client. I have written copy for them. They have sent me checks for my work.
- It's perfectly realistic for my clients in the golf space to claim distance gains off the tee of up to 35 yards. That's a sensible claim provided I can back it up. Sometimes, with proof, I can go over the 35 yard mark.
- A promotion might have a 3% conversion rate. That's a 97% failure rate but verisimilitude tells me to stick to the 3% conversion rate.
- I write resumes for friends as favors for them. If one of my friends has been in charge of a group of people, they have management experience.

You might say, or a critic of direct marketing might say, "There's a fine line between verisimilitude and just plain lying."

Not true. There's a whopping line between the two. The lazy and derelict copywriter makes stuff up. The accomplished copywriter digs and digs for the truth and then he or she puts the truth in the best possible light.

CHAPTER 26

Testing.

A dvanced-level direct marketers are always testing. In the world of branding advertising, there's no way to determine the impact of a campaign with any degree of precision. My clients measure the impact of my copy down to the penny. When people ask me why there are so few direct response copywriters, my answer is usually, "Because it's accountable and you have to write well enough to perform with every promotion." That's pressure.

You've heard the saying, "Failure is not an option." You can ignore this saying when it comes to direct marketing. Failure is always the option. From failure comes success and lots of cash. The clients in direct marketing who test the most and who test intelligently are the ones who make the most money.

Testing is 80 percent science and 20 percent art.

Here's an example of how testing might work.

Let's say I'm selling an information product, specifically a book for single heterosexual women who are in their 50s and want to find a man for a lifelong relationship.

The client/publisher wants to sell the information online. They have a database of prospects plus will advertise online through the networks. Networks are basically companies that let you advertise on various websites like The Weather Channel site. The client will also try advertising on Google and Facebook. The plan is to get the attention of prospects by advertising on the Internet. These ads will send prospects to an advertorial page. The advertorial page will send people to a full-on sales page. The sales page will send prospects to a checkout page along with some upsells.

After the purchase, there will be follow-up emails selling additional products and services. The client will also test a video sales letter against the regular sales page.

Here's the copy I will provide.

- 20 display ads for the Internet.
- 5 advertorial pages.
- 2 versions of the sales letter.
- 2 versions of a VSL.
- Upsell and checkout page copy.
- Follow up emails.

I'll write all the copy then the client will get everything produced and designed. Then it will be time to launch the product.

The client will closely monitor the results of every piece of copy and start directing the traffic to the pieces that work the best. There are several excellent tools to monitor and track results.

For example, one of the display ads might be producing a significantly stronger click-through rate to the advertorial pages. One of the advertorial pages might produce a clear winner. The VSLs might be terrible producers. But one of the sales pages might be generating big revenue and it's the page with the most copy. One upsell works better than another.

Eventually, all the copy and the testing produces what we call a control. Once it's clear we have the control, then it's time to test even more in order to beat that control. As top direct marketer Brian Kurtz says, "The control is the enemy." The most successful direct marketers are always striving to improve and they understand that failure leads to success. Here's what you can test.

- Headlines.
- Photos.
- Price points.
- Video sales letters vs. long-form sales pages.
- Long copy.
- Longer copy.
- Body copy.

- Presentation of the offer.
- Guarantees.

That's just a smattering of what you can test. Everything can and should be tested constantly. My most successful clients let me know about the results of the tests so I can avoid what's failing and replicate what's working.

The above gives you a very basic introduction to testing. Perhaps my next book will be all about testing. But for now, here's what you need to know. You hire a direct response copywriter to help you generate revenue in a measurable way. You will get super-wealthy when you and the direct response copywriter are constantly "feeding the testing beast."

Four additional notes about testing.

One. It's easy to get caught up in some of the technical aspects of testing and start obsessing about things like "conversion rates." It's also tempting to let some of the whizz-bang tools, like heat maps, obscure what's really important: **REVENUE**. You can take revenue to the bank. You can't take conversion rate data to the bank.

Two. If you're advertising and not testing then change that immediately. Many people in advertising...far too many, in fact...want to guide you away from the accountability that comes from testing. Testing can be brutal at times but it will ultimately lead you to the success you deserve.

Three. Bigger companies and direct marketers test constantly. You can discover what's working by looking closely at their work. Don't copy it directly but you can certainly base your testing on what you see.

Four. Things change over time. An advertorial might work for several weeks then start to lose its impact. We call this "fatigue." Keep testing and watch the results closely.

I love writing direct response copy but I get especially excited when the client is testing. We're going to be super-successful with help from testing data.

CHAPTER 27

The Moving Target.

The fundamental principles of direct marketing and direct response copywriting NEVER change. NEVER. Want proof? Then read the seminal book about direct response marketing: *Scientific Advertising* by Claude Hopkins. Yes, it was published in 1923, a few years before we had Facebook, but everything rings true today. David Ogilvy said that everyone in advertising must read *Scientific Advertising* at least seven times before practicing in this field. I agree.

But I digress.

Products change.

Platforms emerge then fade.

Technology changes.

But humans stay the same and thus direct marketing, which is all about humans, stays the same when it comes to the fundamentals.

However, the relationship between humans and products evolves and subtly changes over time. Gene Schwartz writes about this extensively in *Breakthrough Advertising,* another must-read for EVERYONE in direct marketing. I often wonder if *Scientific Advertising* and *Breakthrough Advertising* are required reading in business schools. I fear not.

But I digress again so let's get back to the evolution I just mentioned.

Think about social media. Nobody really knew about social media sites, like Facebook, when it started in 2004. But now, as I write, billions know about Facebook.

If Facebook had asked me to write an ad for Facebook in 2004, my approach would have been totally different than now. In 2004 I would have written copy to explain the basic concept. Today, my copy might emphasize new features and benefits as the platform evolves.

Back to golf. In the mid-1990s, the companies that made golf clubs had an all-new material to work with, mainly for drivers and fairway woods: titanium. I might have written...

The Big Cannon Driver Made from Titanium. An All-New Material to Give You an Extra 27 Yards off the Tee.

Today, as I explained earlier in this book, golfers would laugh at that headline because almost all drivers are made from titanium. So I have to look at another feature, technological advancement, or unique mechanism in order to get the attention of the golfer. Fortunately, the people who design golf clubs are always coming up with something new. They have to in order to sell golf clubs.

Think about the products and services you buy. Products come and products go. Technology changes.

Awareness changes over time. Awareness is essentially the only moving target in direct marketing and direct response copywriting. I must assess the levels of awareness before writing copy.

Right now, I'm writing copy for a brand-new concept in the travel industry. Nobody really knows about the service because it's so new. Fortunately, the service is congruent with an emerging trend in the industry. So I must clearly explain the concept and its many benefits. If all goes well, people will know all about the service in about two years. The copy will have to change.

A direct response copywriter should have a feel for the level of awareness initially then confirm it through studious research. In some cases, I will have to let the client know that nobody really understands what they are selling.

CHAPTER 28

Pricing.

I have read and digested most of the top books about direct marketing and direct response copywriting. You'll find a list in the appendix. You can also visit my website for reviews of many of the books I recommend you read.

There's one book that's not a member of the "usual suspects"...but it should be right up there with the best of the best: *No B.S. Pricing Strategy* by Dan Kennedy and Jason Marrs.

I've read many books in the "No B.S." series and I have two thoughts. First, I'm not sure I like the graphic of Dan Kennedy standing behind a steer with a big smile on his face: it's a bit too "graphic" for me. Second, most of these books are a tad too heavy, for my liking, on the promotion of other products and services. But that's how Dan Kennedy organizes his sales funnel. It's called the ascension model.

However, *No B.S. Pricing Strategy* is NOT heavy on the promotion and it's one of the finest and most informative marketing books I've read. It's right up there with the epic "must reads" of direct marketing. And yet it's a book that many direct marketers have never seen because they don't know it exists.

In direct marketing, we like to focus on lists, copy, proof elements, offers, testing, and the other core elements of our world. But, in my experience, even some of the top direct marketers would benefit significantly by looking more closely at pricing and spending some time learning more about pricing strategy.

Why?

Even a slight tweak in pricing can instantly deliver a 5% increase in revenue. Not too shabby when a company has $100 million in sales. And when a company decides to pursue new pricing strategies, revenue can... and should...explode.

As a direct response copywriter, I have five vital roles when it comes to pricing.

- One. Bring pricing expertise to my clients.
- Two. Justify higher prices for products and services by writing well-executed copy.
- Three. De-commoditize the product or service so that people are not shopping based on price.
- Four. Help organize upsells and downsells in order to drive more revenue.
- Five. Help my clients generate the revenue they deserve for their products and services.

Remember...my goal as a direct response copywriter is to maximize revenue for every client. Pricing plays a vital role. In branding advertising, the goal is to increase awareness and, perhaps, to win awards for creativity. Unfortunately, you can't take awareness and awards to the bank as I have bleated on about in this tome. But you can take money to the bank all day. I have added pricing expertise as a service I provide to my clients.

This chapter could be as long as Dan Kennedy's book about pricing...so read Kennedy's book. But here are some key points about pricing.

- **Test like crazy**. Testing will provide some pleasant surprises. A higher price might beat a lower price for exactly the same product.
- **Upsells and downsells are part of pricing strategy**. You'll be amazed what happens when you offer a lower-priced product when someone says "no" to your initial offer. You'll be amazed at how much people will spend when you keep motivating them to buy with upsells.
- **Use long-form direct response copy**. One of the many reasons to use long-form copy? You can justify a higher price...a *much higher price*.
- **How you break down the price is vital**... $900 becomes "three easy payments" of $300, which becomes "for the price of a double

latte at Starbucks once a day." Notice how you can drive a $45,000 car off the lot for lease payments of just $326 a month.

- **Compare and contrast.** I get giddy when a company has a grid with two or three pricing options. And I get especially giddy when I see the words, "best value" or "most popular" over one of the options...the option that drives the most revenue and/or profit.
- **It's better.** People genuinely believe that when a product has a higher price, it's superior to other similar products. My role as the direct response copywriter is to explain why the product or service is decidedly superior and warrants the higher price.
- **Be ethical.** You don't have to use weird and generally downmarket tactics like "bait and switch" and other such shenanigans, some of which may get you into trouble. No...you can be totally clear about the price of the product or service and the pricing strategy. Why be any other way? Just be totally clear and totally transparent.
- **The bonus.** You can build significant additional value by offering free bonuses to complement and augment the main product. But I must write ample copy for these free premiums. I sell these with the same vim and oomph of the main product.

As a direct response copywriter, it's my responsibility to help my clients with pricing strategy.

And one more thing. I'm sure you've been ready, able, and willing to buy a product only for the salesperson to say something like... "And because you're buying right now, I'm going to give you a discount." Maybe you've thought, on occasion, that you would have paid more for a product or service and that the product or service was underpriced, perhaps suspiciously so.

My clients like it when I help them generate more revenue simply by working on pricing strategy and tactics backed by the power of direct response copy.

Some additional thoughts about pricing and the presentation of the offer.

- In tests, BOGO, which is code for "buy one get one free" is a proven winner. You can create variations on this theme...like *Give One, Get One Free...*
- Present the pricing and the offer so it's so epic enough that the offer is a "slam dunk" even to the most skeptical person on the planet.
- Give a believable reason for a special offer. A fire sale if there's been a fire. A super-low price due to additional inventory. The introductory offer you'll never repeat. I regularly see copy where there's a stupid and non-believable reason for low prices.
- Sell one product at a time. You can have different prices for the same product, or a slight variation, but only sell one product, starting with one main benefit.
- Two versions. Good/better/best. One-year subscription or lifetime. There are lots of ways to provide slightly different prices for the same product.
- Check the competition. How are they presenting their pricing and their offers? If it's been the same for a while, then it's likely working for them.
- A change in format can transform pricing. How much will people pay for a book? Around $20. But they'll pay up to $1,000 for a manual. *Really.* There's only one company I know that's managed to sell a book for $39 and that was Boardroom. It was a huge effort involving the world's top copywriters, elite list data expertise, and more. It's easier to change the format.
- Some copywriters, including Ted Nicholas, had data saying that a price ending in 7 will boost revenue. Test it.
- Want a constant torrent of revenue? *Continuity.* In fact, I like to find clients who have continuity products because I know they are almost always financially solvent PLUS they likely understand direct marketing if they're successful with continuity products.
- You can often charge more when there's a strict limit to the number of products you sell.
- Discounting is for wimps. One reason people hire me? So they don't have to resort to discounts. Also...discounting can change how

people view your product or service. This can happen quickly and it can take a long time to build pricing back up. Just ask anyone in the hotel business.

- There may be certain rules and regulations regarding discounting and presentation of pricing. Check with legal counsel.

My advice to you...

- Read the book about pricing by Dan Kennedy and Jason Marrs.[7]
- Take a close look at your pricing strategy based on the market, testing, and other data.
- Hire a direct response copywriter. They will help you justify a higher price...even when there are similar products in the market that cost less.
- Present options.
- Make sure there's a full-on guarantee.
- Be bold. Way too many people seriously underprice their products and services.

Pricing is one of the most fascinating parts of my work as a direct response copywriter. It's also a part of direct marketing that's overlooked.

---

[7]   The publisher can thank me later.

CHAPTER 29

Speed Is a Strategy.

This saying comes from one of my mentors in direct response copywriting: Andrew Wood, who calls himself "The Legend." The concept also comes from one of the world's most accomplished copywriters, Clayton Makepeace, who sadly passed away in early 2020.

Andrew writes quickly and Clayton wrote super-fast. I strive to write copy quickly.

Some copywriters like to write between three and five major direct mail promotions a year. These might be upwards of 50 pages. It will take a month to research the project. A month to provide a draft. A month to go through revisions. A month to work on the design with the graphic designer. Then a couple of weeks for final changes.

However, most of my clients typically want to move much faster. The faster they get their products and services to market, the faster they generate cash. They're not looking for copywriting perfection. They want copy that will create a positive response and they want it quickly.

One of my clients will contact me on Wednesday. They will need about four thousand words of copy for a product by the following Monday. I'll get them the copy and the promotion will be up and running in 10 days. That's called SPEED. It's easier to move faster on the web. But you can be almost as fast with direct mail.

Some companies like to take their time and take months before sending copy live, either online or offline. Others like to move extremely quickly. I'm happy working in either environment.

I've always written quickly. Back in high school, and even earlier, I was always under some degree of pressure to write a lot, accurately, in a short space of time. This happened every day with homework. Then it happened during exams where I'd have three hours to write four long essays. I also wrote for the school newspaper, regularly writing long pieces in a couple of hours. Earlier in my career, I'd produce a 100-page quarterly magazine without any freelancers. I'd write the ads and write all the articles plus sell advertising and manage the entire publishing cycle.

Speed is great for my clients. I can turn work around quickly so they generate revenue faster. But it's also good for the writer because it means more opportunities.

Speed is a mindset. I eat slowly. I usually ski relatively slowly. But I can produce copy quickly. Where can you speed things up when it comes to marketing?

CHAPTER 30

Why I'm Writing This Book.

I'm writing this book for your success. It staggers me and upsets me that so many people in business give me a blank stare when I tell them I'm a "direct response copywriter."

Why?

Is it my ego?

Not at all.

It's because a direct response copywriter can help you become extremely wealthy. I can't work in a vacuum. You must have a product or service that customers are willing and able to buy. You must have a way to find the people who are going to want your product or service. You must have a way to measure the performance of your advertising. You must develop a passion for direct marketing.

When you have all these in your business arsenal, then a direct response copywriter can help you be extremely successful. I want as many businesses to be successful as possible. This success brings genuine prosperity and this prosperity spreads throughout society. There's a higher calling when it comes to marketing.

One of my clients started by selling DVDs out of his living room. He grew his company to 60 employees and merged with one of the world's largest media giants. Again...he had all the marketing pieces in place. I wrote the copy and he generated millions each promotion. Another client started with just three people and now they have over 40 employees and a sizeable marketing empire. Large companies are usually finding ways to limit the number of employees they hire. Smaller companies are usually hiring.

Perhaps I'm being a smidge philosophical and/or meditative here but I focus on improving my copy and working hard for my clients because they're depending on me to produce results. And when I produce these results, I'm helping to create prosperity and all the good that comes with prosperity.

If you're the owner of a business or you're running a business and you have a great product but you're struggling with marketing and sales, three things are likely happening.

- One. You're not familiar with direct marketing and/or you're not basing your marketing on direct marketing techniques and tactics.
- Two. You give me the "blank stare" when I tell you I'm a direct response copywriter.
- Three. You've fallen prey to the mistake that is called "branding advertising."

There are lots of books out there about how to write direct response copy. There are lots of books about how to execute direct marketing strategies. But this book is the first that explains why every company should find and hire a direct response copywriter.

Perhaps this book will help other direct response copywriters because it will increase the demand for our work and expertise. Perhaps this book will inspire young people to become direct response copywriters. I also hope to convert as many people as possible away from branding gibberish and phoney-ism toward the proven and accountable power of direct marketing.

Yes, there's some ego involved in this book. I want people to understand my work and how I contribute to the financial health of a business. But most of all, I'm writing this book for YOUR success. Now, you know more about the "greatest salespeople you've never heard of" and "the ultimate marketing superpower" and the next step is to start using direct marketing and then you'll want to find a direct response copywriter.

ANOTHER REASON

Here's another reason I'm writing this book. CLARITY IN A CONFUSING WORLD...a world replete with people who claim to know a vast amount about advertising and marketing yet have never actually sold anything.

Not to seem cranky but here's what I regularly see when it comes to writing and marketing.

- In the world of creative writing, the professors and teachers are almost always failed writers who must resort to academia to earn a living. They teach ambitious young writers, many of whom have immense talent. The teachers lead the students in the wrong direction.
- In that same world...conferences and "summer programs" led by failed and mediocre novelists who are simply ripping off the attendees.
- So-called "branding experts" who speak a language I fail to understand yet earn whopping fees for absolutely nothing of any value.
- Pompous farts with C-suite positions who write about themselves in the third person, relish winning awards over gaining revenue, and who look down their noses at direct marketing and direct marketers.
- CEOs who are unable to spot the rancid phoney-ness of the pompous farts and branding experts.
- People who call themselves "direct response copywriters" yet have never sold a thing with their writing. These people speak at conferences, have podcasts, and sell training courses.
- Copywriters who lie.

The result? The truth can be difficult to find. You'll find the truth in this book and the books I recommend in the appendix.

Even better, you will soon discover the truth as you start to get into direct marketing and you start to measure results with extreme precision. This will tell you the truth about your marketing.

When you're deciding who to follow, take a look at the actual results achieved.

- Bryan Kurtz generated over $2 billion in revenue at Boardroom.
- Dan Kennedy could pack a room with two thousand people three times a year at around $2,000 per attendee. And then each event might generate over $5 million in "back of the room" sales.
- David Ogilvy wrote direct mail letters to start his agency and it was up and running and successful in six months.
- Bob Bly has written 99 books, with the 100th on the way and he regularly receives big royalty checks. He's built a list of more than 60,000 writers.

I will not place myself in the same league as the above but I've helped my clients generate over $450 million in revenue over the last eight years plus I've generated over 1,000 leads directly from my website. But people who run events feel they need to book speakers who have achieved precisely nothing.

LOOK AT THE ACTUAL RESULTS NOT THE PRIZES AND FLIM FLAM.

After reading and digesting this tome, you will know how to achieve the success you deserve through the proven power of direct response marketing and direct response copywriting.

I also hope that CFOs in companies read this book and ask the CMO and others, "Why are we spending money on branding advertising when you can assess the results of direct marketing to the penny?" I'd love to be a fly on the wall during that conversation.

So this book is about you, your success, and giving you the raw truth about marketing and selling. I make no apologies to the merchants of branding and others who might be offended. This book is not for them. This book is for you.

CHAPTER 31

Different Types of Media.

S pend a few days really looking and you'll see advertising everywhere. It's in/on the obvious spots, like your TV set, your smartphone, or the radio. But you'll also find advertising in other somewhat bizarre places. I saw advertising on a turnstile in the subway on a recent visit to New York City. Play golf and you might see advertising on the scorecard. What about the top of a taxi? It's all media.

In direct marketing and direct response copywriting, we're more selective when it comes to media. Why? We measure everything to the penny. We know the media that works and the media that fails.

We know, for example, that advertising on Google is more effective than advertising on a t-shirt. We know that advertising through email is more effective, when it comes to what really matters, namely REVENUE, than advertising inside a taxi cab. It's what we call...COMMON SENSE.

As a company owner or marketing manager, there's a dizzying array of media out there. This makes life easier because you can be more targeted. But it can be more difficult to choose.

Right now, in direct marketing, we're primarily using...

- Online advertising through the "networks."
- Email.
- The big online players like Google and Facebook
- Direct mail.
- TV.
- Radio.

- Magazines.
- Newspapers.

I've written copy for all of the above. The fundamentals stay exactly the same. The length differs purely because I can write 20,000 words on a web page while I can only use around one hundred characters in a Google Ad Words ad. But the basics of direct response copy stay PRECISELY the same.

CHAPTER 32

How the Money Works in Direct Marketing.

I'm not an accountant. I'm not a financial analyst. I'm a direct response copywriter and, as such, I must understand how the numbers work in direct marketing. You must apply all you've discovered in this book to your business model and your financial goals. You know yours. I don't know your numbers. I'm making the numbers below up but I'm basing them on experience with clients.

Let's start with cost per acquisition, known in the trade as CPA.

- Let's say you spend $1,000 to get one thousand views for your product. This could be online or it could be in the mail or on TV.
- Fifty people pay attention to your message enough to click through to another web page or call a toll-free number.
- Of those, you'll get a great result if you can motivate 20 of them to make a purchase. You spent $1,000 to bring 20 of these customers into your fold. So the CPA was $50.
- Let's say the product you initially sell costs $50. This brings your CPA to zero, which is where most direct marketers want to be.

"But wait, Scott...that makes no sense at all," you say. "I'm not making any money!"

"True," I answer. "Not yet."

Let me introduce two crucial concepts.

One. Upsells and downsells.
Two. Lifetime value.

Once you've sold that first product, you can sell more, right away. This can significantly decrease the CPA.

But the more important concept for your business is lifetime value. Let's say you take five of those 20 customers and they end up buying $1,000 worth of products in the next 12 months. And perhaps they'll buy even more in the upcoming years. That $1,000 invested in attracting those first clients has produced at least $10,000 plus more on some upsells and downsells.

Producing just five long-term clients or customers out of one thousand touches may seem low from a percentage standpoint but that's how the percentages work sometimes. You have to look at long-term revenue and revenue in general and only use percentages as a benchmark.

You can also mine other streams. Maybe one of those new customers will buy even more products at an even higher price. You can sell the list of people who have purchased products to others. You can send affiliate emails and generate affiliate commissions.

Enter the Experienced Elite-Level Direct Response Copywriter

Now let's look at the example above. It's realistic to believe, provided you have a great list and a great offer, that an experienced elite-level direct response copywriter can triple the response. Let's look at the numbers again, this time measured with the impact of a direct response copywriter on your team.

- You spend $1,000 to get one thousand views of your product.
- One hundred and fifty people pay attention to your message enough to click through to another web page or call a toll-free number.
- Of those, you'll get a great result if you can motivate 60 of them to make a purchase. You spent $1,000 to bring 60 of these customers into your fold. So the CPA is $16.67.
- Let's say you take 15 of those 20 customers and they end up buying $3,000 worth of products. That's $45,000 from the $1,000 invested.

Yes...the numbers are made up but a three-fold increase in conversion is realistic when the copy is just OK at first...then written by an elite-level direct response copywriter along with some serious testing.

Notice that we're closely measuring response at all times. And notice the emphasis on concepts like cost per acquisition and lifetime value.

So, the point of this chapter is to clue you in when it comes to how the numbers work in direct marketing. Take the numbers above and go to a spreadsheet and start goofing around. Add a few zeros. Apply them to your model. Dream a little. Many direct marketers have enjoyed whopping success over the years with this basic framework plus they've had an elite-level direct response copywriter on their team, most likely.

Again...I'm not a numbers person. If you're not a numbers expert, find someone who is. The top direct response copywriters have this person on their team. And their numbers people are not branding people: they understand direct marketing.

Why Do Top Direct Marketers Hire Top Direct Response Copywriters?

Let's say a company is selling a product and it costs $10. The company could have someone write the copy who doesn't understand how to write copy. The company might sell 10 units and generate $100 in revenue.

Maybe someone in the company knows how to write copy at a very basic level. The company might sell 50 units and generate $500 in revenue.

When that same company hires a top direct response copywriter, they'll help them sell 1,000 units at $100 and help them generate $100,000 ... plus they'll help with upsells and other products to drive additional revenue.

My clients hire me because I help them generate massive additional revenue, provided the company has great products and a way to drive traffic.

CHAPTER 33

Yes, You Can Have Your Branding Cake and Eat It Too...

I have extensively, thoroughly, comprehensively, gleefully, and expansively bashed branding advertising in this book and I make no apologies. There's no reason for any company to use branding advertising when direct marketing produces accountable and eventually predictable results. I've hammered branding to help you, not me. I actually take no huge pleasure giving the branding world a solid kicking because I wish that group would see the folly of their ways and embrace direct marketing.

Companies spend hundreds of thousands, even millions, on branding consultants and branding image advertising. You'll get hours of meetings with people who are scratching their chins and asking things like, "How does this product look when it comes to engagement?" or saying things like, "We have to work on brand authority and brand equity and make sure the story and messaging is on-brand," or some such piffle.

There's nothing wrong with a well-designed logo and I understand why companies want the logo to look consistent everywhere from company trucks to letterhead and from pajamas to bicycle locks. I understand this, especially in larger companies. Some branding specialists strive for this consistency and also try to align the company with similar brands. But I know a company that just hired a branding expert for around $200,000 a year. I'm not sure what she's doing and there's no way to assess the ROI on this hire. The same company could spend $100,000 to hire an accomplished direct marketing specialist and this would likely generate more than $10 million in revenue in a couple of years.

Oh well.

Here's something else the branding people do not want to hear.

YOU CAN BUILD YOUR BRAND THROUGH DIRECT MARKETING.

That's precisely what my clients have achieved. They have pursued direct marketing excellence AND built a brand. How?

Because people are not interested in your brand. They are interested in themselves and what they want to achieve. These companies built their marketing around this concept and thus built brands with a reputation for... you guessed it...**HELPING THEIR CUSTOMERS GET WHERE THEY WANT TO GET**.

Dan Kennedy said that branding might be 10 percent of your marketing world. I disagree and it's not often I disagree with Dan Kennedy. Branding should be about 1 percent of your marketing world. Yes...hire a great graphic designer like Lori Haller to create a logo for you. But then hire Lori to help you with your direct-marketing-related design needs.

In my experience, the best way to build a brand is to get the product to people who will benefit from that product.

The most successful direct marketers I know are NOT interested in branding advertising and yet they've built huge brands. They have their branding cake and eat it too.

Part 5

FINDING AND WORKING WITH A DIRECT RESPONSE COPYWRITER

CHAPTER 34

Finding Direct Response Copywriters.

"It's not easy to find direct response copywriters."

That's not me bragging so that I can charge higher fees. It's something I hear from the serious direct marketers who hire experienced direct response copywriters. These serious direct response marketers are typically business owners, marketing managers, and account representatives.

One thing to remember...you're looking for a direct response copywriter, not just a copywriter. There's a HUGE difference as I have detailed extensively in this tome. Finding a copywriter is extremely easy. Finding a direct response copywriter is extremely difficult.

In the latter case, you have to look for a record of actual results. "Regular" copywriters might have won awards and might have a portfolio full of pretty ads but there will be no way to measure the revenue these ads generated. Ask about ROI and you'll get a mumbled, "The client reported a spike in sales and we won some acclaim." The direct response copywriter generates actual revenue and, without breaching an NDA, gives you a general sense of actual revenue generated.

So your first step when trying to find a direct response copywriter is a mindset. You have to say to yourself, "I want a direct response copywriter with a proven track record generating tangible results."

Where Next?

There are several ways to find a direct response copywriter.

Online search. Google "direct response copywriter." In full disclosure, my website will likely be one of the first in the 'organic' search results. You'll find other copywriters, too.

Ask people in direct marketing. You might also ask people in general advertising and marketing but they might not send you to a direct response copywriter. Ask someone who works in direct marketing.

LinkedIn search. Sometimes a search for "direct response copywriter" will yield about four hundred people. Sometimes many more. Sometimes fewer. This tactic will send you to some excellent direct response copywriters. It will also send you to some total beginners, people who call themselves direct response copywriters. You can also advertise an opportunity on LinkedIn.

Conferences and seminars. Many direct response copywriters go to conferences and direct marketing seminars either as attendees or speakers. For example, there's a seminar for financial newsletter publishers every year in Orlando. Several excellent and accomplished direct response copywriters attend. AWAI has their famous "boot camp" every year, now in the spring. You can set up a booth at "boot camp" to look for copywriters: you'll get a few really experienced copywriters there but most will be 'newbies.'

Headhunters. You might have some success in larger markets like New York, London, and Los Angeles. But once again, remember, you're not looking for a "regular" copywriter.

Online job sites. Direct response copywriters, myself included, have a resume indexed on the online job sites.

Commodity sites. Tens of thousands of copywriters are registered on sites like Upwork. It's a great place to look if you must have the lowest price and you don't care a lot about the quality of the work. I use the word "quality" very loosely here. I'm actually listed on Upwork but I make it totally clear I'm only looking to work with serious direct marketers.

Message boards. There are several message board communities dedicated to marketing. Some direct response copywriters check these message boards fairly frequently. Watch out, though. It can be The Wild, Wild West.

Perhaps you've had success finding talent in other ways. There's no need to limit your search to your local area. You can work with direct response copywriters around the world.

Finding the Best

In his magnificent book about direct marketing, *Overdeliver,* Brian Kurtz lists the seven traits of the successful direct response copywriter.

I'm going paraphrase what Brian writes but only if you promise to buy his book. Brian and his associates at Boardroom found the world's top direct response copywriters. They paid them hundreds of thousands of dollars. I will detail why in the next chapter but here's what Brian and his associates at Boardroom looked for in serious direct response copywriters.

1. **HUNGER**. It's more, much more, than simply wanting to be a great direct response copywriter. It's a willingness to put in the hours and hours to become a highly productive direct response copywriter. This also requires persistence because persistence and the hunger to be excellent are closely related.

2. **CURIOSITY**. This trait is connected to research but curiosity is simply a general interest in people, places, products, and how things happen in our world. I enjoy the research phase of a copywriting product because I'm going to learn a lot. I never assume I know the answer to a question. I ask someone who will genuinely know.

3. **SMARTS**. Brian Kurtz defines smarts as a willingness and desire to learn from the best. I agree but I'll take this one step further. Elite-level direct response copywriting is for people who are brainy but in a street-smart way. Is it for the person who can operate a nuclear reactor on a submarine? Probably not. Is it for someone with a BA in English from Harvard? No. It's for people who are smart enough to understand what motivates people and it's for people who are smart enough to understand the need for constant improvement.

4. **PASSION**. Client success. Becoming great. The subject matter. Putting words together. Selling. Direct marketing. A direct response copywriter must have passion for every part of this work. I hope my passion for direct marketing and direct response copywriting, and

the success of people in business, comes across in this book and at all times. I also have a passion for skiing and helping people become stronger skiers.

5. **UNDERSTANDING DIRECT MARKETING PRINCIPLES**. I can say, "I have proof my copy works" based on actual revenue generated. And I can even say, "I'm a direct marketing expert" because I've worked with some of the world's top direct marketers and I've spent significant sums on my direct response education. To be a direct response copywriter who produces, you have to understand the fundamentals of direct marketing at a professorial level, even though you won't find many professors who genuinely understand direct marketing.

6. **HUMILITY**. I never met David Ogilvy, sadly, but in his books, and in the videos of him I've watched, he seems humble. Gary Bencivenga is humble. Not all copywriters are humble, though. One copywriter writes they are "the most ripped-off writer on the Web" and "the most respected writing teacher alive." Another bleats, "America's top copywriter." Hmmmm. Take a look below. You be the judge. Maybe you'll agree. Maybe you won't. I took out the original copywriter's name but you get the point.

Who The Hell Is Dennis?

Dennis   slyly refers to himself as "the most ripped-off writer on the Web", and no one on the inside of the online business world disagrees.

Other marketers also call   *hi*   "the most respected writing teacher alive"... and the list of well-known marketers who freely reference   *hi*   as their primary mentor for

There's nothing wrong at all with pointing out success backed by proof... It's what potential clients want to see. I point out my successes but I totally admit my failures and professional mistakes. Copywriting can, and should be, extremely humbling. I have confidence in my work and my ability and I genuinely believe my best work is ahead of me but I rarely boast and, when I'm perhaps guilty of boasting, I back up my claims with proof. At some stage, David Ogilvy and Gary Bencivenga, when discussing engagements, had to say, "Yes...I'm really good at this," then I'm sure they said, "Here's proof." Some copywriters will say, "All the success is due to my copy," but they're totally wrong. Success in direct marketing comes from a great product and a large number of prospects. The copy simply puts the prospects and the products together. Ted Mahon is one of the most accomplished people I know. He's climbed Mount Everest and climbed and skied the highest 100 mountains in Colorado. He writes about his trips on his blog (Stuckintherockies.com), but he's one of the humblest people you'll ever meet. Same with the extremely accomplished direct response copywriter and author, Bob Bly.

7. **SHARING SUCCESS.** Yes, I've written copy that's helped my clients generate millions in revenue. But I'm just one member of a team. My clients have the prospects and the products. They're the ones taking all the risk. You can blame the copywriter for a failure when the list and offer are excellent. But when there's success, the copywriter should be thinking, *How can I beat the copy that just worked? and How can I help my client generate even more revenue?*

It's not easy to find a direct response copywriter. But it's worth the effort. The top direct marketing companies are always looking for direct response copywriters who can generate revenue.

The Agora Factor

Agora is a publishing company based in Baltimore, Maryland. They also have offices in Florida and other locations around the world. They primarily publish health and financial newsletters and related information products. They also organize events and sell dietary supplements. The founder of Agora, Bill Bonner, is a direct response copywriter although he spends more time today working on running the overall business.

This company might give an organizational specialist a migraine. Why? From the outside, Agora looks like a disorganized collection of independent entities with little or no structure. It may not have a classic organizational chart but it's a company that generates tens of millions in revenue every month thanks in large part to the quality of its direct response copywriters.

Agora is the only company I know with anything that even vaguely approaches an apprenticeship program for direct response copywriters. They hire young or relatively young talent, provide some training, and ask these nascent copywriters to write various promotions. They pay around $40,000 a year for the first couple of years plus a royalty. If a copywriter produces results that are acceptable or above, they stick around. If the results aren't there, they get the boot. Direct response copywriters who are successful at one of the Agora entities can make high six-figure or even "two-comma" incomes per year.

I don't know anything about the training. I'd like to. But here's what I know about Agora... They have cornered the market for the top direct response copywriters. I estimate they currently have 200-300 direct response copywriters on their roster. That's a guess. It's yet another reason it's so difficult to find direct response copywriters who can actually produce revenue. Agora keeps them inside their fold by providing the potential for significant paydays. They don't care about the copywriters who fail. They're kicked out the doors. Brutal, perhaps, but remember that direct response copywriters are salespeople and salespeople have to produce.

Other Challenges When It Comes to Finding Direct Response Copywriters

If they're not working with Agora, many of the top direct response copywriters in the world have exclusive contracts with one client. That's because these companies understand the importance of having a direct response copywriter on their team, whether it's a freelance or full-time employee.

The number of available freelance direct response copywriters who can actually produce revenue is extremely small, probably around two hundred. But there are thousands of people who want to become a direct response copywriter. This means that many copywriters become copywriting coaches, charging up to $500 an hour for advice and coaching. It's usually a rip-off, but aspiring copywriters are only too happy to pay these crazy amounts. I've taken this so-called "instruction" and it was a dreadful experience. I provide coaching, I have to admit, through a video instruction series I make available through my website.[8] I know one famous copywriter who told me, "I don't want to write copy anymore. I'm just coaching now. I work four hours doing nothing and get $2,000. Why go through the hassle of writing copy?" I know one direct response copywriter who simply bypassed actually writing copy because she couldn't produce results and now she is now coaching aspiring direct response copywriters. Hmmmm.

Some copywriters work extremely hard generating results and revenue for their clients. They get paid. But then they realize they're helping someone else get wealthy. So they start using their "superpower" to sell their own products and services. Dan Kennedy and Jay Abraham are two well-known direct marketers who started as copywriters then built speaking and information marketing empires.

I love writing direct response copy. But I know several direct response copywriters who are tired, jaded, fed up, and generally bored. These copywriters retire or take up another trade.

There's nothing linear about being a direct response copywriter. It's not a "typical" career. So there's nothing linear about trying to find direct response copywriters. But keep looking. A direct response copywriter can, and should, generate huge revenue for your business provided you have prospects plus something those prospects will want to try.

What I'm Looking for in a Client

You might be checking me out when you look at my website or we speak in person. But I'm checking you out, in a good way. You're interviewing me. I'm interviewing you. I listed what Brian Kurtz looks for in a copywriter. Now I'm going to list what I'm looking for in a client. David Ogilvy wrote, in *Confessions of an Advertising Man*, about how to be a good client. Remember...if you're a great client, you're going to get the best possible results from your copywriter. Make life difficult for your direct response copywriter and you'll minimize your revenue. Your direct response copywriter will walk out the real or virtual door as soon as you start to become difficult.

---

[8]   TheAspenSchoolofCopywriting.com

Passion for direct marketing. I can tell, in the first two minutes of a conversation with a potential client, whether they're on the direct marketing bus, or want to be. I can help a client get on the bus but it's time intensive and expensive. Sometimes, I work with companies with a huge love for direct marketing. Other times, I get a call from a prospective client who is just getting started on their direct marketing journey. I sometimes hear, "I went to a Dan Kennedy seminar and he told us to find a direct response copywriter." I love it when I hear these magical words.

Desire to learn about direct marketing. The top minds in direct marketing are constantly striving to learn more about the art and science of direct marketing.

Realistic time frames. I write quickly. In fact, I might be the fastest direct response copywriter. But I still need realistic time frames in order to be successful. I especially need research time when I'm beginning an engagement with a new client or working on a large project like a magalog.

Organized and responsive. I'm not always the most organized person on the planet and I don't necessarily ask for organizational perfection from clients but it's hard to help a client when they're not responsive. Organized clients get stronger results from their direct response copywriter.

Understanding of the power of the investment. On my website, I make it totally clear I'm not the least expensive copywriter. I work with companies that understand that paying a direct response copywriter can provide a huge ROI.

Trust. When I'm speaking with a potential client, I want to get a sense of whether they will trust me or not. My clients trust me to generate millions in revenue for their company. If someone does not trust me, what's the point?

Willingness to provide information. You, as the client, know more about the business than me, the copywriter. So, for me to sell your product successfully, I need as much information as possible from you and your team, especially when I'm just getting going.

Testing. Testing = success in direct marketing. Will the client allow me to fail on the way to discovering what works? I look for testing freaks who are constantly striving to "feed the testing beast."

Ethical approach to everything. There are scallywags and numpties in every vertical, including direct marketing. Fortunately in direct marketing, most of the people I know are totally above board. Don't ask me to lie. Ask me to find the truth and tell the truth. There are lots of copywriters who will say anything and blatantly lie. I'm not one of them.

Track record of success...and failure. I sometimes work with startups but I'm usually looking to work with companies with an established business. Yes, I'm looking for success. But I'm also looking for some failures. It shows the company has a direct marketing mindset.

Great offers and products. I can't sell your sunlamps in the Sahara. But I can sell golf balls to golfers. In fact, my copy has sold well over 300,000 boxes of golf balls.

The constant need to sell products and services. This type of company will always need copy and they will regularly need my expertise.

Traffic. Does the potential client have a great list of responsive buyers? Can they get that list? Can they buy traffic successfully? Who is the traffic buyer and what is their track record?

A generally pleasant demeanor. There are some generally disagreeable people in business. I avoid them. I have much more fun and success working with people who are pleasant and polite, like you, I'm sure.

Continuity products. Some clients sell individual products successfully. But the most successful companies have continuity-based products in their portfolio.

I don't have an official checklist when I'm speaking with a potential client. Perhaps I should. But these characteristics are in the back of my head. Other top direct response copywriters will be looking for the same from potential clients. I'm not a prima donna. I'm not trying to be demanding. I'm simply looking for a good fit so the partnership generates huge revenue and success for all.

CHAPTER 35

Cost or Investment? How to Compensate a Direct Response Copywriter.

The Most Powerful and Measurable Investment You'll Ever Make in Your Business.

Marty Edelston, the founder of Boardroom, one of the most successful direct marketing companies in the history of direct marketing, built his empire around finding the top experts in the world to help his business grow and prosper.

As such, he sought and found the world's top copywriters, including Eugene Schwartz, Gary Bencivenga, Clayton Makepeace, Mel Martin, and many others. These and other copywriters usually wrote magalogs. These are multi-page advertising pieces that also look like magazines. Boardroom used these to sell newsletter subscriptions and books. Some magalogs were up 64 pages while most were 32 pages. Either way, these worked. They brought Boardroom over $2 billion in revenue.

Boardroom paid its copywriters an upfront fee of around $25,000 for each project. And that was in the 1990s. But they went one step further, providing a royalty based on the number of times Boardroom mailed the magalog.

Whenever Boardroom mailed a magalog, the direct response copywriter would receive five cents, maybe ten. This might not sound like much but it adds up. If a magalog was performing above a certain metric, Boardroom would keep mailing that magalog until it stopped performing.

This could mean mailing up to 50 million of that magalog. This can add up to a royalty of $2.5 million for the copywriter for that one piece.

A compensation arrangement like this might make you gasp. But whenever Marty Edelston sent out a royalty check to a copywriter, he added a personal note thanking the copywriter for such great work.

Crazy?

Not at all.

Let me quote Brian Kurtz from *Overdeliver.*

When people asked if paying huge royalties bothered us, Marty and I would simply say, "No! If our copywriters are making that much, can you imagine how much we are making?"

This compensation arrangement also attracted and kept the world's greatest direct response copywriters writing for Boardroom.

A quick admission: I don't know the precise payment arrangement between Boardroom and its copywriters. That's obviously private information. But here's the point: one of the most successful direct marketing companies of the last 50 years paid their direct response copywriters a ton of money.

Other companies in the same space as Boardroom sought to emulate Boardroom's success and they quickly realized they needed top direct response copywriters. So they used the same compensation model. I recently met the head of one of these companies. He told me about the massive royalty checks they sent to some copywriters. One check was over $2 million. The CFO almost fell over when he saw the amount. But the head of the company gleefully signed the check.

Why? He understood the following...

The bigger the royalty checks I'm sending to my copywriters, the more money I'm making!

It's rare for company owners and managers to have this mindset. But it's a mindset that helps these companies generate massive revenue.

Here are your choices when it comes to compensating a direct response copywriter.

Pay the lowest possible fee. You can achieve this through "commodity" sites like Upwork and Fiverr where freelance direct response copywriters race to the bottom to bid for work. You will pay very little for copy and you'll get copy that's unlikely to generate much revenue. It's a great model for the people who run these sites but you're wasting your time here. None of the top direct response copywriters go anywhere near these sites. And serious direct marketers who try these sites are almost always disappointed. Yes that's harsh and maybe you'll find some exceptions but when price is the only factor, you stand zero chance of maximizing your revenue.

Pay a sensible, straight fee for copy. A client will ask me to write some copy and pay me a fee. Projects range from a series of emails to advertorials to direct mail letters. Pay the fees and you'll get a solid direct response copywriter. If you want the top direct response copywriters to work with you, then you'll need to pay a higher fee.

Pay a monthly retainer. If you have regular needs and especially if you want to test like crazy, which is a great thing, then you'll get the best value when you pay a monthly retainer. You'll need to define the deliverables but this can be an excellent way to keep a direct response copywriter generating regular results for you.

Hire a direct response copywriter full-time. It's a similar arrangement to the retainer but this can work if you need a lot of copy. The salary will likely appeal to a younger direct response copywriter who wants to learn and needs the financial stability of a regular gig. Copywriters like the predictability.

Offer an upfront fee plus a royalty or percentage of the increase in revenue. This arrangement will attract the world's top direct response copywriters. You'll have to pay a significant fee to start the project. And when the copywriter's work starts to generate massive revenue, you'll have to pay significant compensation. This arrangement will help you secure the services of a top direct response copywriter, plus it can keep someone from working for the competition. However, if you're seriously ambitious, this arrangement is the one that's most likely to help you earn significant revenue.

There are no right or wrong ways to compensate a direct response copywriter. The models I just detailed simply provide a guideline. You have to apply the methods above to your model and your mindset.

Remote or In-House?

If you want to bring the work of a top direct response copywriter to your world, you will need to hire a freelancer and they will work remotely. Agora is the exception but they pay their copywriters vast sums.

A younger copywriter with some talent will be happy to work in a specific location but established direct response copywriters want the geographical freedom that comes from freelancing.

● ● ● ●

I want to quote more from *Overdeliver* about compensating direct response copywriters.

> "Feeling bad because a copywriter makes too much money is shortsighted, because it shows you're not thinking about the growth of your business. I maintain that is scarcity thinking. A mediocre copywriter will hold you back. Despite all I said previously about being your own best copywriter, good copywriters have a unique talent, and it's one that should never be shortchanged.
>
> Don't believe what you read about the toughest job for a copywriter being how long it takes them to count their money while hanging out at their beach house in the south of France. The best copywriters are relentlessly disciplined, and we can all take many lessons from them as we study how they work and what makes them tick; and if they are able to buy that château it's because they deserve it."

● ● ● ●

Remember...Brian Kurtz, author of *Overdeliver*, organized massive success at Boardroom in part because he found the world's top copywriters.

CHAPTER 36

Working Successfully with a Direct Response Copywriter.

I work with a wide variety of clients. Some clients are sizeable companies with an in-house marketing department. I also work with people who run their own businesses, like the rookie real estate agent near Orlando, Florida who hired me to write a postcard. She sent the postcard to 250 people and she got a phone call. This led to a listing and this listing launched her career. I'm just starting a series of projects with a group with just four people.

Whatever their size, my clients have two things in common:

- One. They understand the potential impact a direct response copywriter can have on their business.
- Two. They work successfully with a direct response copywriter.

Let's talk about the second item. Why? Because I want you to get the most out of what can, and should be, a significant investment in a direct response copywriter.

Provide as much research as you can at the beginning of the engagement. Keep feeding research and information as you get it.

Test like crazy. The more you test and the more you allow your direct response copywriter to fail and succeed, the more money you make.

Give your copywriter enough time to complete the work but also expect drafts and revisions to arrive at the deadline.

Communicate in a timely fashion and also expect the same from your copywriter. I like to get off the grid but I usually respond to client emails within one business day.

Trust your copywriter's work. Change facts that are wrong but trust your direct response copywriter's copy. You trust your plumber. You trust your doctor. You trust your gardener. So trust your copywriter.

The big picture. Give your direct response copywriter a sense of goals, short-term and long-term.

Ask your copywriter to provide guidance for graphic designers and ask them to work with others in your business, especially traffic buyers and people putting together offers.

Pay on time and be easy to work with. I ask for 50% at the project start and 50% at project completion. I also give the "red card" to clients who become total jerks. I bend over backwards and do back flips for friendly, amenable, wonderful clients.

Think long-term. I have worked successfully with clients who have hired me for one project but the best results come when I have a longer relationship with a client.

Ignore the naysayers. There might be times, especially in a larger organization, where people will question the decision to hire a direct response copywriter. It might be an internal accountant. It might be someone with the title "Senior Vice President of Marketing" who looks at the copy and starts wondering about the impact on brand equity or some such guff. Stick with your plan. Stick with direct marketing.

Focus on revenue generated, short-term and long-term. There are lots of ways to test copy. There are lots of online tools to test everything from where people click on a page to CPA. Ultimately, I recommend you focus on revenue generated. And in a perfect world, you can measure short-term value and long-term customer value.

Get your copywriter to help with strategy and tactics. I'm not a traffic expert. I'm not a list expert. I'm not a graphic designer. But I know enough about every aspect of direct marketing to help my clients with strategies and tactics. I also have a sub-specialty in pricing strategy.

Keep reading and learning. If your direct response copywriter is like me, they are constantly striving to improve and learn more about direct marketing. You'll get epic results when you have this same passion for direct marketing.

It's extremely rare for me to give a client the "red card" like I detailed above. Here are the reasons/occasions this will happen.

- Missed payments.
- Not sharing the same passion for direct marketing.
- Not trusting my work and expertise.

Many of my clients come to my front door, figuratively, through my website. There's a page titled, "Are We a Good Fit?" and this page and my entire website attracts strong potential clients and repels potentially bad clients.

This might seem rude or condescending but I simply want to work with wonderful clients and help them become fabulously successful. It's a relationship.

Managing The Project

Here's how you organize a project with a direct response copywriter.

Let's say you have a product or products you currently sell. Plus you have a database of prospects or you know how to get to prospects. Then you decide to hire a direct response copywriter. GREAT DECISION.

Let me detail how the workflow gets organized.

CREATIVE BRIEF. You provide the direct response copywriter with clear direction for the project. This includes the type of copy, the media, deadlines, and other information about the project. All this information goes into what's called a creative brief.

RESEARCH. I provide my clients with a checklist to start the research process. Provide your direct response copywriter with as much information as possible about the prospects, your products, your benefits, what you know about why people buy...EVERYTHING.

LET THE COPYWRITER WRITE COPY. Your direct response copywriter will then produce a draft. You and your group review the copy. In a perfect world, you fix any factual errors but mostly leave the copy alone. The smartest direct marketers ask for two or three versions of the copy for testing purposes.

RENDER THE COPY. Organize the video or the sales page or the direct mail piece. The direct response copywriter should be involved in this process.

SEND THE COPY LIVE and closely measure the results. Share the results with your direct response copywriter.

That's a super-simplified version of how a project works.

CHAPTER 37

The Real Reason to Hire a Direct Response Copywriter.

W hen you meet someone and they say, "I'm a direct response copywriter," you will now know exactly who they are, what they can
do, and the powerful skill they possess. It's a skill I, and others, call a
superpower.

You will know to avoid the merchants of branding, and why. You will
now have a basic understanding of direct marketing and why you MUST
use direct marketing and avoid branding advertising and all the forms of
advertising that are not measurable. You should also understand that your
direct marketing journey has just begun. There's so much more to learn
and so much fun to be enjoyed. I love direct marketing and I love writing
direct response copy.

But most of all, I love helping my clients become wildly successful.
Everyone should constantly strive to reach their full potential. I'm a freelancer in part because there will NEVER be a limit on what I can achieve.

You hire a direct response copywriter because he/she will help you
reach your full potential in business. We'll help you reach your business
goals, whatever these might be...however lofty.

As such, you'll achieve the goals that lie beyond simply making a lot of
money. These goals? They vary. It could be to provide for your family...live
where you want to live...travel to bucket-list destinations...enjoy certain
experiences...give back to people you really want to help...have a lot of free
time...and so on.

Are you greedy for wanting to be successful? No. Greed is the constant and occluding desire to make as much money as possible purely for the sake of making money and reaping the material gains. I admire people who have been whoppingly successful in business but only when they have a sense of the real impact of their achievements. These people create jobs. They provide opportunities. They elevate our communities.

The real reason to hire a direct response copywriter? To fulfill your potential and enjoy the success you deserve. To help you reach your full potential.

CHAPTER 38

A Superpower? Really?

D an Kennedy, the super-famous direct marketer, has called direct response copywriting a "superpower." He might have heard this from someone else. It might have been an original thought. It might have been because he was on the hunt for copywriting gigs at $50,000 an engagement.

Either way, Kennedy is totally correct. Direct response copywriting is a BUSINESS SUPERPOWER. Let's say you wanted to sell 50,000 units of a product you offer. A direct response copywriter could write copy to help you achieve this goal, provided you have the right prospects and the right product/offer. And let's say you didn't have a direct response copywriter involved. How else could you sell the product? Door-to-door? Telemarketing? Through stores? An army of salespeople who must have leads?

No need for any of that. You hire an experienced direct response copywriter and you can achieve your sales goals. A direct response copywriter SIMPLIFIES the sales process dramatically. Direct marketing also makes it much, much easier to measure everything and make changes so you increase revenue and avoid mistakes.

A SUPERPOWER? **Yes...TOTALLY**. I'm biased. But I'm biased based on actual revenue and results. People right now are reading what I've written and they are pulling their credit cards out of their wallets and buying what I'm selling. That's a powerful skill and it's a skill that can totally transform the fortunes of a business.

CHAPTER 39

How to Create a Direct Response Copywriter.

Maybe you have a copywriter on your team but they're a branding copywriter. Maybe you can't afford to hire a top direct response copywriter, but you want to hire someone with potential. Maybe you believe you can be a direct response copywriter to sell your own products and services...and you want to learn.

This leads to the question... How do you create a direct response copywriter? How can someone learn to write powerful direct response copy?

It's not easy, as I've mentioned earlier in this book. Direct response copywriters come from a wide variety of backgrounds.

- Sales
- Writing
- Journalism
- Medicine
- Teaching
- Engineering
- Speaking

If you look at the early careers of top direct response copywriters, you'll see that every journey is totally different. It's almost always peripatetic and rarely linear. It's not like the career path of, say, a doctor or airline pilot.

So...if you want to become a direct response copywriter or you want to turn an employee into a direct response copywriter, here's my advice.

- Learn how to sell and actually sell products. A direct response copywriter is a salesperson.
- Practice. Write copy for "pretend" products to get a feel for how direct response copywriting works.
- Write classic copy long-hand. This technique works for many freshly-minted direct response copywriters.
- Have a direct marketing mindset. Ignore the branding people.
- Read all the books and study the great copywriters.
- AWAI has some excellent training products.
- Get the "Quick Start" program/manual that Clayton Makepeace wrote...if you can find it.

Plus...I would be remiss if I failed to mention my training course, which is a series of videos where I write copy and reveal how it works.[9]

Just about every university or college offers some type of marketing course. But there isn't a single course I know that really teaches direct marketing or direct response copywriting, as I mentioned earlier.

A WORD OF WARNING

I regularly see this promise and slight variations.

LEARN TO BE A WEALTHY DIRECT RESPONSE COPYWRITER IN JUST SIX MONTHS!!!!!!!!!!!!

Someone who is bright and driven can write somewhat competent direct response copy in a short period. I define "short period" as three years.

It takes well over a decade of dedication to direct response copywriting to become "OK" and have the ability to generate decent revenue. It took Gary Bencivenga approximately 20 years to get to the top. It's also extremely difficult for someone who is relatively young, under 40, to write really high-powered direct response copy.

Why?

Because a big part of writing successful copy is understanding life and the dreams/aspirations of the people you're trying to reach. Another

---

[9]   AspenSchoolofCopywriting.com

reason? Direct marketing tends to skew to an older demographic. It's hard for a younger person to understand what an older person is really going through.

What are they going through?

They're worried about retirement. They're worried about constant pain. They're worried about death. It's pretty much impossible for someone who is 25 to understand what someone who is 65 is experiencing.

Every year, thousands of people think, I want to be a direct response copywriter, but there are only around four hundred direct response copywriters who can really generate significant revenue consistently. One reason: it's REALLY hard to learn to write direct response copy.

● ● ● ●

LIFE is the Greatest Teacher...

I mentioned all that training. But the greatest trainer by far is…LIFE.

Let me explain. I was at an event a few years ago and met an extremely accomplished yet totally non-famous copywriter. He actually mentored under Gary Bencivenga. How many copywriters can say that? Not many. How I wish I had had that opportunity.

I started talking with that copywriter in the area outside the large ballroom. What's that area called, by the way? I have no idea. But the carpet is almost always really ugly.

Anyway, the copywriter told me a couple of things that were especially interesting.

First, he sold encyclopedias door-to-door as a teenager IN ORDER TO SUPPORT HIS FAMILY. No pressure there. Second, he would often just sit in a coffee shop, look at the people, and imagine what they were going through.

I lived in London as a teenager. I didn't have a car so I rode The Underground all the time. I would sometimes look around the carriage and start to imagine who I was looking at and what their lives were like.

I would make up names and backstories for them. Right now, as I write, I'm in a coffee shop.

There's a big man sitting in the corner. He's about 45 but looks older and needs to lose around 70 pounds. I imagine he manages the water system for the local government but he loves chess and is playing a game with someone in Borneo on his laptop.

Next there's a bald guy, fit and trim, looking at his tablet. How old is he? He's around 40. I imagine he's about to inherit around $250 million from his great uncle, who owns a chunk of a Fortune 500 company. To this point, he's been struggling to make ends meet as an electrician. Now he's thinking about where he's going to travel and the house(s) he's going to build.

There's a family of five at the next table with three children aged ten, eight, and eight months. They're eating some donuts. What's the father thinking about? I imagine he works for a company in the accounting department. He works hard for his family but he just got bypassed for a promotion because they gave the job he wanted to a person with an MBA.

In the next corner, there's a young woman on her laptop. She's on Facebook (wild guess, I know) and thinking about a trip to Australia and New Zealand. She's also chatting with some friends who might make the trip. Or maybe she's a medical student starting to figure out what she's going to specialize in.

And what about the five employees working behind the counter? I don't know their names. I don't really know anything about them, other than their place of employment. Why are they here? It's hard work with strange hours. Almost all the customers are pleasant, I'm sure, but what about that 1 percent who are jerks?

Are the baristas here for the pay? The health insurance? The tuition reimbursement program? The stock options? The free shift beverages?

I can only imagine.

I will NEVER be right when I imagine what people are going through and what they're thinking. How can I ever get this right? It's an exercise.

But I know, with total certainty, all these people have the following...

- Dreams, goals, and aspirations.
- Feelings.
- Skepticism.
- Days of confusion and days of clarity.
- The ability to love.
- The same motivators that ultimately motivate everyone on this planet.

I would add A LOT OF TATTOOS, but that's probably going a bit far.

There are lots of copywriting courses and events making a lot of crazy promises...like...be a world-class copywriter in six months.

It's not hugely difficult to find ways learn the skill of direct response copywriting. The techniques and so on. Headlines...bullets...writing a guarantee. That's not impossible for a decent writer.

But here's the difference between the copywriter who generates $50,000 from a promotion and the one who generates $500,000... **THEY UNDERSTAND PEOPLE**.

Claude Hopkins touched on this in his book *My Life in Advertising*. He said that young graduates from expensive universities rarely make good copywriters. But it's the hustling, street-smart person who writes direct response copy that converts.

That was in the 1920s, but it's the same today, essentially. I'm fortunate in that I was very well educated but I was never part of the "ivory tower" club.

I've been writing copy for over 30 years now but I had a wide variety of jobs before I wrote copy. Here are just a few...

- Application screener in an HR department.
- Quality control specialist in an ice cream factory in West London. AKA Ice Cream Taster. Really!
- Filing clerk.
- Publishing salesperson.
- Magazine publisher.
- Ski instructor.
- Waiter.
- PR specialist.
- Reporter.
- Soccer coach.
- Published author.

That's just a few of the gigs.

The result?

I understand people and what motivates them. No training in the world can give you this vital perspective.

People who are brand new to direct response copywriting? They rarely have this. They can write some clever branding ads but they can't write direct response copy that generates results because they just don't fully understand people like I do...like that copywriter I mentioned earlier in this chapter.

There's no training course for this part of being a direct response copywriter. It's something that happens over time but it's a skill, if that's what it's called, that can be fostered.

Here's something interesting. With all those jobs I've had and all the varied experiences, and especially all that selling, you might call me a hustler.

In fact, I was at a meeting of the mastermind group I was in and there was a famous copywriter there. He said, after hearing about my work, "Oh... you're a hustler." I'm not sure precisely what he meant, derogatory or otherwise, but I'll take it as a compliment.

I'm a hustler, according to that guy. So I understand how human beings work. OK. I'll take that, I suppose. It's one reason I'm a successful direct response copywriter.

CHAPTER 40

The Rise of the Direct Response Copywriter and the Inevitable Death of General Advertising and Branding.

There's a publication out there called Digiday. I don't know if it's just digital or available in print as well. In fact, I'm not sure how I found it.

Either way, it's unpleasant reading for those in the branding or "big agency" world. There's a lot of bad news in the publication plus a lot of really unhappy people. All is not well in the world of "general" advertising.

One piece caught my attention because it was about a professional copywriter at an agency. The copywriter lamented the lack of respect for copywriters. This comes from a changing agency culture but also from a change in the "big agency" business model.

I don't work in the branding agency world, thankfully, but it seems the "agency of record" model is heading out the window. Companies want a project model. They're also bringing a lot of work in-house, essentially creating their own internal advertising agency.

Here's something else I've noticed in Digiday...the increasing influence of accounting and consulting firms in the decision making. I have no proof, but here's what I imagine is happening.

The "consulting" firms are telling their clients, "There has to be some sort of measurable ROI on the ad spend."

Put this another way... Where's the accountability?

So companies of all sizes are looking at their agencies and asking for more defined results. The agencies are making the usual excuses like, "It's all about brand authority and it's really difficult to measure." Or they're pointing to awards. Or they're blaming Brexit or something silly like that. Some agencies have tools they claim measure the impact of branding ads. They can't measure direct revenue generated.

Here's my fearless prediction. The branding agencies are going to HAVE to be more oriented to direct marketing. They're going to need more direct marketing experts and they're especially going to need highly skilled direct response copywriters.

The most intelligent agencies will understand the importance of the direct response copywriter because this importance will become apparent in actual measurable data. Agencies will find that a top direct response copywriter brings much more revenue while a really bad copywriter will bring no money. Over time, copywriters will gain more respect and will once again be at the top of the creative ladder.

Branding copywriters like the one in the article I read will have to make the switch to direct response copy. Some will hate this. Others will love the opportunities.

There will be some branding stuff around but the advertising world is finally moving toward the model that David Ogilvy so accurately predicted so many years ago in the video I mentioned and transcribed: "We Sell or Else."

CHAPTER 41

Clarity Is King.

A lot of direct response copywriters will talk about the importance of the headline, bullets, the guarantee, and so on. But the most important fundamental of direct response copy is CLARITY. Yet it's rare for anyone in direct marketing to talk about clarity.

The reader MUST understand, instantly, what you're providing. Every single part of every communication with current and prospective clients MUST be totally clear. In the branding world, many copywriters try to be subtle, witty, clever...obtuse even. Their thinking: the reader/viewer will have to think and therefore they will like the product and be salivating for it. Absurd.

Unfortunately, I even see direct response copy that's not totally clear. Confused people will NEVER buy your product or service if the message isn't totally clear at all times. Or let me put this another way. When the copy and the presentation of the copy are totally clear, money will start flowing.

Here's a famous ad, written and produced in the 1930s for/by advertising agency Young and Rubicam.

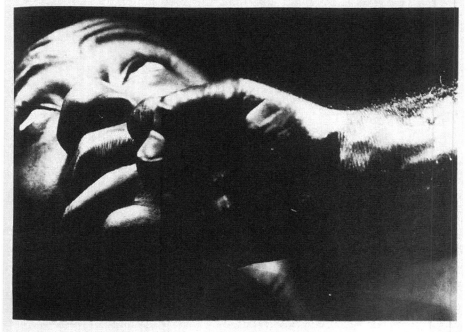

IMPACT

ACCORDING TO WEBSTER: The single instantaneous striking of a body in motion against another body.

ACCORDING TO YOUNG & RUBICAM: That quality in an advertisement which strikes suddenly against the reader's indifference and enlivens his mind to receive a sales message.

YOUNG & RUBICAM, INCORPORATED · ADVERTISING

NEW YORK · PHILADELPHIA

· 81 ·

Here's the question about the ad above. What am I receiving for my money? Impact? If I'm a CEO or a marketing decision maker, how will impact help? I need revenue and I'm certain Young and Rubicam could help me generate some but the connection between impact and revenue is not TOTALLY clear.

The next time you see an advertisement, ask yourself this question: How clear is it?

I build every advertisement I write around this...

WHEN YOU HAND OVER YOUR MONEY/INFORMATION...
HERE IS EXACTLY WHAT YOU ARE GOING TO GET...

When I'm writing copy for a product or service, I make sure I describe PRECISELY what the customer/client will receive, often introduced with the copy...

HERE IS WHAT YOU RECEIVE WITH (name of product/service)...

Then I make sure I detail, with extreme clarity, absolutely everything the customer/client will get. For example, I was just writing a promotion selling a golf-specific video camera. The camera comes with some accessories, including a stand and carry bag. I made sure I detailed these complementary items. Why? Because I want to make it TOTALLY CLEAR that you get all the items as part of the package.

What about complimentary items that might come with a product or service? I describe these in great detail as well. Why? There's a segment of potential buyers who will want to know about every single item they receive for their hard-earned money.

Here's some copy I recently wrote for a successful promotion.

● ● ● ●

Here's what you receive with **THE IZZO SWAMI SWING CAM** package.

- The rugged and easy-to-use **IZZO SWAMI SWING CAM** that shoots in high-definition video...the quality found on video cameras costing hundreds more.
- Durable and strong camera mount so you can attach **THE IZZO SWAMI SWING CAM** to your golf bag... No more trying to balance your smartphone on the ground or on top of your bag...or asking another golfer to video your swing.

- 8GB Memory card so you can download videos directly to any computer and not take up valuable memory space on your smartphone.
- USB charger so it's easy to keep **THE IZZO SWAMI SWING CAM** fully charged...and not use up your smartphone battery
- Full wireless capacity so you can quickly transfer video to your smartphone or share your swings with others...including your golf teacher if you have one.
- Free App so you can fully assess your swing on your smartphone... just like a professional golf instructor.
- Handy-dandy carry bag so **THE IZZO SWAMI SWING CAM** fits in your golf bag.

Here's What You Receive with **THE IZZO SWAMI SWING CAM.**

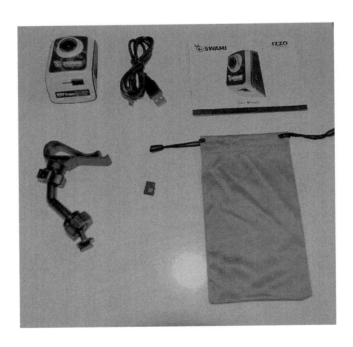

● ● ● ●

The company didn't give me an official photo of the package...so I took a photo myself as a placeholder.

Here's my process for providing all this clarity.

- ONE. Detail all the elements of the product or service. Everything.
- TWO. Describe the features.
- THREE. Get into the benefits the features provide.

Every copywriting book I have read, and I've read a ton of them, touts writing about benefits. "The prospect buys the lawnmower," states the writer of the marketing book, "not for the lawnmower itself, but for the feeling of general bonhomie that comes from a beautifully manicured lawn that drives the neighbors bonkers with jealousy."

Absolutely correct.

But if I'm selling that lawnmower, I'm making it absolutely crystal clear that, for your money, you're getting a lawnmower with an engine, blades, a grass catcher, beverage holder, and everything else...even the instruction booklet. Remember...there might be a feature, however insignificant it might seem, that's extremely important to that potential buyer.

Then I'm going to include all the benefits. Sometimes I list the associated benefits right away...sometimes I leave them for later. I could write a list of bulleted features and I could include this feature...

"Electronic ignition"

Or...

"Electronic ignition, which means you don't have to destroy your shoulder by pulling on one of those old-school and totally horrible starter cords for the better part of eight miserable minutes."

Whatever the order of features and benefits, I just want to make it super clear... TOTALLY CLEAR...

WHEN YOU HAND OVER YOUR MONEY/INFORMATION...
HERE IS EXACTLY WHAT YOU ARE GOING TO GET...

Here's a still frame from a Ginzu knife TV commercial from the 1970s.

People in the world of direct response TV advertising make it TOTALLY CLEAR what you're going to receive. When I write copy, clarity of the offer is king. And if I sold physical products in a store, I'd make sure I provided the customer with total clarity about the products in the store. In fact, I used to work in a store that sells outdoorsy stuff and clothes. I remember making sure I told a customer everything I possibly could about a backpack...every feature and every benefit. I was really good at selling backpacks and related gear.

Gary Bencivenga wrote with total clarity.

Let's take a look at some examples.

```
***********************************************************
*                                                         *
*       Announcing a Private Seminar in Great Neck on     *
*       TAX REDUCTION AND RETIREMENT PLANNING             *
*          ...Exclusively for Investors                   *
*       With Portfolios or Pension Plans                  *
*          Worth $500,000 or More.                        *
*                                                         *
***********************************************************
```

* Admission is free for investors, professionals and business owners
  with a portfolio or pension plan worth $500,000 or more.

* Your spouse and business associates are also invited free.

* An "information only" seminar; no financial products will be sold.

* A unique opportunity to discover today's most powerful opportunities
  to reduce your taxes, multiply your wealth tax-free, and increase
  your investment income with great safety.

* Complimentary refreshments will be served.

* Offered on several dates in the near future, to give you every
  opportunity to attend.

* Limited seating. Attendance by reservation only. To guarantee your
  place, or be notified of the next available dates, please call or
  return the enclosed card immediately.

Age-Reversing Secrets

of America's youngest-looking women

Announcing a direct response advertising agency that will guarantee to outpull your best ad.

If you are a direct response advertiser, here is a no-risk offer from Callas, Powell, Rosenthal & Bloch . . .

We'll guarantee to outpull your best ad by at least 10% in a split-run test.

If we don't pull at least 10% more responses, you won't owe us a penny for any work we've done — creative or production. We'll even refund half your media expense, to cover our half of the test.

If we do beat your best ad by at least 10%, you simply pay us an agreed upon creative fee. Should the test results be impressive — and we both wish to enter into a full-service agency agreement — this creative fee will be refunded to you in full.

In effect, we offer you a risk-free trial of our advertising pulling power. Our work will cost you absolutely nothing — no creative, production or media costs — unless we beat your best

panding our capacity and can offer guaranteed results to more advertisers.

How Can We Guarantee Results?

We're willing and able to guarantee results because of our *total approach* to direct response. To be sure, few of the ideas in this approach are original with us, but the total combination seems to be — and makes for unusually powerful advertising. Here are the key points:

1. Advertising Is Salesmanship. Our whole creative approach is built on this fundamental premise. Every word, every picture in our advertisements must justify itself in sales.

Of course, most agencies in direct response fully agree with the idea that advertising must sell. But we don't believe most of them live by it as religiously as we, and would shrink from the thought of guaranteeing their work.

2. Building on a Strong Product.

more their ads sell, the more money they can make, with no limit. If you think this motivates copywriters to work hard and create the best ad they can for you — you're absolutely right!

5. A Principal on Your Account. During and after the initial test period, an agency principal will supervise all work on your account, and have day-to-day responsibility for anything done for you. You gain the experience of — and have immediate access to — one of our key people at all times.

6. Bringing It All Together. Bringing this all together is an esprit de corps that makes work a joy at CPR&B. You'll find our copywriters working until 7, 8 and 9 o'clock, night after night, brainstorming and trying to smash someone else's control ad to smithereens. The creative excitement is exhilarating.

The president of a major competitor, himself a famous copywriter, recently confided to us, "I'd join you for the fun of it all—if I were 25 years younger."

A Local Bookstore: We did a "quickie" self-mailer for these friends who tell us it set all-time records for store traffic and cash sales.

A Guard Service (supplier of uniformed guards): Our first ad for leads outpulled their basic control ad by better than 7 to 1. On a small test budget, we generated more leads than they could effectively handle.

A Commodity Dealer: Our advertising helped play a part in their "cinderella" success story. Four years ago, when we began doing their advertising, their annual sales were $7 million. Sales have since more than doubled every year. Last year, their share of market was probably above 50% and their sales surpassed $400 million.

A Financial Advisory Service: This is a new client, and our advertising is still in early stages. In their two most frequently used media, our advertising has brought in subscribers at 40% below their former average cost. Tests in other media show we may have opened

Here's what I see in all those examples: CLARITY.

I see a lot of branding advertising that conveys a message with some degree of clarity. Here's an excellent example, written by David Ogilvy.

The Rolls-Royce Silver Cloud—$13,995

"At 60 miles an hour the loudest noise in this new Rolls-Royce comes from the electric clock"

What makes Rolls-Royce the best car in the world? "There is really no magic about it— it is merely patient attention to detail," says an eminent Rolls-Royce engineer.

1. "At 60 miles an hour the loudest noise comes from the electric clock," reports the Technical Editor of THE MOTOR. Three mufflers tune out sound frequencies—acoustically.

2. Every Rolls-Royce engine is run for seven hours at full throttle before installation, and

years. With a new network of dealers and parts-depots from Coast to Coast, service is no problem.

7. The Rolls-Royce radiator has never changed, except that when Sir Henry Royce died in 1933 the monogram RR was changed

12. There are three separate systems of power brakes, two hydraulic and one mechanical. Damage to one system will not affect the others. The Rolls-Royce is a very safe car—and also a very lively car. It cruises serenely at eighty-five. Top speed is in excess of 100 m.p.h.

And another from Ogilvy.

How direct response advertising can increase your sales and profits

Even if your company has never used direct response, read what Ogilvy & Mather has learned from half a billion coupons

Ogilvy & Mather has created more than $150,000,000 worth of direct response advertising—in mail and media—for the American Express Company, Burpee Seeds, Cessna Aircraft, Nationwide Insurance, Shell Oil, Sears, Roebuck and other clients.

In the process, we have learned that direct response advertising can help sell $750,000 jet airplanes as well as 25¢ packets of flower seeds.

Here are a few of the ways Ogilvy & Mather uses this most *accountable* form of advertising as part of our clients' marketing programs. Some of them may be useful to you.

1. Direct response can be your "secret weapon" in new product introductions. Cessna Aircraft used direct mail in its introduction of "Citation," a new $750,000 business jet. Ogilvy & Mather began mailings to a list of key corporate executives and their chief pilots long before the first "Citation" was in production.

Sales leads in response to these mailings helped "Citation" become the world's largest selling business jet in just one year.

2. A remarkably efficient way to reach your best prospects. Today Mercedes-Benz diesel-engine cars sell well in America. But ten years ago, it was difficult to identify and reach the limited number of high-potential prospects for diesel cars.

Ogilvy & Mather compiled a list of people who matched the demographic profile of *existing* diesel car owners, then sent them an 8-page letter. As a direct result of the letter, Mercedes-Benz sold 716 diesel cars within eight weeks.

3. How to land your most profitable new customers. Ogilvy & Mather has developed special acquisition programs designed to acquire new credit customers for our clients on a highly selective basis.

These programs combine sophisticated list segmentation techniques with a remarkably precise formula that identifies the profitable customer; establishes his real value; and reveals how much should be spent to acquire him.

PRESENT VALUE FORMULA

$$PV = \int_0^s (a r x p_t^{-t/s} - a n d e^{-t/t} - a C_g C^{-t/b}) e^{-\rho t} dt - Sc^{-\rho t} - M - RC_p$$

This is an example of a "present value" economic model. This model—programmed with new results and appropriate up and downside risks—reveals the true cost of improving a new credit customer and predicts the net profit he will return over the next 5 years.

4. How to build a bank of localized leads for your sales force. The pinpoint accuracy of direct mail makes it the ideal medium for obtaining sales leads exactly where you need them most.

Our computerized "Commodity Futures List Bank" supplies *localized* leads to Merrill Lynch representatives from Saskatchewan to San Francisco.

5. Direct response can make television dollars work harder. Television commercials for American Express Credit Cards end with a request for a direct response by phone. This produces tens of thousands of applications for the Card.

Ogilvy & Mather has also improved response to direct mailings by timing mail drops to coincide with television advertising.

6. Direct response is an indispensable element in successful travel advertising. Direct response, in mail as well as other media, has proven to be a key ingredient in marketing travel.

The secret is to close the sale by mail—or to obtain a highly qualified lead—instead of wasting a fortune mailing expensive booklets and pamphlets.

Ogilvy & Mather coupon advertisements for Cunard have paid out four times over in immediate ticket sales.

A direct mail offer of free London theater tickets produced response rates as high as 26 percent for the British Tourist Authority.

7. You can now sell high-ticket items direct by mail. Today's ever-increasing distribution of credit cards has revolutionized marketing by mail.

Credit cards now make direct mail practical for selling sewing machines, calculators, color television sets and many other products costing hundreds, even thousands, of dollars.

As sales costs escalate, more and more manu-

How to capitalize on new profit opportunities in direct marketing.

Today, more and more major corporations are considering direct marketing in their search for new sources of profit.

It pays to look before you leap into this highly specialized business.

Ogilvy & Mather has found that the odds for success improve if you can use your own customer list and retail packages as an entrée into direct marketing.

One mail marketing business we helped develop now does fifty million dollars in annual sales.

facturers will turn to this new way of selling direct to the consumer.

Techniques that work best in direct response advertising

8. Challenge dogma. Ogilvy & Mather has found that it often pays to challenge dogma and test for breakthroughs. Our tests show that:

• An inexpensive offset letter can often out-pull far more costly computer letters.

• "On-page coupon-envelopes" can be more cost efficient than expensive preprint inserts.

• An innovative *letter* can be more important to your success than a big, beautiful 4-color brochure.

Note: These examples are not offered to create new dogma but to emphasize that it *pays to test.*

This innovative "personal" letter from Peter Rich Knitwear—created from hundreds of letters actually written by the great customer—substantially increased response for a new record offer.

9. How to make long copy succeed. Tests show long copy usually, but not always, pulls more orders than short copy in direct response advertising.

Specifics are the key ingredient in successful long copy. Glittering generalities turn readers off. Beware of long copy that is lazy. Supply facts and figures. They impress the reader and help close the sale.

10. The way you position your offer can double your response. We recently split-run three new advertisements against a successful Burpee advertisement that featured a $1 offer in the headline.

All three new advertisements improved

response. The one shown below increased results 112 percent.

Old.   *New: 112 percent more response.*

The reason: The new advertisement offered a free catalog—and clearly positioned Burpee as America's leading breeder of new flower and vegetable varieties for the home gardener.

11. It pays to demonstrate. Product demonstrations are not easy to do in direct mail. But they are worth the effort. They can be exceptionally effective.

Ogilvy & Mather's mailing for Cessna's "Citation" jet enclosed a recording that contrasted the "Citation's" low noise levels with competitive jets—and even an electric blender.

The record proved Cessna's case; words alone could only have made a claim.

12. Asking the reader to quin himself increases response. Inviting readers to take a quiz involves them with your advertising.

This can pay handsome dividends, as this split-run test shows.

WHICH AD PULLED BEST?

The advertisement on the right invited the reader to quiz himself—as we are doing here by asking you to guess which ad pulled best. (The "quiz," of course, by 250 percent.)

13. The "close" is crucial in direct response. The reader who makes a mental note to "mail the coupon later" usually never does.

One survey showed that less than a third of the readers who *intended* to send in a coupon actually did so.

Ogilvy & Mather uses a four-point checklist to ensure that our copy does all it can to get the reader to tear out the coupon before he turns the page.

14. The position of your advertisement can make the difference between profit and loss. Tests show that the back page of a publication, or the back of one of its sections, can pull 150 percent better than inside pages.

POSC—page opposite third cover in magazines—is another winning position. You can often buy it without paying a premium.

15. New direct mail techniques. The efficiency of mailings can be substantially improved through new techniques.

These techniques—"merge-purge," "hotline" mailings, timing sequence—produce more response for every dollar invested.

16. Separate the wheat from the chaff. List segmentation concentrates your dollars where they will do the most good.

List segmentation—by both demographic and psychographic factors—becomes critical to profit as direct mail costs go up and up.

Take full advantage of computer technology and sophisticated segmentation procedures—zip code analyses and consumer criteria grids.

They now make it practical to single out your best prospects.

Separating the wheat from the chaff is the secret to successful direct mail.

17. Pretesting copy can reduce costs and improve response rates. Ogilvy & Mather's Research Department has developed inexpensive techniques that rank copy promises *before* mail or media testing.

This saves time and money—and increases your chances for success.

COPY PROMISES CAN VARY WIDELY IN APPEAL

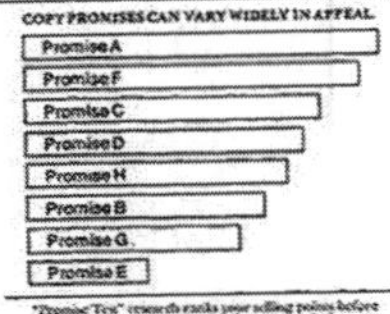

Promise A	
Promise F	
Promise C	
Promise D	
Promise H	
Promise B	
Promise G	
Promise E	

"Promise Test" research ranks your selling points before mail or media testing. In the above example from an actual test the winning promise proved to be about three times more accepted than the weakest one.

18. Success can be exported. Ogilvy & Mather has found that direct response principles which work in the U.S. are frequently just as effective when applied abroad.

We export these principles to 57 Ogilvy & Mather offices in 30 countries, and coordinate international campaigns through New York.

Example: A series of new direct response advertisements and mailings, initiated in New York and carried out by our Paris office, tripled response for one of the leading book clubs in France.

19. The most accountable form of advertising. Claude Hopkins titled his famous book "Scientific Advertising."

He emphasized that coupon feedback makes direct response the most *accountable* form of advertising. It allows you to measure precisely what every dollar invested returns in sales and profits.

We use coupons and sales conversion rates to evaluate the specific contribution direct response advertising makes to our client's marketing programs. Results show direct response has increased sales and profits in almost every case.

An Invitation

Ogilvy & Mather's Direct Response Division employs three dozen people who specialize in this demanding discipline.

The body of our experience—which can only be hinted at in the space available here—is revealed in a slide presentation: *"What Ogilvy & Mather has learned about direct response advertising and marketing."*

To arrange a presentation, please mail the coupon below.

Ogilvy & Mather

Barry Blau, Managing Director
Ogilvy & Mather, Direct Response Division
2 East 48th Street, New York, New York 10017

I would like to arrange for a special presentation of *"What Ogilvy & Mather has learned about direct response advertising and marketing."*

Name_____
Company_____
Title_____
Address_____
City_____State____Zip____
Telephone_____

Note how both Ogilvy and Bencivenga wrote advertising successfully selling their services. How many copywriters and advertising agencies successfully achieve this? My competition, with only a few notable exceptions, is routinely awful at copy for their sites. The copy on my website has generated over a thousand leads for me over the last six years.

A digression. Apologies.

I see a lot of advertising where I scratch my head and genuinely wonder what the company is actually selling. SERIOUSLY.

I know...I'm perhaps getting a touch obsessed with being as clear as possible when writing copy, to the point where I consider TOTAL CLARITY to be an advanced copywriting technique. Why this focus?

The answer is simple: THE CLIENT.

Let's say I write a super-clever advertisement. It's witty. It makes people laugh. It has a beautiful photograph of people enjoying the product. The advertisement has some degree of clarity. Other copywriters shower the advertisement with praise to the point where it wins a highly coveted copywriting award. I gleefully collect the award at a black-tie dinner and receive hearty pats on the back. Another copywriter, a girl, gives me a big smack on the cheek.

The next day, I tell the client the good news about the award, and the client is delighted.

At first.

Then the client starts to ask questions about the revenue the advertisement actually generated.

"But there's no way to measure the actual results," I might say. "Plus, remember...the ad won a prestigious award."

The client is not happy, and with good reason.

Now, just for the record, I have NEVER won an award for copywriting. I hope this NEVER happens. I want to write advertising that maximizes revenue for my clients and to achieve this goal, my ads must have the TOTAL CLARITY that's only found in direct response marketing.

Why do I exist?

A big question in the universal sense, for sure. So let's be more specific.

What is my role, in the business space/time continuum, as a direct response copywriter?

My job is to help my clients sell their products and services and maximize their revenue.

What did Claude Hopkins, in *Scientific Advertising*, say about the subject of total clarity?

"Don't try to be amusing. Money spending is a serious matter. Don't boast, for all people resent it. Don't try to show off. Do just what you think a good salesman should do with a half-sold person before him.

No one reads ads for amusement, long or short. Consider them as prospects standing before you, seeking for information. Give them enough to get action.

Ads are not written to entertain. When they do, those entertainment seekers are little likely to be the people whom you want."

Going to argue with Claude Hopkins? Go ahead.

Testing and measured results tell us that TOTAL CLARITY motivates potential customers to buy once...and then keep buying. TOTAL CLARITY comes from direct response copy. I fail to understand why any company that's serious about maximizing revenue would head in any other direction. Hopkins expressed the same frustration.

Ads are planned and written with some utterly wrong conception. They are written to please their seller. The interest of the buyer is forgotten.

Ads are not written to entertain. When they do, those entertainment seekers are little likely to be the people whom you want. This is one of the greatest advertising faults. Ad writers abandon their part. They forgot they are salesmen and try to be performers. Instead of sales, they seek applause.

Writing copy is salesmanship. Think about the last time you were in front of a salesperson and you were interested in the product or service being sold. Was the salesperson trying to entertain and make you laugh and be witty and essentially act like a clown? If so, did you buy the product or service? Or was the salesperson explaining the features and benefits with total clarity so you could make a fully educated decision based on the facts?

When I write direct response copy, my #1 goal is TOTAL CLARITY... based on this simple premise.

WHEN YOU HAND OVER YOUR MONEY/INFORMATION...
HERE IS EXACTLY WHAT YOU ARE GOING TO GET...

Let's keep going with clarity because it's such a powerful yet under-appreciated aspect of copywriting.

Syntactical Clarity

What is writing?

Writing is, at its core, the selection of words and the placement of these words with the goal of communicating something.

That's not a dictionary-like definition...so...let's actually consult the dictionary.

"The activity or skill of marking coherent words on paper and composing text."

Bit limp, isn't it? I like my definition better but I'm biased.

In copywriting, writing revolves around providing clarity that motivates the reader to take the action you want him/her to take.

Here's some copy I recently wrote for a golf product, specifically a rangefinder.

● ● ● ●

Today's professional golfers are ultra-precise with every club...so they must have yardages to... well...the yard.

You see...to the professional golfer, there's a HUGE difference between 157 and 153 yards. The correct yardage can mean the difference between winning and coming second—and that could mean a difference of $600,000 in prize money ...

So, naturally, professional caddies who work for these golfers demand the absolute "best of the best" when it comes to rangefinders. They must provide

their golfers with totally accurate yardages every hole…every round…every day.

● ● ● ●

I could have written…

● ● ● ●

The contemporary golfer who receives remuneration for their performances in the competitive realm strives, with every golfing implement they use, to be extremely accurate. They demand yardages that are within a yard when it comes to accuracy of salient yardage information.

For the golfer who receives compensation for their efforts, there's a notable difference between 157 and 153 yards. In fact, the accurate yardage can create a difference of being placed first or being placed second in the competitive arena. This could create a pecuniary differentiation of $600,000…significant remuneration.

Thus it's no surprise that professional caddies demand absolute excellence when it comes to the selection of yardage information. These caddies must provide their golfers with precise yardages to the target, which is a hole, during all rounds played in the sporting arena.

● ● ● ●

Now…that's clear to me, probably because I wrote the other version. But it's probably not clear to a chunk of readers who are going to wonder what on earth "pecuniary" means.

Here are some guidelines when it comes to syntactical clarity.

1.   Use a conversational style, like you're speaking to someone in a bar.

2. Break up long sentences. Long sentences are OK in copy, provided they are broken up.
3. Use the ... a lot... As you can see, I like to use the ... to the point where people make fun of me. I don't care.
4. It's perfectly acceptable to start sentences and paragraphs with clauses like, "As you can see..." and "Before you try this..." It's conversational English.
5. Start each paragraph with a different word from the last paragraph...unless you're starting each paragraph with the same word for effect. If one paragraph starts with the word "the," then start the next paragraph with a different word.
6. Look at the tabloid newspapers for excellent examples of simple and super-clear syntax.
7. Break up copy by using lists, subheads, and bullets.

If I'm not clear that a paragraph is clear, I read it aloud to myself.

Here's what marketing specialist and experienced copywriter Jay Abraham wrote about copy.

> **"Make your copy straightforward to read, understand, and use. Use easy words; those that are used for everyday speech. Use phrases that are not too imprecise and very understandable. Do not be too stuffy; remove pompous words and substitute them with plain words. Minimize complicated gimmicks and constructions. If you can't give the data directly and briefly, you must consider writing the copy again."**

And here's John Caples.

> **"To impress your offer on the mind of the reader or listener, it is necessary to put it into brief, simple language. No farfetched or obscure statement will stop them. You have got to hit them where they live in the heart or in the head. You have got to catch their eyes**

or ears with something simple, something direct, something they want."

Clarity of Graphical Presentation

Gary Bencivenga sells a set of copywriting DVDs using a sales page with 30,000 words of copy and there isn't a single photo, save for the image of Bencivenga in the masthead. But even though the copy gets a bit dense in spots, the simple layout is clear, thanks, mostly, to the liberal use of Johnson boxes, sidebars, bullets, and lists.

You can write super-clear copy that won't be super-clear to the reader unless the graphical presentation follows some basic direct response rules.

- Serif type for printed materials.
- Sans-serif type for web and email.
- Black type on a white background.
- Enough leading for readability.
- Plenty of subheads and other elements to break up the copy.
- "Less is more" when it comes to color.
- Keep the layout in a narrow corridor.
- Use of copy doodles and related graphical elements.

The experienced copywriter takes charge when it comes to the clear graphical presentation of the copy and the copywriter almost becomes an art director. I know a large number of graphic designers. But I only know THREE graphic designers who genuinely understand graphic design for direct marketing.

Clarity of Proof

I detailed and described proof elements earlier in this book but I want to mention proof again in this chapter.

Want to see proof of excellent presentation of proof? It's not complicated; watch an infomercial or one of those three-minute ads with a lot of "before and after" examples.

It's one thing to provide a lot of proof to back up statements, but the proof must be presented with TOTAL clarity.

Clarity of Common Sense... Clarity of Thinking and Logic...

One successful copywriter once said that "good writing is good thinking, clearly expressed." I love this statement. In fact, it's up on the wall next to where I work.

I vacillate somewhat on how to achieve this type of clarity. Sometimes I think it's difficult to achieve, especially with a complex subject. Other times, I wonder why clarity of logic and presentation needs to be so complicated.

Increasingly, though, I strive for clarity through simplicity. Why? It's extremely easy to complicate copy to the point where the reader is scratching their head going, "What on earth are they talking about?" At this point, the sale is lost, and the reader/viewer/listener has moved on to something they deem more important in their life, like where they are going to have dinner that evening or how to get a cable channel they're not currently getting.

Does clear logic have to be complicated? Of course not. Does getting to clarity have to take weeks of research? Not always.

Getting to this simplicity can be complex. For example, as I write, I am studying for my Level 2 certification from the Professional Ski Instructors of America. I'm a part-time ski instructor. Part of the exam requires looking at skiers and assessing their skills. It's called "Movement Analysis," and I initially found it extremely difficult. Thankfully, the people who are training me are making it simpler and easier.

Over and over, my trainers stress keeping things simple...just 15 words instead of a five-minute, jargon-filled description. The trainers have been performing movement analysis for upwards of 20 seasons, and I've been learning this new language for about three months. So I understand why achieving simplicity here is challenging.[10]

Here's another quote I like.

> "The most important job advertising can do
> is to clarify the obvious."
> —Jay Chiat.

---

[10] Update: I since passed my Level 2 movement analysis ... and with flying colors thanks to the instruction I received.

It helps that I've been writing copy for over 30 years. Why? Because this helps me keep my copy clear and simple and the experience helps me with clarity of the logic in the argument.

Clarity of the logic and common sense is a vital. I use these tactics...

ONE. Discover what's really important to the majority of potential customers and focus on this benefit up front. Include all the other benefits later. For example, if you're selling a dietary supplement targeted at those who struggle to move their bowels, perhaps you might try this headline...

ARE YOU FED UP WITH CONSTIPATION?
Discover the Solution Trusted by 3.2 Million People...

This headline took me precisely 30 seconds to write. Some copywriters might take a week to write a headline out of a desire to be clever or subtle or witty. Why not just be super-clear and totally focused on what the potential customer really wants? Then you can pile on the additional benefits.[11]

TWO. Go with your gut. What does common sense tell you about marketing the product and writing copy for the product or service?

THREE. Take a look at how others are marketing and selling similar products and services, especially when you can find out exactly what works. It's highly likely the company that's selling the most is being straightforward and simple. Don't plagiarize, obviously, but, instead, gain some inspiration from their clarity.

FOUR. Discover what testing tells you. Your testing data will lead to you to TOTAL clarity and simplicity of logic...when you let it.

FIVE. Make keeping things simple and focusing on TOTAL clarity the foundation of your approach to marketing. Why would anyone make things complicated? Yet I routinely see bizarre messaging, complex

---

[11] Get it, farmers?

headlines plus super-complicated arguments that only 3 percent of the population would ever understand,.

SIX. Who, in your world, keeps the messaging simple? Maybe you should emulate them. Life will be a lot easier.

SEVEN. Remember why people buy. People usually, as Andrew Wood told me, buy products for emotional reasons backed by logic. So provide them with the logic, clearly stated. They also buy products so they can feel better about themselves.

EIGHT. Learn to write quickly. The more I write copy, the faster I get. And the faster I write, the clearer the copy because I don't give myself the time to get complex!

When I'm teaching skiing, I strive to keep my instruction short, logical, and straight the point. My students DO NOT want to stand around, especially when it's super cold, listening me to describe the finer points of rotating the femurs under a stable upper body.

It's the same with my copy. I strive for simplicity, relevancy, and clarity of the sales argument and proof. Works for me...over $400 million in sales over six years for my clients.

Maybe clarity and simplicity come to me because I've been writing professionally for 30 years. Maybe it's because I have a degree in English and comparative literature and the work required for that degree entailed simplifying a lot of complex information. Maybe it's because I spent most of my young life reading and writing.

Can you gain this knack for simplicity of presentation? Let's head back to the world of the ski instructor. I regularly ski with instructors who have been teaching for 30, 40, and even 50 seasons. They make even complicated skiing moves look super simple. They make teaching look simple. I'm catching up, but it's going to take several seasons to come close to their simplicity. This knack for copywriting simplicity will come to you with practice and testing. Take advantage of the latter if you have that luxury.

Defenestrate Subtlety and Cleverness and BE DIRECT! Embrace TOTAL CLARITY!

Ah...defenestration...one of my absolute favorite words. It means, roughly defined, to throw something or someone out the window.

The Thirty Years War (1618–1648) started with The Defenestration of Prague. Several dignitaries were thrown out of a window by people who were not supposed to throw people out of windows. A long war ensued that claimed the lives of eight million people.

If you're a copywriter...or if you're a marketer of any type...or if you're a business owner and you want to maximize the impact of your marketing, then ban cleverness and subtlety and "award-winning" advertising and focus on TOTAL CLARITY.

Let me explain, perhaps, by going back to 2002 when I lived in Charlotte and I was publishing a magazine, writing books, and writing copy. A friend contacted me. A relative of my friend, a young woman just out of college, wanted to get into the advertising industry. "Would you speak with her?" was the question. "Of course," I replied.

I met with the young woman and discussed her goals and described the advertising business and how it works. I recommended books she could read. She seemed flustered during the conversation and ended the meeting by saying, almost in tears, "I JUST WANT TO DO SOMETHING CREATIVE."

What is creative? What is creativity?

In most marketing departments and advertising agencies, based on my experience, creativity is...

- Witty ads/funny ads
- Pretty advertising
- Originality
- Flowery language

...all to win awards and make people in the advertising agencies and marketing departments feel great about their creativity.

Here's the dictionary definition of creativity, for what it's worth.

"The use of the imagination or original ideas, especially in the production of an artistic work."

To me, as a direct response copywriter contracted to help my clients sell products and services en masse, creativity is...

Understanding the needs and desires of customers and presenting, with TOTAL CLARITY, these customers with products and services that meet these needs and desires so the customer can feel better about themselves and reach their life goals.

I value clarity over creativity—yet presenting products with clarity requires creativity. Think about the ad for Ginzu Knives where they show the knives slicing through a can then slicing through tomatoes. That's clarity... That's creativity...

I can't think of anyone in direct marketing, and certainly not in branding, who really discusses clarity, yet it's a powerful copywriting weapon in my arsenal. If you look at all the most successful direct marketing campaigns, there's one commonality: TOTAL CLARITY...usually coupled with simplicity.

Let me go one step further and remind you about the basis of TOTAL CLARITY...

WHEN YOU HAND OVER YOUR MONEY/INFORMATION ...
HERE IS EXACTLY WHAT YOU ARE GOING TO GET ...

Embrace and implement clarity in all your marketing and you will soon generate a torrent of revenue while your competitors flounder around trying to be clever.

AFTERWORD

I just finished reading the final draft of this book and it's ready for the printing press. It's a touch chaotic in places, and it's not going to win a Pulitzer prize, and it's not going to win the American Marketing Association Foundation's Berry-AMA Book Prize for the best book in marketing. Why? Because it's not "thought leadership" although I give you the raw truth about marketing. There's nothing new here.

But...I have to admit I'm really happy with the result.

Why?

Because, even if it helps ONE company become super successful, it will have created a positive impact.

Maybe that's YOU.

- If you're the owner of a company, or its CEO, or its chief marketing officer, then you'll know what a direct response copywriter is and you'll hopefully hire one, or several, and watch your revenue grow.
- And if you're one of the above and you've been thinking "branding is the way to go," then you'll be thinking twice about your marketing strategy. YOU HAD BETTER BE! You will fire the branding consultants and move toward direct marketing.
- If you're an MBA candidate, or if you have an MBA, you will say, "Forget what the marketing professors are telling me... I'm using direct marketing."
- If we meet in person or if you meet another direct response copywriter, you will no longer have the "blank stare."
- If you're a branding copywriter or if you work in a branding agency, you will understand the pure folly of branding creative and

head to direct marketing. You'll have the potential to make a lot more money.

- If you're relatively young and searching for a career, you will consider being a direct response copywriter.

I will not be getting thank you notes from branding consultants, gurus, and others who routinely lead their clients down the wrong path. I get this.

Hopefully, this book makes the world a better place for all direct response copywriters. But I primarily wrote this book for ambitious business owners who want to be more successful. Now you know...

A. What a direct response copywriter is.
B. How a direct response copywriter can bring you massive revenue.

What are your next steps?

- Look around and understand the difference between branding advertising and direct marketing. This will become super-clear.
- Train yourself to spot the work of a direct response copywriter.
- Watch the David Ogilvy video, "We Sell or Else" three times a week. Make everyone in your company watch it too.
- Read the books I recommend in the section titled "Recommended Reading."
- Get all branding advertising and non-measurable marketing TOTALLY out of your life. This could mean making some massive changes.
- If/when you hire marketing professionals, make sure they are direct marketing people.
- Get an experienced and proven direct response copywriter on your team.
- MEASURE EVERYTHING and be willing to fail. Success will follow.
- Strive for constant improvement and demand this from your marketing people.
- Understand lists and offers.
- Find a company in your space that uses direct marketing strategies and take a close look at what they're doing.

- Orient your entire company around direct marketing...from the person who drives the forklift to the CFO.
- Tell the truth and treat your customers like royalty.
- Attend direct marketing conferences but closely scrutinize the qualifications of the speakers.

And most importantly...

HAVE A LOT OF FUN WITH DIRECT MARKETING.

When you get going, you may struggle to understand direct marketing and direct response copywriting. Be patient. You're going to have a great time...especially when all that revenue starts pouring in and the value of the business explodes.

I wish you all the very best with your business and your direct marketing adventures.

ACKNOWLEDGEMENTS

I have so many people to thank for so much that I don't even know where to begin.

Brian Kurtz, in his book *Overdeliver*, has several pages of acknowledgements.

If I even try to list everyone, I'm going to leave someone out so I'll just say a deep "thank you" to mentors, friends, clients, associates, family, and the people I've never actually met who helped me by providing their sagacity. You know who you are.

APPENDIX

Recommended Reading. I've mentioned several books I recommend you read. Other copywriters will provide other suggestions in their books or on their websites. I provide free reviews of these books on my website.

Please order these through your local independent bookstore. These stores help to support reading and writing in local communities.

Scientific Advertising. Claude C. Hopkins. 1923.

Secrets of Successful Direct Mail. Richard Benson. 2005.

The Ultimate Sales Letter. Dan Kennedy. 1997.

Bencivenga Bullets. Gary Bencivenga. Available online for free.

Open Me Now: Direct Mail Envelopes That Work ... and Those That Don't. Herschell Gordon Lewis. 2006.

The Golf Marketing Bible. Andrew Wood. 2009.

Ogilvy on Advertising. David Ogilvy. 1985.

Words That Sell. Richard Bayan. 2006.

Million Dollar Mailings. Denny Hatch. 1992.

How to Write Sales Letters That Sell. Drayton Bird. 1994.

My Life in Advertising. Claude C. Hopkins. 1927.

The Ultimate Guide to Direct Marketing. Al Lautenslager. 2005.

Tested Advertising Methods. John Caples.

The Advertising Solution. Craig Simpson and Brian Kurtz. 2016.

NO BS Price Strategy. Dan Kennedy and Jason Marrs.

On Writing Well. William Zinsser. 1976 to 1990.

Mindset: The New Psychology of Success. Carol Dweck. 2007.

Overdeliver. Brian Kurtz. 2019.

The Copywriter's Handbook: A Step-by-Step Guide to Writing Copy That
Sells. Bob Bly.
Confessions of An Advertising Man. David Ogilvy.

Most of these books include recommendations for additional reading.
Read those books.

● ● ● ●

Even More Reading

Every entry on Clayton Makepeace's blog. It's not up as I write. Hopefully
that will change.

I recommend you read everything that Bob Bly has written about copy.
He has several books plus some great info-products on his site.